YALE STUDIES IN ENGLISH

Yale Studies in English publishes books on English, American, and Anglophone literature developed in and by the Yale University community. Founded in 1898 by Albert Stanburrough Cook, the original series continued into the 1970s, producing such titles as *The Poetry of Meditation* by Louis Martz, *Shelley's Mythmaking* by Harold Bloom, *The Cankered Muse* by Alvin Kernan, *The Hero of the Waverly Novels* by Alexander Welsh, *John Skelton's Poetry* by Stanley Fish, and *Sir Walter Ralegh: The Renaissance Man and His Roles* by Stephen Greenblatt. With the goal of encouraging publications by emerging scholars alongside the work of established colleagues, the series has been revived for the twenty-first century with the support of a grant from the Andrew W. Mellon Foundation and in partnership with Yale University Press.

UNCLOSETING DRAMA

american modernism and queer performance

nick salvato

Yale UNIVERSITY PRESS
new haven and london

Published with assistance from the foundation established in memory of Amasa Stone Mather of the Class of 1907, Yale College.

Yale University Press books may be purchased in quantity for educational, business, or promotional use. For information, please e-mail sales.press@yale.edu (U.S. office) or sales@yaleup.co.uk (U.K. office).

Set in Minion and Franklin Gothic types by The Composing Room of Michigan, Inc. Printed in the United States of America.

Library of Congress Cataloging-in-Publication Data

Salvato, Nick, 1978–
    Uncloseting drama : American modernism and queer performance / Nick Salvato.
        p.   cm. — (Yale studies in English)
    Includes bibliographical references and index.
    ISBN 978-0-300-15539-6 (paperbound : alk. paper)   1. Gays' writings, American.
2. Modernism (Literature).   I. Title.
    PS627.H67S25 2010
    810.9'920664—dc22

                            2010003128

A catalogue record for this book is available from the British Library.

This paper meets the requirements of ANSI/NISO Z39.48-1992 (Permanence of Paper).

10 9 8 7 6 5 4 3 2 1

CONTENTS

ACKNOWLEDGMENTS

Of the many people whom I would like to thank for making the writing of this book possible, I must begin with my dissertation advisers, Joseph Roach and Michael Trask. The earliest close readers of this project, during its formative stages, they are also the ones to whom I owe the greatest debt for their counsel, encouragement, and wisdom. For symmetry's sake (and for so much more), I think that it is only appropriate to thank, in the same breath, my other two "earliest close readers": Annette and Nicholas Salvato, the parents who read indefatigably to and with me when I was a child and who instilled in me the lifelong habit of critical inquiry that makes my work imaginable. My critical work on this particular book was also conceived with generous fellowships from the Andrew W. Mellon Foundation and the Beinecke Rare Book and Manuscript Library at Yale.

For their willingness to read drafts of many pages, to help me clarify various ideas, or just to sustain me with their brilliant and nurturing conversation, I thank the friends whom I consider my closest interlocutors: Rebecca Berne, Jane Carr, Maria Fackler, Carlynn Houghton, Kamran Javadizadeh, Eric Lindstrom, Megan Quigley, and Tristan Snell.

Other colleagues and friends have read (or heard) and commented on various parts of this project at various stages of its development. Without the generous insights of the following individuals, whether or not they recall those insights in their particularity, the book could not have taken its present shape (barring, of course, its errors, which are entirely my own): Alan Ackerman, Robin Bernstein, Michael Cadden, Marvin Carlson, Lara Cohen, Wai Chee Dimock, Craig Dworkin, Laura Frost, Diana Fuss, Langdon Hammer, Amy Hungerford, Pericles Lewis, Douglas Mao, Jeff Nunokawa, Tavia Nyong'o, Julie Stone Peters, Linda Peterson, Amy Reading, Marc Robinson, Karin Roffman, Mark Scroggins, and Robert Stepto.

I have omitted some readers and auditors from the previous list because they deserve to be mentioned, alongside other colleagues and friends, in their equally special capacity as the intellectual companions who have made Cornell University such a wonderful place to work, share ideas, and bring this project to fruition. These companions include Jeremy Braddock, J. Ellen

Gainor, Andrew Galloway, Sabine Haenni, Ellis Hanson, Philip Lorenz, Jenny Mann, Masha Raskolnikov, Byron Suber, Amy Villarejo, Sara Warner, and Haiping Yan, among others.

My extremely thoughtful editor, Alison MacKeen, in concert with Jennifer Banks, the anonymous readers who provided so much valuable advice, and the hardworking staff at Yale University Press, has made it a pleasure to publish this book as part of the series Yale Studies in English. I thank Dan Heaton especially for his meticulous, clever, and cheerful copyediting.

A book is made for as many possible readers as it may hope to attract, but I would nevertheless like to dedicate this one to two readers in particular: Bethany Mito, without whose example, friendship, and inspiration I would never have dreamed of beginning it, and Samuel Buggeln, without whose love, patience, and support I could never have thus completed it.

UNCLOSETING DRAMA

introduction: "half in and half out"

"CUMBROUS NONDESCRIPT"

In the introduction to *Trash Trio*, a collection of three of his early screen-plays, the filmmaker John Waters explains for his readers, with typical cheekiness, the use value of a printed edition of his work:

> Finally, in the best Mickey Rooney–Judy Garland tradition, you can now put on my movies like little plays in the privacy of your own home. Some rainy Saturday afternoon, just call all your friends together and yell, "Hey, kids, let's do *Pink Flamingos!*" Every hideous word of these films is right here in black and white, so you don't have to rely on a vague memory of some midnight show you staggered into years ago in a questionable state of mind. In the light of day, on the printed page, these "celluloid atrocities" may seem even ruder than you remember. Say the dialogue out loud, even yell it like the characters do—you'll feel better. Do Divine's psychotic monologues and feel the tensions and distractions of everyday life melt away. You could even read along with the videos, getting the inflection just right, playing your favorite part in front of the mirror. Or, what the hell, play every single part yourself and watch your friends run from your house in a panic.[1]

If we were to take at all seriously, and with only slightly exaggerated innocence, the filmmaker's imperative to "put on [his] movies like little plays in the privacy of [our] own home[s]," or even if we were simply to read *Pink Flamingos* in a suitably beat-up and tackily upholstered armchair, we would validate Waters's effective transformation of his films into closet dramas —that is, into plays written for private reading or coterie performance, but not for public staging.[2] Of course, the project that Waters proposes to his readers throws into relief the fundamental instability at the heart of any such secure and mundane definition of closet drama. Just as a screenplay explicitly intended for public consumption—indeed, one that has been produced and watched by millions of viewers worldwide—can turn into a closet drama "in front of [our] mirror[s]," so, too, can a director hold up a mirror (perhaps from the funhouse) to a supposed closet drama and reflect it onto the stage. Waters's imagined scene of Divine recreation also gestures toward the uncannily queer implications that seem to haunt so much closet drama, where the pun on *closet* is firmly intended: performing *Pink Flamingos* with our friends, we could not help but turn into camp queens participating "in the best Mickey Rooney–Judy Garland tradition"; and performing it by ourselves, we would come to resemble Bottom, that queerest of Shakespearean clowns who wants, like the demented Waters fan, to "play every single part [himself]."

Though Waters belongs more obviously to a cinematic tradition including directors like Kenneth Anger and Luis Buñuel than to a literary tradition comprising authors like Ezra Pound and Gertrude Stein, I find that his remarks frame neatly—and in an appropriately perverse spirit—the key issue that animates this project: the interpretations, both critical and performative, of queer closet drama. Alongside the work of Pound and Stein, I also examine the dramatic writing of Louis Zukofsky and Djuna Barnes —and, with equal importance, the staging of their respective plays by such diverse performance practitioners as the Classic Stage Company, the Wooster Group, the language poets, and Jackson Mac Low. Together, Pound, Zukofsky, Stein, and Barnes represent an important and cohesive strand of American modernism. Pound was not only the author of what is arguably the most iconic modernist long poem, *The Cantos,* but also an editor (most famously of T. S. Eliot's *The Waste Land*), publisher, mentor, and promoter of the work of other, often younger modernists, including Zukofsky. As Zukofsky developed a close relationship with Pound and worked on his long poem "A," indebted to but self-consciously departing from *The Cantos,* he also drew inspiration from what small part of Stein's corpus was being published in the early twentieth century. Indeed, though Stein was a prolific writer, she received little attention (or negative notices) for her work until her best-selling sensation, *The Autobiography of Alice B. Toklas,* brought her explosive popularity and fame. That ventriloquized memoir capitalized on Stein's role as a salon hostess and leading collector of modernist visual art in Paris, where her fellow expatriate Djuna Barnes, most celebrated for her novel *Nightwood,* traveled in sometimes overlapping circles of American and European artists.

Given the rich literary and biographical connections among these four authors, each of whom knew or read the works of all the others, an exploration of their more or less contemporaneous dramatic experiments illuminates not only aspects of their respective works but also trends in the modernist era. One such modernist trend was a turn, made by these authors and others, to the writing of closet drama, which had last fully flowered roughly one hundred years before Barnes, for instance, wrote her long verse play *The Antiphon.* A genealogy of the European closet drama begins with early modern dramatic verse modeled on Senecan dialogues; after further development in the seventeenth and eighteenth centuries, the closet drama enjoyed its greatest vogue in the nineteenth century, particularly in the hands of Romantic writers in England, France, and Germany. At the most basic level of commonality, each of the modernist authors under consideration here was aware of the tradition of loosely grouping these diverse efforts, and they all situated their work in response to earlier plays recognized as closet drama. Pound calls his translation of one of Musset's short closet dramas a "play modelled on the Noh," and he implies that his simultaneous translations of actual Nō plays belong also to the camp of closet drama. In moves that similarly hark back to Romantic predecessors, Stein writes a closet drama about the great closet dramatist Byron, and Barnes cites Shelley's *The Cenci* as a model for *The Antiphon* in that work's final monologue. Gesturing to an earlier moment in the closet drama's history, Zukofsky's translation of Plautus's *Rudens* recalls the Elizabethan closet dramatists' interest in Latin precedents.

Despite the capability—the modernists' and our own—to trace such a genealogy, it would be a mistake to treat the closet drama as a stable genre or to forgo questioning the meanings of the term that designates this supposed genre. Such neglect characterizes, nevertheless, most of the small body of critical literature on closet drama. Addressing early modern closet drama, mostly by women, Karen Raber notes that the "wide variety of plays" that she considers share essential common features, as "compositions intended for reading or private recitation rather than for theatrical performance."[3] In so defining the plays as closet texts, Raber assumes the legibility of intention, privacy, and theatrical publicity and uses this assumption, in turn, to make the definition of closet drama itself a legible and untroubled one. Writing more recently on similar material, Marta Straznicky observes with greater nuance that the authors that she investigates do not share a common set of intentions, and she likewise makes clear that "private and public are shifting rather than fixed points of reference" and that "early modern closet plays are in general not opposed to theatricality, even if most of them would not have aspired to or hoped for performance in a commercial venue."[4] But as Straznicky admits the complexity of such key terms for her study as *privacy* and *playreading*, she does not put pressure on the term *closet drama* itself as a placeholder for the various and variegated plays that she cites. Even Evlyn Gould, who coins the term *virtual theater* to describe with admirable sophistication a relationship among optics, philosophy, and "the writing of [plays] that cannot be staged," makes occasional use of the term *closet drama* without questioning either its relationship to her own more precise coinage or the status of closet drama as such.[5]

These critical omissions have the cumulative effect of leaving closet drama intact as a genre and of leaving the impression that the genre is a transparent one. Alternatively, I use *closet drama* not as a designation of a genre with distinct boundaries but as a conceptual tool that can fruitfully guide an analysis of texts with complex relationships to drama and theater; and part of what makes the tool a fruitful one is the elasticity, rather than the givenness, of closet drama as an indexical term. Indeed, and in contrast to the recent critical tendency to deploy *closet drama* as if it had a clear and definite meaning, closet drama was understood rather as an extremely vague category in the early twentieth century, the period during which the modernists would have begun reckoning with it. In the most pointed and dismissive assessment of this categorical vagueness, William Archer called the closet drama a "cumbrous nondescript";[6] more elusively and productively, Thomas Hardy wrote in the preface to his closet drama *The Dynasts*, "To say, then, in the present case, that a writing in play-shape is not to be played, is merely another way of stating that such writing has been done in a form for which there chances to be no brief definition save one already in use for works that it superficially but not entirely resembles."[7] Embracing the qualities of difficulty, slipperiness, and refusal to conform easily to class or kind suggested (if belittled) by the phrase "cumbrous nondescript," I situate closet drama, as Hardy does, as a marker for texts whose nominations as such can never be "brief" and whose "resembl[anc]es" to one another should not elide the strength of their differences. In so doing, I take a cue, too, from prominent scholars of melodrama, another category that was likewise and for a long time marginalized or denigrated by critics. In contrast to earlier authorities who dismissed melodrama, later generations of theorists have made its study central to literary and performance studies (among other disciplines) by reconceptualizing the so-called genre as a *mode*. Drawing upon the pathbreaking work of Peter Brooks and Christine Gledhill, Linda Williams exemplifies this conceptual move best and explains it admirably when she writes that "the noun *melodrama* functions to denote a certain form of exciting, sensational, and, above all, moving story that could then be further differentiated by more specifications of setting or milieu and/or genre. It is this basic sense of melodrama as a *modality* of narrative . . . to which we need to attend if we are to confront its most fundamental appeal."[8] Like melodrama, best understood not in its limited sense as a genre but as a mode of storytelling (and, indeed, of apprehending and explaining the world), closet drama could and ought to denote a mode of expression that disrupts or exceeds generic distinctions. But what makes closet drama a trickier mode to analyze is that "to confront its most fundamental" aspect is not a matter of identifying its affective qualities, strategies, or effects, as in the case of a melodramatic mode marked by the simultaneously "sensational" and "moving" features to which Williams refers. Rather, closet drama's most fundamental or constant feature is, ironically, its contingency as the mode at the threshold between writing and performance—a threshold that is always, or at least always in danger of, moving.

This observation raises a salient question about the instability of closet drama as a category. If closet drama is not intended for performance, is unperformed, or is at least "unsuitable" for performance, does it cease to be closet drama when brought to the stage? Or does a resistance to performance registered in the dramatic text linger even in or after performance? Rather than take one side or another of this issue, I would describe the central feature of closet drama as precisely its undecided—and undecidable—relationship to performance. Like the visionary Saint Therese in Stein's *Four Saints in Three Acts,* "half in and half out of doors,"[9] closet drama is always half on and half off the stage; and like the fisherman Greave in Zukofsky's *Rudens,* whose "alien" desires are "incompressible," closet drama opens a window onto energies that refuse containment by any single performative iteration.[10]

In making these claims about closet drama's undecidability and its unsettling of fixities, I align my position with that of Kenneth Cox, who warns of the danger of viewing the closet drama as a singular form with a coherent or linear historical trajectory. "The closet drama is a contingent category," he writes, "for it measures the ever changing distance between a dramatist's expectations and theatrical realities. Many romantic works that were published as closet dramas—Shelley's *The Cenci* or Musset's plays, for example—later met with some theatrical success. In a few cases, the closet drama represented not an armchair drama but bold dramatic experiment. . . . The closet drama sought the theatre of the future."[11] Whether or not closet dramas necessarily envision a theater of the future, they have tended to resist in some way the theatrical constraints and conventions of their present. Because these conventions are themselves historically contingent, so, too, will the impetus to write a closet drama change from one time and place to another.

In the twentieth century, this schematic relationship of closet drama to theater is complicated by the fact that modernist drama and theater as such are also marked by the kind of resistance and experimentation that Cox attributes more singularly to an earlier period's closet plays. Peter Szondi elaborates this paradox—modernist drama's refusal of the "dramatic"—in his foundational *Theory of the Modern Drama,* in which he identifies the quintessentially dramatic (in the West, and since the early modern period) as interpersonal, dialogic, focused on the present, and driven by event; he then proceeds to trace the ways in which late-nineteenth-century drama, in a transition marked by crisis, and early-twentieth-century drama, resolving the crisis in its various guises as expressionist play, political revue, epic theater, montage, and metatheater, reject these values and replace them with their opposites: alienation, monologue or narration, memory- or dreamscape, and an emphasis on psychic interiority.[12] In their introduction to the recent anthology *Against Theatre: Creative Destructions on the Modernist Stage,* Alan Ackerman and Martin Puchner continue, refine, and extend this argument as they stake the claim that "in no period before modernism [is] the theatre . . . more ready to take to heart the arguments and obsessions of its detractors," with the result that "literature and theatre, anti-theatre and theatre, are not simply opposed to one another but multiply intertwined."[13] According to this line of thinking, modernist closet drama, then, would manifest the most extreme version of energies already at play in other modernist dramas and on actual modernist stages. This resonance of modernist closet drama's attributes with the agendas and ambitions of modernist drama in general is echoed linguistically in Szondi's account, which contrasts the "disclosures" of traditional drama (8), "the art form par excellence of dialogic openness and frankness," with modern drama's fondness for "*enclosing* others within the character's frame of reference" in the service of "presenting secret psychic events" (25, emphasis added). The enclosing tendency of this dramaturgy draws it closer to the closet than, say, to the drawing rooms of nineteenth-century realism.

Just as modernist closet drama can be understood not as entirely exceptional but rather as posing an exaggerated version of its sister plays' relationship to theatrical staging, so, too, should its relationship to the *page* —typically, if superficially, recognized as closet drama's special provenance —be placed on a spectrum that takes into account the emergent meanings and importance of textuality and publication to modernist playwrights on the whole. W. B. Worthen addresses this issue in his recent book, *Print and the Poetics of Modern Drama,* in which he observes that print, previously "a deferred form of the drama's identity," becomes "by Shaw's day . . . the condition of drama"; he argues, as a consequence, that "the action of modern drama, whether immediately and effectively stageable or apparently just 'literary,' arises in the conflict between the materialities and mutabilities of the stage and the page."[14] If, as Worthen suggests, modernism's shift in equilibrium places much more priority than ever before on the often conflicted exchanges between stage and page, then the page of the modernist closet drama—and its ostensibly tortuous relationship to the stage—tells only a hyperbolic version of a story otherwise playing out (literally) in the period. This claim prompts a revisitation to and revision of one of the central questions raised in Austin E. Quigley's *The Modern Stage and Other Worlds,* which addresses what Quigley calls the "horizons" between theatrical "domains" that seem radically different and rigidly separate but that, in fact, overlap, merge, and even mutually constitute one another.[15] When Quigley speaks of such domains, he has in mind chiefly the sphere of the stage and its interaction with the sphere of the audience, and he is surely right to consider this complex interaction with the nuance and care that he lavishes upon it; but what if, following Worthen and thinking of closet drama, we change frames and attend to the horizons between stage and page? How would this difference in emphasis force, for instance, a recalibration of Quigley's observation that as "the degree of difference between domains increases, the lines between domains move steadily towards barrier status, and as they do so, there is an ever more urgent need . . . *to find new ways to draw attention to horizons, and to find new ways of showing how they can be transcended"* (32)? Quigley wants to think through the ways in which modernist drama, whose worlds seem to differ radically from the lives of its audiences, makes itself felt by those audiences, but the perhaps even greater hurdle consists in getting that drama intelligibly onstage in the first place (arguably, "the degree of difference" between a strange text and bodies onstage is more substantial than that between strange bodies onstage and bodies in an audience). That hurdle was often surmounted by the various innovators who forced renovations of the stage and created, in Ackerman and Puchner's compelling formulation, "ever-new theatres" (14). When the hurdle was not met, whether because of the incapacity, the indifference, the failure, or, most aggressively, the determination and design of modernist playwrights, closet drama resulted—but a closet drama that is intimately related to its staged counterparts.

QUEER CONTORTIONS

These observations about the contiguities between modernist closet drama and companion plays that were realized in the theater raise the question: what *is* exceptional and distinctive about modernist closet drama, as it relates both to contemporaneous plays and to the closet drama of earlier periods? This is a question deliberately deferred by Martin Puchner in his noteworthy book *Stage Fright: Modernism, Anti-Theatricality, and Drama.* When Puchner identifies the modernist closet drama as a period-specific, uniquely ambivalent response to the theater and locates the ambivalence of this dramatic writing squarely between a more traditional antitheatrical prejudice and what he calls the "(pro)theatricalism" of contemporaneous avant-garde movements, he does not associate this ambivalence exclusively with closet drama.[16] Rather, he contends that modernist drama *in toto* inaugurates "a theater at odds with the value of theatricality" (7) and that closet drama merely "takes this resistance [to theatricality] to an extreme" (15). Where, then, do we locate the special quality of modernist closet drama? Puchner himself suggests what I take to be the most promising path when he cites the queer resonances of modernist closet drama as a fruitful area for further exploration. "Because closet dramas use their freedom from the normativity of the theatre to create worlds characterized by various forms of ambiguity and deviance," he writes, "it is possible to adopt Eve Kosofsky Sedgwick's project of an epistemology of the closet for the closet drama" (17). Puchner proceeds to analyze briefly such literary phenomena as Leopold Bloom's sex change in the "Circe" episode of *Ulysses* (88), but these analyses remain incidental rather than fundamental to his emphasis on modernist drama's diegetic strategies as a critique of mimesis (5) and as a resistance to the (Wagnerian) idea of the total work of art (55).

In turn, I contend that the queer potential of closet drama, treated only in passing in *Stage Fright*, belongs prominently among the reasons for its modernist renewal and for its distinction on the spectrum of modernist drama. When Puchner recommends "an epistemology of the closet for closet drama," he has in mind largely modernist closet drama, but he allows for the possibility that such a project could take a broader and more sweeping historical view. It is true that the "ambiguity and deviance" that he identifies as symptomatic of the closet drama as such inform plays like *Manfred* and *The Cenci,* both of which explore homoerotic and incestuous subjects. I would argue, nevertheless, that only in the twentieth century, when sexual discourses are ubiquitous and sexual identities are codified, does the queering of closet drama become a truly significant phenomenon. Pound translates Sophocles' *Electra*—and translates Electra herself into a palpably queer figure—as could only a post-Freudian writer concerned intimately with questions of modern psychology and psychiatry (as Pound was in the late 1940s). Stein's drama often owes its inspiration—and sometimes its outright content—to the Parisian lesbian community in which she, Barnes, Natalie Barney, and numerous other American women participated. For Barnes's part, her writing on the American family depends entirely upon her upbringing in a distinctly modern kind of American family, as the granddaughter of a late-Victorian free-love proponent and the daughter of an open polyamorist. And when Guy Davenport suggests that Zukofsky's *Rudens* reimagines Plautus's Rome as modern New York City, we must remember that the city in question is, among other things (and in George Chauncey's words), a *gay* New York.[17]

Or at least a queer one. In describing modernist closet drama as distinctly queer closet drama, I revert, perhaps unfashionably, to the formulation of queerness most popularly espoused by academics in the early and mid-1990s. As I intend it, the word *queer* designates not so much a category as a border-crossing between categories, if not the contestation of categorization altogether. As Eve Sedgwick has observed, "One of the things that 'queer' can refer to [is] the open mesh of possibilities, gaps, overlaps, dissonances and resonances, lapses and excesses of meaning when the constituent elements of anyone's gender, of anyone's sexuality aren't made (or *can't* be made) to signify monolithically."[18] Following this cue, I use the concept of queerness not to designate a static site of lesbian and gay identity but to gesture toward transgressive *movements* between and among different positions of sex, gender, and desire. In so doing, I put my project in sympathetic dialogue with the work of other critics who have recently explored the queer contours of modernism. Most prominent, Joseph Allen Boone's *Libidinal Currents: Sexuality and the Shaping of Modernism* explores the ways in which the expression of sexuality in modernism "escap[es] rigid categorization even as categories devised to contain [sexual] energies proliferate."[19] The "theatricalized play" of "queer alterity" that he finds at work in modernist fiction—both in overtly gay, subcultural texts and "within canonical modernism"—is equally well at work in modernist closet drama and deserves the kind of further attention that puts simultaneous pressure on the concepts of queerness and theatricality and on the relationship between them (15). Where the former concept is concerned, other critics of modernism have rightly reminded us of early-twentieth-century valences of the word *queer* and their potential usefulness to us in our scholarly analyses. Anne Herrmann, for instance, notes that "in the modernist period queerness still means 'strange, odd, peculiar, eccentric; suspicious, dubious; not in a normal condition,'" with the implication that queerness's "resistances to regimes of the normal," while rooted in issues of sex, gender, and sexuality, need not conform to "post-Stonewall lesbian and gay identity politics"; indeed, one of the strengths of the term's deployment might be its ways of "mak[ing] strange the relations between identities."[20] A scholar might even risk and take pleasure in queerly laying waste to the mechanics and goals of identity politics, as Scott Herring does when he invokes the "earlier [twentieth-century] 'self-conscious' usage of 'queer' as an active process of spoiling or ruining or making rotten" precisely in order to ruin "the 'undertaking' of sexual communitarianism" rooted in identity formation.[21] While such an agenda is not my own explicit undertaking, I do want to emphasize the ways in which critical inquiry can challenge, if not spoil, both the truisms about sexuality obtaining in the early twentieth century and those with which we tarry and toil.

In some quarters, queerness has come under fire for precisely the definitional disruptions that I describe here and that I take to be a methodological strength. Leo Bersani exemplifies the resistance to queer theory when he criticizes it for "de-gaying gayness."[22] Even when critics continue to use the word *queer,* many, unlike those cited above, have moved away from its more radical implications; instead of connoting an interrogation of sexual coherence, queerness now seems more often than not to serve simply as a substitute for *lesbian* or *gay,* especially in the academic study of theater and performance.[23] Thus when Alisa Solomon recently declared that "theater is the queerest art," she cited chiefly examples of lesbian and gay theater to account for "the kind of *mimetic experience* offered in theatre [that] can by its very process disrupt conventional patterns of seeing, of knowing, and, especially, of seeing and knowing bodies."[24] But "mimetic experience" may be exactly one of the conventional patterns that a queer theater can disrupt, if queerness is understood not as a transparent representation of sexual identity but as an affront to the transparency of both sex-

ual identity and its representations. Laurence Senelick rejects this very possibility when he states summarily and succinctly that "Martha Wilson is
queer theatre, Robert Wilson is not."[25] In a similar move, a critic might want
to distinguish Pound and Zukofsky, two ostensibly straight men, from Stein
and Barnes, a lesbian and a bisexual woman. Conversely, I argue that the
works of all four unleash queer energies, and I seek to reinvest the term
queerness with its resistant force as I explore the queer dimensions of modernist closet drama.

Such a method is required to attend to the nuances of the works of the
four authors highlighted in this book, because they, too, resisted or rejected
certain conceptions of sexual identity taking hold in the late nineteenth and
early twentieth centuries. Most notoriously (and oft-cited) among them,
Barnes declared about her relationship with her longtime female lover, "I'm
not a lesbian. I just loved Thelma"; but in myriad and arguably more subtle ways, Barnes and the others all used their dramatic work to interrogate
received notions about sexuality. Nor is it an accident that the work in question should take the form of closet drama. Just as the closet drama approaches the stage (if it does so at all) ambivalently and ambiguously, so
does the queer refuse to fit neatly into stable sexual roles. Thus queerness
produces confusions and contortions akin to those of closet drama, and
closet drama provides a uniquely suitable space for the expression of queer
sensibilities. Modernist authors exploit this suitability as they seek simultaneously to challenge sexual normativities and dramatic conventions. Julie
Stone Peters observes that "modern drama, steeped in the work of Richard
von Krafft-Ebing, Otto Weininger, Havelock Ellis, [and] Freud . . . gave embodiment to the strange new figures created by modern sexology" and that,
concomitantly, sex "became *the* problem for modern culture."[26] In turn,
sexology, its figures, and the limited and limiting kinds of embodiment and
expression that they entailed became the problem for modernist closet
dramatists. If, as Peters notes provocatively, one etymology for *obscene,* "*ob*
[against] and *scaena* [stage]," suggests that "obscenity is that which is against
or off the stage" (214), then modernist closet drama does truly obscene
work, insofar as it resists or refuses the stage in order also to ignore, deny,
or derail the categories and values of the new sexual sciences.

CLOSE CALLS

Both the sexual and dramatic challenges of modernist closet drama have a
specifically temporal dimension. As early-twentieth-century authors look
backward for models—to the plays of ancient Greece, Rome, and Japan,

or to Romantic verse drama—so, too, do they look forward and imagine sometimes utopian possibilities for theatrical and erotic representation that have yet to come into being. Returning to Kenneth Cox's conjecture that closet drama seeks the theater—or, more broadly, the *polis*—of the future, I argue that modernist closet drama remained closeted until the end of the twentieth century because the conditions of the theater had not yet caught up to the drama's vision. As RoseLee Goldberg says in an essay on the history (and historicization) of twentieth-century live performance: "Imagine starting out as a painter and having no recourse to twentieth-century paintings: no Matisse, no Pollock, no Guston. Now, imagine starting out as an artist who thinks of sound, space, movement, and the body as raw material and who lacks access to the works of Yves Klein, Joseph Beuys, or Joan Jonas. It's unimaginable for the artist who works in paint but standard for the artist who works in performance."[27] Imagine, in turn, writing an experimental play like *Doctor Faustus Lights the Lights* when Yves Klein was only ten years old. After the efflorescence of performance art in the 1960s, new generations of theater practitioners could bring to bear techniques and styles of staging—indeed, perverse media—uniquely suited to the adaptation of notoriously difficult modernist works. Modernist closet drama required (and, in a sense, anticipated) the advent of innovations in postmodern performance, through which it could be, as it were, uncloseted.[28]

Importantly, the respective backward- and forward-looking qualities of modernist closet drama that I describe are not easily separable. In fact, modernist closet drama's utopian drive explains both its sometime reliance on or reference to earlier eras' modes and models of dramatic composition and its longing for a theater of the future; for, as Joseph Roach observes, nostalgia always has "designs on . . . the future."[29] Further, this utopian quality of closet drama jibes with Elizabeth Grosz's claim that utopia is "usually an enclosed . . . space"—that is, a closet.[30] In turn, what I want to emphasize about the uncloseting of closet drama is not merely that it is an unfolding in time of the utopian impulses figured in the space of the dramatic text but that those utopian impulses, even (and especially) in performance, are always deferred. As Jackson Mac Low allows a computer program, in part, to generate "his" voice, or as the performers in the Wooster Group interact with filmed images and laptop-generated noises, their mediatized bodies are performing beyond the limits of what Barnes or Stein could have imagined in or as embodied performance; but such performances are not, as a consequence, unqualified fulfillments of closet drama's potential energies. Philip Auslander is overtly skeptical of the idea that the interaction of stage and screen, for instance, "can convey a fuller idea of what it is to be human" and sees instead in the simultaneity of the two a strong lure for audiences away from the human and toward the filmic or otherwise mediatized elements of performance.[31] But what if stage and screen working together do not mean to convey a fuller sense of what it is to be human? Rather, what if they aim to gesture momentarily beyond the current possibilities of being human—not toward the post-human, exactly, but toward another incarnation (the next, if you like) of being human? In this case, performance has "caught up" to closet drama's vision not because it can envision what the theater previously could not but because it continues to postpone such questions as what humanity might entail and to posit the future as the place where such questions might be answered. Thus the uncloseting of closet drama is utopian in the sense that Jill Dolan imagines the utopian in performance, "as an index to the possible, to the 'what if,' rather than [as] a more restrictive, finite image of the 'what should be,' [which] allows performance a hopeful cast, one that can experiment with the possibilities of the future in ways that shine back usefully on a present that's always, itself, in process."[32]

To juxtapose Auslander's and Dolan's claims about performance is no innocent enterprise, since Dolan states plainly that she "believe[s] in all the things that Auslander disparages . . . [and has] experienced them all: . . . the magic of the theater; . . . the palpable energy that performances that work generate; and . . . the potential of the temporary communities formed when groups of people gather to see other people labor in present, continuous time, time in which something can always go wrong" (40). For his part, Auslander, in the preface to the revised edition of *Liveness,* writes that to see his position as a disparagement of the value of these experiences constitutes a misreading, and that he questions rather the availability in the first place of such experiences, "given the current cultural standing of live performance and the continued domination of mediatized forms" (xii). The tension between Auslander's and Dolan's positions is a tension, at root, about the place of the body in live performance; Auslander doesn't think that we can see it through the various technological manipulations to which it is routinely subject, whereas Dolan sees and feels nothing so clearly as this body when she goes to the theater (hence her emphasis on the "palpable" effect of live performance). While this impasse may seem, at first blush, to amount to little more than a difference of temperament, sensibility, or disposition between two critics who are unafraid to foreground their own experiences in their critical accounts of performance, I think that assessing their divergent points of view has a more significant purchase than that—and that assessing it through the lens of modernist closet drama can offer a fresh perspective on the important issues that they raise.

The body that belongs at once to a twentieth-century man and a fourteenth-century woman (who is also a fourteenth-century boy); the body whose very orifices mutate, unstably; the body that calls into question the distinction between the human and the animal, the living and the dead; the body whose desire becomes, retrospectively, the source of its own oxymoronically female paternity: these are some of the bodies, imagined in modernist closet drama, that I will examine more fully. And this (by no means exhaustive) catalogue of such bodies suggests a powerful resistance to the actor's body in real space and time and the limits of what that instrument can accomplish, or be made to seem to accomplish, through the various techniques of theatrical illusion. But the utopian deferral that I described above—both the deferral of concretely realizing utopian affect and the utopian as an affective deferral of concrete realization—is the complementary resistance that the actor's body brings to bear in the performance of modernist closet drama. Far from opposed to modernist closet drama's ambivalent relationship to embodiment, the bodies that uncloset this drama reproduce and even exceed such ambivalence in their own complexly gendered and sexual positions—and they achieve this reproductive capacity in part through the ways in which they are mediatized, just one subset of the ways in which the performing body is always *mediated*. Indeed, "the magic of the theater" that Dolan salutes depends upon the mediation of live bodies in performance, the mark of difference that tells us that such bodies belong to "other people" and not to the "groups of people" who watch them (and who might, unlike Auslander, be enthralled by these mediated bodies for all the ways in which they gesture to an elsewhere past themselves and their mediation). In so gesturing, these bodies that uncloset drama are not unlike the subjects who come out of the closet, because, as Amy Villarejo (following Judith Butler) suggests, "what is disclosed [in coming out] is to remain permanently unclear through the deferral of the signified."[33]

Thus performance often clarifies closet drama's meanings (and especially its queer meanings) precisely by identifying certain notions of clarification as untenable or phantasmatic; and the kinds of performance that can do this work are as intellectually sophisticated as more recognizable methods and models of cerebral inquiry. Underscoring the imbrication of *thinking* and *doing* in her analysis of British Romantic closet drama—and offering a useful corrective to narratives of the period that overlook women's

contributions to theater theory—Catherine B. Burroughs writes: "The opposition between closet and stage as it appears in the theoretical discourse
of the British Romantic period points us to a[n] . . . obstacle that has prevented us from recovering women's theatre theory written before 1900. This
is the tendency to associate the closet with reading only, to oppose it to theatricality, and to forget that, during the early nineteenth century, not only
did the phrase serve as a metaphor for privacy and intense intellectual engagement, but it also identified a literal space in which a variety of theatrical activities—many particular to women—took place."[34] I am interested
here in Burroughs's astute challenge to the faulty critical opposition between
"intense intellectual engagement" and "theatrical activities" because of the
almost uncanny ways in which her diagnosis can be mapped onto critical
prejudices and blind spots that sometimes emerge in my own period of
study. To be sure, modernist dramatic experiments reward close(t) reading, and many of their opaque meanings begin to become clear only to the
industrious student who pores over their words. Yet the most industrious
students have often been the actors, directors, and other performance artists
who have paid attention to these challenging texts, many of which have been
almost entirely overlooked by the academy—and the proof of their nonaca-
demic but serious and rigorous "reading" is in the traces of their performances. In other words, theatrical activity *is* an intense intellectual engagement that demands our attention not only as a historical phenomenon
worthy of study in its own right or in isolation from texts but also as a kind
of critical interpretation that reveals to us aspects of texts that would otherwise remain obscure in our own versions of criticism.[35] Reading modernist drama through the lens of performance offers a corrective to those
literary scholars who would privilege the former over the latter—to the
detriment, in my view, of richer understanding. Our understanding of the
queer textures of modernist closet drama is, in particular, enriched by a consideration of such drama's performance history. In performance, sexed and
gendered embodiment—or, more aptly, embodiment that calls into question the categories of sex and gender—constitutes an interpretive dimension that mere reading (or at least our fantasy of disembodied reading) does
not usually accommodate. Alert to this crucial, interpretive dimension of
performance, I identify this project with work in performance studies that
has emphasized the ways in which "the value of [some writing is] *contingent
upon* performance"[36] and, as Dwight Conquergood has observed, the ways
in which "enclosures"—such as those of dramatic texts?—"are poached"
in oral communications that resist regimes of body-discipline.[37]

At the same time, a project such as this one may offer a corrective, in the other direction, to those scholars of performance who would de-emphasize traditional forms of textuality. I take a cue here from W. B. Worthen, who writes compellingly of the ways in which performance study may, in its own authorizing gestures, be as guilty of certain kinds of occlusion as literary study:

> Stage vs. page, literature vs. theatre, text vs. performance: these simple oppositions have less to do with the relationship between writing and enactment than with power, with the ways that we authorize performance, ground its significance. . . . From the "literary" perspective, the meaning, and so the authority, of performance is a function of how fully it expresses the meanings, gestures, themes located ineffably in the structures of *the work,* which is taken both as the ground and origin of performance and as the embodiment of authorial intention. . . . The performative perspective generally avails itself of the same emphasis on origins: stage production is, in a sense, the final cause for writing plays, which gain their fullest, their essential meaning only in the circumstances for which they were originally intended: theatrical performance.[38]

Closet drama necessarily complicates and disrupts the notion that performance is the sine qua non of playwriting—although, as I have attempted to suggest through a nuanced examination of its contingencies, closet drama does not necessarily deny performance. Rather, this project demonstrates my conviction that—at least in cases where a written text hovers in the background of a performance—the latter cannot be thought through properly without a sophisticated consideration of the former. In no way does this mean that I prioritize textual authority over performance. Indeed, many of my readings of closet dramas will, in a limited sense, "de-authorize" the texts, as I reveal the ways in which multiple and sometimes contradictory meanings inhabit them—or impinge upon them from outside. Unlike Worthen, who makes a Barthesian distinction between the work and the text to which I do not strictly adhere, I do not want to bracket "intention" entirely—but I do want to suggest that intention is a complicated, unstable, often unavailable, and sometimes chimerical feature of a text. And when the text in question is a play, I read it, nonhierarchically, alongside other texts, among whose number the "text" of a given performance always figures prominently.

That close reading, even in a renovated guise, should be pursued at all requires perhaps, in our current critical climate, some further justification and contextualization. In *Libidinal Currents,* Boone claims for close textual reading a status as a practice not at odds with but working toward the same goal as cultural criticism—if both enterprises are predicated upon the use of focused analysis "to spot (and thereby slip through) the loopholes . . . of hegemonically legislated discourses," and when close reading is disarticulated from "the traditionally conceived formalist enterprise of upholding the autonomy and superiority of the art work" (24–25). With specific regard to the study of modern drama, Alan Ackerman makes a similar case for the compatibility of close reading, "theoretical generalization," and "moral obligation," as he traces the ways in which the rejection of the form/content division opens a space for rigorous examination of language (and other signs) in the service of philosophical investigation, social critique, indeed anything but the "privileging [of] an 'autotelic' text."[39] Enacting a version of these related assertions, I elaborate in this book the ways in which close reading is a necessary precondition for making visible modernist sexual politics and sexual ethics, their limitations and lacks, and the strategies of compensation for and supplementation to these limitations and lacks, in both theatrical and academic performance.

Attempting to serve multiple masters as a scholar of modernist, performance, and queer studies—and feeling, something like Saint Therese, "half in and half out" of each discipline—I have found an anchor through work in two kinds of archives. One is the sometimes intangible archive of experience, as I have attended performances as different as a reading by Jackson Mac Low and a production by the Wooster Group, or as I have conducted interviews with such figures as the director Elizabeth LeCompte and the poet and performer Bob Perelman. This lived and living research can be a welcome change to those of us who are accustomed to spending long hours in musty libraries, but the more conventional archive has proven exhilarating for me as well. Examining documents both at Yale University's Beinecke Library (home to the papers of Ezra Pound and Gertrude Stein) and at the University of Maryland's Hornbake Library (for the papers of Djuna Barnes), I have made discoveries that directly inform my understanding of modernist closet drama. Among Barnes's typescripts, I have considered and written extensively about two of her unpublished plays, on which no other scholars have yet written for publication. Stein's letters, manuscript drafts, and collections of books and other ephemera—some of them heretofore overlooked—have integrally guided and shaped my readings, as have some previously unconsidered manuscripts and letters in the Pound collection, particularly his early correspondence with Zukofsky.

The university library's archive is itself a kind of closet, where the closet is understood as both "the place of private study or secluded speculation" and a "private repository of valuables or . . . curiosities."[40] More generally, such spatial implications of the closet for closet drama must be considered alongside the temporal strategies of its enactment already discussed. We are used to conceiving of "the closet" as the site of homosexuality's (open) secret, but this formulation needs to be complicated. While I find useful and powerful Sedgwick's claim in *Epistemology of the Closet* that the closet's centrality has organized "a whole cluster of the most crucial sites for the contestation of meaning in twentieth-century Western culture," we must take care to avoid speaking of the closet anachronistically when thinking through such contestations of meaning as they pertain to modernism—and the meanings of the closet for modernist drama.[41] As George Chauncey reminds us (and as even a cursory glance at the *OED* entry for *closet* and its idiomatic uses suggests):

> Given the ubiquity of the term today and how central the metaphor of the closet is to the ways we think about gay history before the 1960s, it is bracing—and instructive—to note that it was never used by gay people themselves before then. Nowhere does it appear before the 1960s in the records of the gay movement or in the novels, diaries, or letters of gay men and lesbians. The fact that gay people in the past did not speak of or conceive of themselves as living in a closet does not preclude us from using the term retrospectively as an analytic category, but it does suggest that we need to use it more cautiously and precisely, and to pay attention to the very different terms people used to describe themselves and their social worlds.[42]

When I draw attention to the various closets configured in and by modernist closet drama, they may sometimes appear as cloisters, but a cloister is not necessarily the site of prohibition; indeed, these cloisters often transform into—or are at least juxtaposed with—bedrooms (another early meaning of closet), and bedrooms, too, may afford a space of privacy and (sexual) intimacy without necessarily setting the scene for secrecy or repression.

Of course, secrecy and repression do also abound in modernist closets. But we might remember at the same time that the word *closet* was once figuratively used to describe the "den or lair of a wild beast," for wildness and excess are as prominent in modernist closets as are restraint and constraint. Nor are these opposites always easily separable. The wildness of restraint and the excess of constraint have their own erotic appeal; or, as Cary Howie says of claustrophilia (the love of enclosures), "To be inside . . . is not to be sealed off: it is to be summoned, paradoxically, into a more concrete, ecstatic relation to what lies not just beyond but *within . . . boundaries.*"[43] To consider this claim in the specific context of twentieth-century sexuality, we might recall what D. A. Miller says of the bifurcated understanding that gay audiences have brought to bear on musicals like "*Gypsy* and its closeted kind," which simultaneously hide queer content and produce the spaces in which such queer content can find hiding places: "To perceive the closet was always also to perceive the multitude of conditions under which closeting was possible, to glimpse, even as it was being denied, *the homosexual disposition of the world.*"[44] Sometimes modernist authors produce proleptic versions of this closet and ask us to use a similar double vision to see its spaces clearly; at other times, they ask us to see through the double bind of the gay closet and appreciate a space unconstrained by its logic. In short, modernist closet drama's precarious and sometimes turbulent alternations (as well as blurred distinctions) between sexual secrecy and disclosure, between desire's impossibility and its realization, paradoxically anticipate both the gay closet and the performances that have sought to undo the closet's effects. As a series of related texts that resemble both the historical gay closet and the putatively liberating acts and gestures that oppose that closet, modernist closet dramas, to echo Whitman, contain multitudes; and this multitudinous capacity is the feature that has drawn performance practitioners to the texts that I, like them, read closely.

LITTLE BOXES

Alongside the idea of the closet, other spatial metaphors have helped me to articulate both the positions—conceptual and erotic—that modernist authors assume in their closet dramas and my own orientation toward those positions. In Chapter 1, "Fronting Pound," I consider Pound's various "fronts" or personae as I make my own frontal assault on his homophobia (as well as an assault on the idea that his writing is unilaterally homophobic). Chapter 2, "Bottoming Zukofsky," challenges the notion that modernists are preoccupied in any simple way with mastery, as Zukofsky proves himself the master of submission—only for Stein to reassert the modernist ego in Chapter 3, "Topping Stein," where I consider the ways in which the acquisition and maintenance of power inform Stein's erotic and dramatic writing. Finally, in Chapter 4, "Backing Barnes," I trace the logic by which Barnes looks backward to the family as the source and site of sexual cathexes, at the same time as I "back" her against the critical charge of mere sexual victimization.

Top, bottom, front, back—and on the side(s)? Here a word about chronology is necessary. Each of these four authors led an exceptionally long life, and many of the plays that I consider here postdate the period that we usually associate with so-called "high modernism." Nevertheless, a drama completed by Barnes, for instance, in 1958 or by Zukofsky in 1967 bears a closer aesthetic and theoretical resemblance to one of his or her own (or each other's) earlier works than it does to certain contemporaneous works by a younger generation of American writers. On the side, then, we find developments in the closet drama that I do not discuss but that are certainly worth attention and that could be fit into a complex genealogical schema, which would put such "newer" closet drama into dialogue with its modernist "predecessors." To cite one instance in passing, the dramatic experiments of Frank O'Hara can be read as an outgrowth of and response to modernist closet drama. Like Pound, O'Hara is interested in Nō drama (and even subtitles his short piece *Try! Try!* "A Noh Play"); and like Stein and Barnes—whose works challenge the notion of "modernist impersonality" —he draws upon personal experience to craft his drama. But the largely colloquial idiom in which he does so differs so markedly from the repetitive, quasi-Cubist diction of Stein's work or the dense, quasi-Jacobean style of Barnes that he must be considered a very different sort of queer writer and person. Unlike in any dialogue we encounter among the modernists, the character Kenneth says, in the unfinished play *Kenneth Koch: A Tragedy* (co-written with Larry Rivers), "I used to go and meditate in our oldest building which was built in 1938, it was so cool and restful. They called me 'queer' and I thought they meant I was a poet, so I became a poet. What if I'd understood them? Moses! what a risk I was running. I know one thing today, I have my roots, just like anybody else."[45] Like its title character, this play may have its roots in earlier closet drama—and O'Hara may know it—but the play has sprouted different branches. In addition to its formal dissimilarities, the joking invocation of the word *queer,* used by O'Hara with a slangy specificity (distinct from, say, Stein's more ambiguous line "Doctor Faustus a queer name"), locates his play in another world.[46]

In some respects. Among O'Hara's plays, I am drawn to this one in particular because of its "ending," when the other characters, tired of Kenneth's prattle, "*knock him down, drag him outside, and tar and feather him*" (132). This sudden eruption of aggression yokes O'Hara's play to those of his modernist forebears, whose works are all intimately, if not obsessively, concerned with various kinds of violent and sadistic display. When I first conceptualized this project, I had not expected the theme of violence to figure so prominently in modernist closet drama or to feature so heavily in my discussions thereof—and when, in the course of research and meditation, I realized that this preoccupation was an important one, I could not immediately formulate an overarching explanation to account for it. While it is certainly true that violence intersects with sexuality in nearly all of the works that I consider, the relationship between the two terms changes in subtle ways from one author's corpus to the next. For Pound, violence stands in metaphorically for sexuality that cannot, for one reason or another, be expressed explicitly, whereas for Barnes violence erupts as a *result* of unexpressed sexuality. Zukofsky figures homoerotic desires and encounters as violent ones in contradistinction to heteronormative placidity, as Stein vacillates between a critique of heterosexual violence and a recognition of the inescapability of similar violence in homosocial and queer contexts. Ultimately, the common feature of these negotiations is the inability of modernists to think sex apart from violence.

While this conflation may represent nothing new in the course of human history, I do want to suggest that there is some specificity to the modernist yoking of sex and violence. The level of carnage in the two world wars of the twentieth century was unprecedented, as was the immediacy with which it was seen or reported to and by people removed from explicit military engagement—and much of the drama that I examine in this project comments directly or obliquely on war. Pound translates Nō plays about combat during the First World War and Sophocles' *Electra* on the heels of the Second (and after his own incarceration at a Pisan detention center). Stein writes *Doctor Faustus Lights the Lights* in 1938 and loses the composer Lord Berners as a collaborator because of his crippling depression over the state of European affairs. Similarly, Barnes, writing after 1945, sets *The Antiphon* during World War II, and Zukofsky turns to projects like *Bottom: On Shakespeare* and *Rudens* after that same war leaves him disenchanted with more explicitly Marxist undertakings of the 1920s and 1930s. In an era during which brutality seemed to touch all aspects of life, even the most personal or quotidian, closet drama—a form that is itself associated with privacy—imagined sex and sexuality as perhaps inevitably violent affairs. It should be no surprise that we can identify similar cultural trends and phenomena in the early twenty-first century.

It should also be no surprise that this explanation of the modernist preoccupation with violence is, at best (and as any would be), a partial one.

Looking for other partial explanations to provide its supplement, I am drawn, appropriately enough, to a fragment: lines composed by Pound in 1924 for Canto XX, ultimately rejected for inclusion in his long poem, and recently discovered and discussed by Alec Marsh. The fragment is not a closet drama, but its preoccupation with sex and violence, and its "closeted" status as a scandalous piece of writing excluded from the published *Cantos,* make it a useful synecdoche for the kind of work more generally under consideration here:

> And coming back to the cabin (Sambo) unexpectedly
> Dinah having company , Sambo ,
>> (Dinah , who dat in yo' bed)
> St[r]uck unexpectedly.
>> Mah glory , Gawd my glory ,
>> boh, you dun cut Massa Washin'tun .
> George died of a hemorage , that is, throat trouble
> At Mt Vernon ,
>> and they put up a symbolic monument ,
>
> AGAMEMNON[47]

In this imagined scene of national origins, Pound exposes, in Marsh's words, the "forbidden sexuality" that constitutes, in its inseparability from slavery, "our true and secret history" (127). Of equal importance, the apposition of this scene with a mention of *Agamemnon* (a play that Pound would begin but never finish translating) indicates the pull toward closet drama as a space well suited to the exploration of such forbidden sexuality —and its distinctive Americanness. Indeed, passages such as this suggest the extent to which much queer closet drama in the early twentieth century has a national specificity; American history influences the violent nature of Pound's and others' sexual imaginations, and the political skeletons in the American closet make of it an especially rich stage for unconventional, furtive, and at times queer representation. To borrow a turn of phrase from Stein, the making of queer closet drama may be, among other things, the making of Americans.

My use here of such terms as *distinctive Americanness* and *the making of Americans* requires some qualification and clarification. Of course, modernism is an international phenomenon, and the transnational affinities and affiliations of modernist closet dramatists are well explored by Puchner in *Stage Fright.* As a complement to that work, I propose that, for a certain cluster of modernists, the writing of closet drama is inflected by their reckoning with—and ambivalent feelings about—the United States, both as a place and as an idea. National identity was negotiated in complex ways by the authors on whom I focus, three of whom were longtime expatriates and one of whom, Zukofsky, experienced Americanness in the crucible of his family's immigrant experience. If, as I have suggested, modernists' resistance to sexual ideologies shapes and is shaped by their resistance to dramaturgical conventions, then this nexus of resistance must also include the resistance to mythologies of "America"; for much queer modernist closet drama emerges from cathexes on sexuality, theatricality, *and* the nation.

As a group of authors marked by their profound ambivalence about these three concepts and their interrelations, Pound, Zukofsky, Stein, and Barnes are all inheritors and reshapers of the sensibilities of Henry James, a figure whose impact on these modernists has been well documented and whose influence palpably haunts their work (and the pages of this book). James, who is often and justly foregrounded in studies of American and British modernist fiction, is not, however, a modernist closet dramatist. As Nina Auerbach has convincingly argued, James's relationship to the theater is eminently Victorian, for he, like many prominent mid- and late-nineteenth-century contemporaries, "wrote for the theatre, longed to write for it, [and], failing to achieve theatrical success, transplanted theatrical values into the works that made [him] famous."[48] James does, nevertheless, prefigure significantly many of the concerns of modernist closet dramas and the key issues animating my treatment of them. Despite his firm desire to write for the existing mainstream theater on its own terms and his apology to his readers, in the prefatory note to his first series of *Theatricals* (1894), that the "humiliating confession of defeat" entailed by publishing unproduced plays is "the consolation—poor enough, alas!" of the failed, would-be commercial playwright, James did not believe that the public performance of plays was their only or even greatest purpose.[49] Demonstrating Worthen's notion that, in the late nineteenth and early twentieth centuries, print was the ever more prominent proof of a play's success, importance, and very substance, James lamented, "on more than one occasion, . . . the failure of the English-speaking audience to demand the text of a play with the same insistence as did the Continental audience,"[50] and wrote determinedly in "After the Play," "A play isn't fully produced until it is in a form in which you can refer to it."[51] Perhaps more important, James sometimes conceived of that written form "in which you can refer to" a play as a kind of closet. As he wrote in an 1875 review of Tennyson's *Queen Mary*, "The five-act drama—serious or humorous, poetic or prosaic—is like a box of fixed dimensions and inelastic material, into which a mass of precious things are [sic] to be packed away."[52] This definition of the drama recalls the meaning, discussed earlier, of closet as curio cabinet, and James's ensuing account of the "precious things" inside that closet sounds, to my ear, like a veiled description of the erotics of enclosure explored by Howie in his study of claustrophilia: "The precious things in question seem out of all proportion to the compass of the receptacle, but the artist has an assurance that with patience and skill a place may be made for each. . . . [The box] closes perfectly, and the lock turns with a click; between one object and another you cannot insert the point of a penknife" (181–82). What are these "things," after all, but the imaginary bodies of the fictional characters that populate a play and the interactions between them as the play's events unfold? In the thrillingly packed closet of the play text, which upon second thought seems more like a bedroom than a cabinet, those imaginary bodies, queerly "out of all proportion" to their environment and to one another, might enjoy the pleasures of tightness, touch, and friction conjured by the overdetermined language of James's prose.

Except that characters do not enjoy such pleasures, at least in any of the plays that James actually wrote. Rather, as James strove to create unobjectionable plays in the popular styles of the late nineteenth century, his kinkier energies—as well as the anxieties induced in part by his failure to meet with theatrical success—found expression instead in queer fictions. David Kurnick argues that, in *The Awkward Age* (which he all but calls a closet drama) and in response to the "dramatic fiasco" of *Guy Domville*'s poor reception, James creates a "phantom" or "'impossible' theater," liberated from the constraints of both dramatic realism and novelistic logic, in which "erotic permission" and "vibratory pleasure" enjoy a "robust," if elliptical, elaboration.[53] Chronologically speaking, we do not, however, have to look as far forward as *The Awkward Age* (1899) or even the equally twisted "The Turn of the Screw" (1898) to locate James's queer closets. In "Owen Wingrave" (1892), James opposes the queerly coded title character, whose good looks he keeps emphasizing for no apparent reason other than his own desirous investment in them, to a series of intertwined values: military glory, familial duty, and marital attachment, all of which Wingrave rejects when he refuses the army career that his family has chosen for him (as it has been chosen for all his male forebears), is threatened with disinheritance, and thus loses the affection of and economic means to wed Kate Julian, a friend and unofficial ward of his aunt.[54] In establishing this opposition, James also opposes two closets: the secluded space in which Wingrave enjoys the private pleasure of reading Goethe's poems, a pastime about which the narrator concludes that "there was no doubt that he was perverse" (70); and the White Room, a "dull, old-fashioned bedroom" in the Wingrave family's house haunted by the ghost of Wingrave's great-great-grandfather, who "struck [dead] in a fit of passion one of his children" in that room and later died there himself (88–89). Kate Julian taunts Wingrave into entering the White Room and confronting the ghost in order to prove his courage, and Wingrave, like the beaten child, dies there as a consequence of the confrontation. In acquiescing to the challenge that Miss Julian hurls at him, Wingrave abandons his queer closet, the site of his solitary "perversity," and submits to the White Room's "dull, old-fashioned" purity, symbolized by its name, and to a conception of manhood that is heteronormatively conditioned (his act is advocated by and will render him worthy of a suitable female companion); his literal death represents in part the death of queer possibility that flies in the face of this heteronormative compulsion.

The particular genius of the story lies in its limitation of point of view, as a consequence of which the precise content of the argument between Wingrave and Miss Julian remains unknown to the other characters and to the reader—closeted, as it were. One effect of this closeting is the creation of a space in which the queer reading of the story that I have sketched remains more strongly available than it would be, for instance, if we learned that Wingrave loves Miss Julian romantically and is invested in her sexually, and that such an investment (rather than a more complicated affective allegiance to her) motivates his decision to enter the White Room. This less vague—and thus less richly suggestive—version of the story is exactly the one that James produced when he uncloseted "Owen Wingrave" and rendered it as a one-act play, The Saloon (meaning "salon"), in 1908. Just as Owen Wingrave sacrifices himself in the face of Miss Julian's pressure, so, too, did James sacrifice the most interesting aspects of his story when faced with the pressure to make The Saloon dramatically conventional and commercially appealing by translating an ambiguous "offstage" encounter into an onstage lovers' quarrel.[55] (Following Michael Moon's readings of James, we might think of this change as a recentering of the "erotic offcenteredness" of the original piece.)[56] In turn, James was outraged when, in the play's brief 1911 run as a curtain-raiser at a London little theater, the producer chose, contrary to the playwright's wishes and intentions, to materialize the ghost dimly rather than plunge the stage into total darkness at the moment of Wingrave's reckoning.[57] Where the supernatural was concerned, James understood that its embodiment could box something pleasurably mysterious into an extremely limiting and thus dissatisfying package; whether he felt the same about the embodiment of Wingrave as a typical lover remains unclear, but the parallelism of the two moves invites the speculation that James may have channeled his disappointment about both compromises into his indignation over the one that he did not engineer or license. In any event, a theater that realizes boyfriends and phantoms is far from the phantom theater that Kurnick describes as a site for the "proliferation of . . . erotic possibilities" (115).

While the particular cautionary tale constituted by *The Saloon,* obscure in its day, would not have been available to the next generations of modernists, the larger patterns and lessons of James's engagement with the theater, of which it is an index, surely made an impact on them as they turned to the composition of queer closet drama. Wagner, against whose ideas of theatrical totality some modernists turned explicitly when they turned to closet drama and related kinds of dramatic expression, is for this reason the presiding nineteenth-century spirit of *Stage Fright* (32). Given the authors and issues that I have chosen to highlight, James may, more modestly but no less powerfully, stand here as an alternative, negative model through whom to understand modernists' suspicions and fears about the theater and their varied but related embraces of closet drama. Those queer embraces and the later performative embraces of the works thus engendered are the subject of this book.

1

fronting pound

PERSONAE

To propose a queer reading of Ezra Pound is, frankly, a little queer. Or to propose a recuperative queer reading of Pound, at any rate, must seem like a curious move, since homophobia can be easily, though somewhat anachronistically, linked to the more familiar burdens of fascism, anti-Semitism, and misogyny with which critics have rightly charged Pound. Indeed, we might go so far as to claim that Pound's palpable aversion to same-sex desires and practices cannot be thought *apart* from his aversions to capitalism, Jews, and at least certain kinds of women. As Jean-Michel Rabaté has compellingly argued, sodomy—a particular thorn in Pound's side in the early *Cantos*—is a so-called crime against nature yoked invariably to usury, and both are, for Pound, merely two egregious symptoms of a more comprehensive plague of deviance.[1] Language, for instance, like flesh and money, is also susceptible to the infectious and warping effect of deviance; as Rabaté underscores, "the progressive link . . . between blasphemy, sodomy, and usury is condensed by Pound into the term 'perversion'" (191).

Of course, it is Pound's own perverse, if not perverted, language that invites such speculation about his ideological proclivities. His overt intention, in such passages as his Hell Cantos, may be to purge culture through a serial accusation of its worst poisoners—and his proposed method of treatment may be the use of clear and searing language—but the result is far more ambiguous and confused than such an account would allow. Consider the spectacle that Pound makes of the anus in Canto XV:

skin-flakes, repetitions, erosions,
endless rain from the arse-hairs,
as the earth moves, the centre
  passes over all parts in succession,
a continual bum-belch
  distributing its productions.
Andiamo![2]

Sometimes, as the saying goes, the cure is worse than the disease. *Let's go,*
Pound may implore his reader in ostensible disgust, but he can't, in fact,
let go of the abominations in which he seems finally to revel more than he
reviles them. What begins for Pound as a mere catalogue of affronts ends
as an obsessive fixation on the objects of his contempt. The "repetitions"
that he identifies here are presumably the repeated acts perpetrated by—
or upon—the belching bum, yet it is Pound himself who can't help but repeat, and keep repeating, his pronouncements on sodomy in an overwrought stammer. "The great arse-hole" cited in Canto XIV is reinvoked
in Canto XV as "the great scabrous arse-hole," which is in turn juxtaposed
with "legs waving and *pus*tular" and a "condom full of black beetles" that
recall "Episco*pus,* waving a condom full of black-beetles" a mere page earlier (63–64, emphases added). Such repetitions don't read as carefully calibrated variations designed to register shades of nuance; rather, they suggest that Pound's raging voice has become contaminated by the very sex acts
whose noxious influence he purports to contain. As critics like David Savran
and E. Patrick Johnson claim, such language testifies to the ways in which
"the compulsory heterosexuality of [the] rather pathetic—if tyrannical—
[normative male] subject is always ghosted and disrupted by its forbidden
other,"[3] a homosexual specter who incites "not only . . . disavowal but also,
at the very least, . . . psychic mourning"[4] of the homosexuality being ambivalently disavowed.

This is queer, indeed. But the posture of a railing sermonizer whose ser-
mons betray his own preoccupation with sin (it is no small irony that "the
arse-belching of preachers" turns up on Pound's list of perversions) is just
that—a posture, and only one among the many postures, personae, or
"fronts" that Pound assumes. I imagine that a reading much more system-
atic than the one outlined here could expose any number of so-called deviant investments lurking within the agendas of *The Cantos,* but I invoke
these brief examples simply as a reminder that even at his most unctuous,
Pound is never as transparent or single-minded as we might suppose. More

important, the sensibilities expressed elsewhere in his corpus offer a much more direct counterbalance to the homosexual panic of *The Cantos* than can be generated by reading that poem against the grain of its own pieties.[5] In particular, I would cite the personae in Pound's closet dramas, *"Noh" Plays* and *Elektra*, as queer figures with whom Pound's equally queer identifications must challenge any monolithic understanding of his aesthetics and politics.

Pound's translations of Nō and ancient Greek drama, accomplished near the beginning and end of his career, respectively, are best understood as closet dramas chiefly and most simply because they were composed as literary exercises rather than as prompts for the stage. *"Noh" Plays,* published in 1916, was undertaken at the request of Mary Fenollosa. Her late husband Ernest, a scholar of political economy and philosophy who developed an interest in ancient Japanese art during a professorship at the University of Tokyo, had begun translations of and essays about Nō drama, for which his widow enlisted Pound as a literary executor and co-author. The final work, which intersperses Pound's translations of the plays with extensive commentary and annotations adapted and expanded from Ernest Fenollosa's notes, is meant to introduce an elite readership to "one of the most recondite" arts of the world, with the hope of inspiring further interest in and research of Nō.[6] "If one has the habit of reading plays and imagining their setting, it will not be difficult to imagine the Noh stage," Pound writes, with the assumption that he is addressing precisely the sort of audience who reads rather than produces plays and for whom his work would constitute exactly such a theater of the imagination (214). The translations' status as closet dramas is brought into even bolder relief when they are considered alongside the Nō-inspired plays of Yeats, to whom Pound introduced Nō while working simultaneously as Yeats's secretary and with Fenollosa's notes.[7] As Martin Puchner makes clear, Yeats's attraction to Nō was motivated by an antitheatrically marked desire to renovate modern performance, and particularly the Western actor's disposition in modern performance; but a performance space whose alteration is governed by "a specifically theatrical orientalism" is, nonetheless, still a performance space (125). In contrast, Pound's closet orientalism takes the form of savoring and fetishizing the book that encloses supposed Eastern secrets, which can be disclosed only to the properly oriented reader—in this case, ironically, one as queerly oriented as Pound proves in his approach to Nō material.

In the case of Pound's *Elektra,* written during the period of his confinement in St. Elizabeths Hospital and in collaboration with the scholar

Rudd Fleming, the text was literally closeted for nearly forty years. Pound's friendship with Fleming led to the collaboration not only because of Fleming's knowledge of ancient Greek language and culture, but also and more pragmatically because Pound wanted the translation to be published in Fleming's name. As Richard Reid summarily explains, "Pound did not wish it to appear that he was 'sane' enough to translate Greek," given his "precarious legal situation":[8] as a consequence of pro-fascist radio broadcasts made during World War II, Pound was first confined to an American detention camp near Pisa (initially in a cage), then transferred to the United States to be tried for treason. In response to Pound's controversial plea of insanity, a special federal jury found him incompetent to stand trial, and he was sent to St. Elizabeths, a public psychiatry facility in Washington, D.C., where he remained for twelve years—and where work like the translation of *Electra* could call into serious question his supposed incapacity to face criminal charges.

Ultimately, Pound did not seek publication of the translation, and the surviving copies of the manuscript remained unpublished until Carey Perloff unearthed and produced the play in 1987 for the Classic Stage Company, an off-Broadway theater founded in 1967, housed on East 13th Street since the 1970s, and "committed to re-imagining the classical repertory for a contemporary American audience."[9] Following this production, both a popular and a scholarly edition of the text appeared. Exactly why Pound chose never to publish the play in his own lifetime remains unclear; after his release from St. Elizabeths, he no longer had to fret over legal complications that might ensue from his authorship of the translation. Whatever the reason, *Elektra* was, until Perloff's production, a closet drama in the narrowest senses of the term. Cloistered in his room at St. Elizabeths, Pound could share his work only with a coterie of one—Rudd Fleming—as "the two men took turns reading the Greek aloud, discerning each rhythmic choice and then devising English equivalents."[10] After Pound's death, the readership increased only barely and by the thinnest thread of connections: James Laughlin passed Carey Perloff a Xerox of the original manuscript's sole duplicate, access to which was limited to patrons of Yale University's Beinecke Library—somewhat like visitors' restricted access to Pound himself in the late 1940s.

The likeness of sequestered manuscript to sequestered author is not the only parallel to be drawn between the life of the translator and his (and Sophocles') art. Richard Reid astutely locates Pound's attraction to *Electra* in the particular and precarious position that he occupied in the supposed time of peace following the devastation of the Second World War; he also links the project to Pound's unfinished translation of *Agamemnon* in the early 1920s:

> The choice, too, of Sophocles' *Elektra* instead of, say, the *Libation Bearers* of Aeschylus is equally revealing. That is, in yet another postwar period, why should Pound not pursue his earlier interest in the *Oresteia* and just reëmphasize the destructiveness and futility of a seemingly endless series of bloody recriminations? For such would have been consistent with his proclaimed view of both the first and second World Wars, that indeed the history of our century continued what is a single perennial war interrupted by the mere "parenthesis of peace," as he put it. . . . But to follow upon the *Agamemnon* with a *Libation Bearers* would be to imply the third play of the Aeschylean trilogy, the *Eumenides,* and [its] recuperative vision. . . . Sophocles' eschewal of the trilogy in favor a single play might be interpreted as one way of ruling out the future. And to a poet for whom the future is very much in doubt, and a trial by jury obviated, Sophocles could well prove the safer bet. (xiii)

As Reid pursues this line of thought, he suggests that "the voice of the poet rings throughout the many various voices of the play, and perhaps in none more so than Orestes'" (xviii). Here I deviate from Reid's otherwise fine reading and would suggest instead that Pound's most intense identification as a translator associates him with Electra—and that the complex and multilayered interplay of his voice with hers creates a node of specifically sexualized disturbance in the already disturbed and disturbing world of Sophocles' drama. Similarly, I will argue that Pound's cross-gender identifications with the unusual female figures in Nō drama—and his willful mistranslation of at least one Nō play—constitute an actively, and at times aggressively, queer approach to his source texts. In what is perhaps a more passive and unwitting role, Pound is also the transmitter, along with more perfunctory information about performance practices in the Japanese theater, of a tradition of same-sex erotic practices inextricably linked to the origins, composition, and staging of Nō drama. Furthermore, in both his active and passive guises as a queer translator, Pound is continually and consistently drawn to material in which eruptions of violence stand in for "unnameable," transgressive sexual confrontations. Ironically, a man who had no trouble naming the "endless rain from the arse-hairs" and "the great scabrous arse-hole" proves queerest in his management of coded expressions and evasive strategies of "perversion." These strategies are reimagined

by Perloff's production of *Elektra*, to which I will turn at the end of this chapter and in which race, as a libidinous category, participates queerly in performance.

"THE BODY IS THERE IF YOU SEE IT"

In the fall of 1913 Mary Fenollosa sent Ezra Pound the following letter, worth quoting at length in order to tease out its many rich implications:

Dear Ezra:—

Please don't get discouraged at the ragged way this manuscript is coming to you. As I said yesterday, it will get there in time,—which is the most important thing.

For instance, chronologically, the lectures taken down hastily by my husband, from old Umèwaka Minoru are so rough, and so many abbreviations are used, that I can't send them until I have time to make quite copious notes to help you understand. It is going to be somewhat of a puzzle, at best.

In these notes the initials, "U. M[.]" are constantly used. Sometimes they are put "M.U.," for, to this day the Japanese are a little undecided whether to place the family name first, according to their own custom, or last. In any case, whenever you see these initials together they mean the old lecturer. He was brought up in the last Shogun's court, and comes from a long line of famous Nōh players. He had all the costumes, masks, literature and traditions. . . . He had two beautiful young sons, still living and acting—whether real or adopted I am not sure, but that doesn't matter in Japan. The son who is adopted for reasons of fitness, talent, and capability of carrying on an artistic tradition is considered more real than a son who is merely of the flesh. All the great artists of old times adopted successors this way. These sons, also very often referred to in the notes, and in the studies of the Nōh plays, were Manzaburo Umèwaka and Takeyo Umèwaka. Both were beautiful,—the former, a tall and rather stout youth, did not look unlike a picture of a cavalier by Franz Hals, and the younger, our teacher in the singing of Nōh, was more like a soulful and very handsome East Indian poet than a Japanese. I hope I come across a photograph of him, but I haven't yet. However I have an excellent one of the old Umèwaka to send.

I shall go over these notes of his lectures, and wherever you see new ink writing you will know that I put it.

I must explain at more length the recurring term "cats." This would surely be a puzzler. At the back of the stage in many,—in fact most, of the pieces, there are always two queer old, old musicians. . . . They have weird little drums, and at intervals, during the perfromance [*sic*], they utter the most astonishing sounds, suppressed wails, throaty gurgles, and muted banshee howls. These sounds are more like the noises of back-yard fence cats than anything else on earth, and the Professor [Fenollosa] and I got into the way of calling them "cats." I didn't realize that he had accepted the term seriously enough to put it all through the notes. . . . You will see also frequent reference to "Mr. H." This always means little Mr. Hirata a pupil of my husband's, who always went to the Nōh performances with us, and did the translations. I don't think much of his literary style. Neither will you. I should suggest that the examples you wish to present in full should be taken only from those pieces where the Professor has written out the Japanese words too, and given the literal translation.

Please remember, from the first, that whenever I say "suggest," I mean just that thing, and nothing more stringent. What I am hoping is that you will become really interested in the material, absorb it in your own way, and then make practically new translations from the Japanese text as rendered into Romanji. It seems going ahead of myself a little, but I might as well tell you the Nōh pieces that have seemed to us most beautiful. I think that first I would place "Kinuta." Old U. M. considered it so, and also said that it took nearly a life-time, and much prayer and fasting, to learn to sing properly. . . . This is a big enough dose for one day. When you get into it, please don't hesitate to ask me questions. I only wish I were there with you and Yeats, working on it. I am homesick for London already.

Mary Fenollosa[11]

Toward the end of her letter, Mary Fenollosa is careful to qualify her many exhortations to Pound as mere suggestions, "and nothing more stringent." The letter is, nevertheless, full of caveats and explanations of the things that Pound *must* understand and *ought* to do: he must understand who U.M. is and what the word *cats* signifies; he ought to disregard the translations of Mr. Hirata and place the play *Kinuta* first in his estimation. What's more, Fenollosa positions herself as the one guarantor able to steer Pound correctly through the difficulties of translation: only she can make "quite copious notes" to render the manuscript legible, and only she can answer the questions that Pound should not "hesitate to ask" her. At last, she incorporates herself into the literal scene of translation, if only as a spectral presence who will haunt the site: "I only wish I were there with you and Yeats, working on it." "There," in the moment of Fenollosa's letter writing, was Stone Cottage in Sussex, where the two writers had decamped to escape the "whirl" (in Pound's formulation)[12] of Bloomsbury and where, as A. Walton Litz observes, "joint work on the Noh gave a sense of common purpose to this and the succeeding two winters."[13] An intense homosociality, shading ever so delicately into the homoerotic, also marked the time at Stone Cottage, where intellectual activity gave way to intimate athleticism as "Pound taught Yeats fencing to improve his health."[14]

In this context, how best to understand Fenollosa's lush and lingering portrayal of two striking Nō actors? Is the image of the Umèwaka youths, one like "a picture of a cavalier by Franz Hals" and the other "like a soulful and handsome East Indian poet," yet another important detail that Pound must keep in mind, and is the photograph of the latter one more crucial artifact that ought to guide his work? Fenollosa emphasizes the beauty of the actors so longingly that her description becomes an implicit request for Pound to identify with her desire. Equally implicit is the suggestion that the desire for the actors is not hers alone. Whether the Umèwakas are adopted is immaterial, she explains, because "the son who is adopted for reasons of fitness, talent, and capability . . . is considered more real" than an actual son, and "all the great artists of old times adopted successors this way." Fenollosa hovers here near an account of a tradition of man-boy love that was integral to the evolution of Nō. Indeed, the sexual allure that young actors held for older men played a foundational role in the earliest stages of the Nō theater; as William MacDuff attests, "In about 1375, it was the physical beauty of the young Zeami (as well as the artistry of his father) that inspired the shogun Yoshimitsu to bring the Kanze troupe to his court —and Zeami to his bed—and set the stage for the development of classical *nō* drama."[15] Thomas Blenman Hare, who corroborates this account, adds that it was not the sex of the young Zeami that troubled the shogun's advisers and other members of the aristocracy but the fact that "Zeami seemed to come from among the lowest classes in society."[16] Class confusion was much more threatening to the imperial old guard than homoeroticism, which played a principal role not only in the private lives and public performances of Nō practitioners but also in the theorizations of the actor's craft by Zeami, who went on to compose the most important plays and treatises of the Nō. His discussions of the *hana* (Flower) and *yugen* (Grace) of Nō actors make clear that the success onstage of young male performers depends more on the sensual charm that they exert on their audiences than on the development of artistic skill. Of boys aged eleven or twelve, he writes: "In the first place, a boy's appearance, no matter in what aspect, will produce the sensation of Grace. And his voice at this age will always sound charming as well. Because of those two strong points, any defects can be hidden and the good points will be made all the more evident. On the whole, it is better not to teach any fine points concerning Role Playing for a child's performance, for such knowledge would make his performances at this stage seem inappropriate and, in fact, hinder further progress in his art. . . . With the appearance and voice of a child, a boy actor, if he shows skill in his performance, can hardly give a bad impression."[17] Just as the boy actor in shogunate Japan was an object of desire both onstage and off, so, too, might the medieval boy undergoing religious training participate in a liaison with an older man. As MacDuff explains, "Noblemen sent their sons, aged roughly from seven to fourteen, to be educated at [Buddhist] monasteries, and it was common knowledge that priests there often fell in love with their young acolytes, or *chigo*. Numerous sources detail the affairs between priests and young aristocrats" (249). By the end of the fifteenth century, such affairs inspired a series of popular stories, called the *chigo monogatari;* but even earlier, this manifestation of man-boy love, coupled with the similar erotic attachment between a samurai warrior and his young companion, or *wakashu,* provided the scaffolding and subtext for a number of Zeami's and others' Nō plays, among which MacDuff cites *Tanikō, Tsunemasa,* and *Atsumori* as chief examples (250–55).

Mary Fenollosa certainly underscores the beauty of young Nō actors, and she seems to intuit the importance of their beauty to their art, but to what extent she or her husband might have understood the rich homoerotic legacy of Nō drama and theater remains unclear. Fenollosa's notes, at any rate, are not explicit on the subject, and Pound seems to have been in the dark about the homoerotic connotations of some Nō plays, even as he transmitted them to his English-speaking audience. Consider his foreword to the play *Tsunemasa,* in which he writes, "The Noh, especially the Noh of spirits, abounds in dramatic situations, perhaps too subtle and fragile for our western stage, but none the less intensely dramatic. Kumasaka is martial despite the touch of Buddhism in the opening scene, where the spirit is atoning for his past violence" (264). Perhaps undetected by Pound, part of the subtlety and fragility that he senses in these plays owes to the delicacy with which desire is expressed; and what lies behind "the touch of Buddhism" at which he seems, ever so slightly, to turn up his nose is the whiff of homosexuality that is indeed implied in the texts of *Kumasaka* and *Tsunemasa*.

Kumasaka concerns the spiritual transformation of its eponymous protagonist, a plundering highwayman who repents his banditry after a fatal encounter with a beautiful young boy named Ushiwaka. In the first part of the play, the ghost of Kumasaka appears in the village of Akasaka and asks a traveling novitiate priest to pray for "[a] certain man [who] died on this day"—none other than Kumasaka himself—so that he can "enter the gates of Paradise" (249–50). The ghost appears not as Kumasaka, however, but in the form of an old priest, and reveals his true identity only in the second part of the play; here he tells the full story of his life and death with the aid of a chorus, which "sometimes speaks what the chief characters are thinking" and "sometimes . . . describes or interprets the meaning of their movements" (249). Kumasaka describes his final mortal night, on which he raided an inn where a great feast had taken place. He explains that he and his men waited for the revelers to fall asleep before attacking, "but there was a small boy with keen eyes, about sixteen or seventeen years old, and he was looking through a little hole in the partition, alert to the slightest noise" (253). As Kumasaka's tale builds in intensity and suspense, the image of a beautiful, sleepless boy, gazing through a chink in the wall, is certainly an eroticized one, but the overdetermination of the figure's desirability isn't complete until Kumasaka's next, breathless revelation: "We did not know it was Ushiwaka." For a contemporary reader, as perhaps for Pound, this may seem like an arbitrary detail, yet for the play's original audience, the utterance of the name "Ushiwaka" would have conjured a host of significant associations. As William MacDuff explains, "Ushiwaka is the subject of epics that note his androgynous beauty as a *chigo,* his devotion to his mentor, . . . his skill with the flute, [and] his supernatural talent for the martial arts"; in his incarnation as "the popular boy-hero of *nō* drama," he emphasizes a "shift in erotic tastes" from the *chigo* to the slightly older *wakashu* as the political power of the samurai class grew at the beginning of the thirteenth century (252–53).

Thus when Kumasaka names the boy who will defend the inn as Ushiwaka, and when the priest responds, "It was fate," we ought not only to be primed for the inevitable, climactic combat between the bandit and the boy but also to read this combat as a metaphor for sexual climax. At this point in the action, the chorus takes over the storytelling as the other actors re-create the duel in a symbolic and highly stylized dance. The chorus's words conjure pointedly the sexual tension between the man and the boy: "What can he do, that young chap, if I ply my secret arts freely? Be he god or devil, I will grasp him and grind him. . . . So he drew back, and holding his long spear against his side, he hid himself behind the door and stared at the young lad" (254). The illicit connotation of Kumasaka's "secret arts"; Ushiwaka's ability to arrest Kumasaka's gaze; the phallic significance of Kumasaka's "long spear" pressed against the side of his body; the coital fury of Kumasaka's intention to "grasp" and "grind" the boy—all of these elements contribute to the erotic intensity of the moment. But ultimately the dance itself, more than the chorus's lavish verbal description, must convey the sexual spark between the two actors. In a later exegetic section of "Noh" Plays, Pound quotes at length from Fenollosa's essays on the Nō, including the following descriptive passage on Kumasaka's dance: "In Kumasaka the boy-warrior, Ushiwaka, fights a band of fifteen giant robbers in the dark. They fight with each other also. One by one, and two by two, they are killed. At one time all are dancing in double combat across stage and bridge. The Noh fencing with spear and sword is superb in line. In the conventional Noh fall, two robbers, facing, who have killed each other with simultaneous blows, stand for a moment erect and stiff, then slowly fall over backward, away from each other, as stiff as logs, touching the stage at the same moment with head and heel" (281). To be sure, Pound was well-versed in enough literatures beyond the classical Japanese to understand the ways in which death often serves as a trope for sexual extinction. And even though Pound had never seen a play of this sort staged, Fenollosa's loaded description of the dancers' carefully choreographed movements, "erect and stiff," "as stiff as logs," could have easily raised his brow. The palpable sexual charge of Kumasaka's fight scene lends a retrospective irony to Pound's macho approval of the play's "martial" elements, "despite the touch of Buddhism"; for even without sufficient knowledge of Japanese cultural history to understand the erotic role of the Buddhist monk's chigo, it is precisely in Kumasaka's overt violence that its covert homoeroticism is most readily legible.

Much less apparent, even to the most discerning eye, is the homosexual subtext of Tsunemasa, which tells the story of a slain boy whose spirit returns briefly to earth to rekindle the joys of his former life. William MacDuff offers an account of the play's provenance that provides a useful context for its atmosphere of loss:

> [The play] is based on an account in the epic Heike monogatari in which the Taira prince, Tsunemasa, refuses to abandon the fallen capital with-

out first visiting his former mentor, the abbot of Ninna-ji temple. Tsunemasa spent the ages of eight to thirteen there, during which time he rarely left the abbot's side; in return, the abbot so favored Tsunemasa above all others that he gave the boy a centuries-old Chinese *biwa* [lute] which had been designated an imperial treasure. The parting of mentor and protégé is highly romanticized in the tale. Tsunemasa at last breaks away with an impassioned promise to the abbot: "Never will I cease to desire / To remain here by your side." (251)

The Nō play based on the tale picks up this thread after Tsunemasa's death in battle. An old priest holds up the biwa with which the abbot—in Pound's mistranslation, "the Emperor"—honored the boy, and "offer[s] this lute to his spirit in place of libation" (264). As a "reward for this service," Tsunemasa's spirit materializes to play the lute once more. After some disbelief on the part of the priest that he has actually invoked Tsunemasa ("O, do I, or do I not see you?"), the spirit prefaces his performance with the following account of his youth: "When I was young I went into the court. I had a look at life then. I had high favour. I was given the Emperor's biwa. That is the very lute you have there. It is the lute called 'Seizan.' I had it when I walked through the world" (265–66). This description of Tsunemasa's "high favour," coupled with his possession of the emperor's phallic lute, is certainly redolent of the *chigo*'s sexual indenture to an older man, but to what extent did Pound, like the incredulous priest, see or not see this aspect of the spirit? Upon Tsunemasa's first appearance, the priest declares, "I see the form of a man, a faint form," and he and the spirit debate whether a ghost's voice can have a corporeal dimension, a proposition to which Tsunemasa responds, "[The body] is there if you see it" (265). Similarly, the current of man-boy love running through the play is there if we see it, but its presence is likewise faint, and it is questionable whether Pound understood the romantic and sexual pining implied by the spirit's departing words: "Pitiful, marvellous music! I have come down to the world. I have resumed my old playing. And I was happy here. All that is soon over" (266–67). In his foreword to the play, Pound praises the directness with which the play evokes a sense of longing, in language "as clear as Dante's. 'Era già l'ora che volge il disio'" (264). Nevertheless, *Tsunemasa*'s clear and simple language ultimately serves indirection more than directness; and Pound's quotation of this famous line from Dante's *Purgatorio*, in which the "desire" expressed is for old friends rather than old lovers, suggests that the erotic dimension of the Nō play may have been lost on him.

In both *Kumasaka* and *Tsunemasa*, bodily violence intersects with sex and sexuality in important ways. In the former play, a violent death stands in the place of a sexual act; in the latter, violent death stands in the way of a romantic attachment's full consummation. Whether representing or impeding sexual union, the martial practices to which Pound is drawn are intimately bound to the sexual practices that inform Nō drama. In a different key, violent passions and actions also inform the Nō drama focused on the roles of women—but here, as in the case of the play *Awoi No Uye,* the violence of the texts themselves is matched and even exceeded by the violence done to the text by Pound in provocative mistranslation.

LOST IN TRANSLATION

In the introduction to *"Noh" Plays,* Pound approves of Nō drama at least partially on the basis of its rejection of mimesis: "There has been in Japan from the beginning a clear distinction between serious and popular drama. The merely mimetic stage has been despised." Though Nō drama is not, by this account, "merely" mimetic, it participates nevertheless in some version of mimesis, as Pound's next comment indicates: "The Noh holds up a mirror to nature in a manner very different from the Western convention of plot" (221). However the Nō may deviate from Western conventions, "hold[ing] up a mirror to nature" seems to conform to the classic definition of mimesis—and indeed, Pound likens Nō drama to the very model of mimesis in the Western theatrical tradition: ancient Greek drama. As Pound explains, both Nō drama and "the Greek plays" present "known [figures such as] Oedipus in a known predicament" (222).

How is it that Nō both is and isn't mimetic, and what is it about the Nō's transcendence of the "merely" mimetic that Pound finds so appealing? Yamazaki Masakazu, who has written an introduction to the English translations of Zeami's treatises, helps to untangle the complicated relationship of Nō to mimesis:

> In Zeami's analysis of actual acting, one notices that he counterposes two basic methods, imitation and becoming. "Imitation" means to copy gestures and facial expressions realistically. It means to observe a human action, analyze it, and reproduce it consciously in detail. On the other hand, "becoming" means that the actor assimilates himself into the emotions of the character. . . . When he has completely assimilated himself into the character, he fills his heart and mind with the emotions of that character alone, and tries to allow those emotions to move his body with their own force. At such times, he has become completely united

with his own body, and he can forget about each specific gesture and facial expression. . . . According to Zeami, ideal acting is founded on the unity of these two methods.[18]

While Zeami's theory of acting involves a balanced interplay of imitation and becoming, it is clearly the idea of becoming that attracts Pound. Indeed, he adapts with admiration from Fenollosa's notes an anecdote that captures perfectly the opposition of becoming to imitation:

> Imitation must not be wholly external. There is a tradition of a young actor who wished to learn Sekidera Komachi. . . . He followed a fine old woman, eighty years of age, in the street and watched her every step. After a while she was alarmed and asked him why he was following her. . . . He confessed that he was an ambitious Noh actor and wanted to play Komachi.
>
> An ordinary woman would have praised him, but she did not. She said it was bad for Noh . . . to imitate facts. For Noh he must feel the thing as a whole, from the inside. He would not get it copying facts point by point. All this is true. (241)[19]

Both Masakazu's and Fenollosa's accounts of becoming as a Nō acting technique emphasize the importance of emotional interiorization, the incorporation of personal qualities that borders on possession—in short, what we might call a deep and powerful identification. Particularly in the case of female roles, identification must compensate for a variety of technical features of Nō that might impede the successful embodiment of a character: the use of masks, the elaborate choreography, and the sheer physical disparities between adult male actors and very young or very old female figures. But it is not simply the case that realistic imitation could not, by itself, guarantee an effective performance within the confines of a highly stylized, all-male theater. Beyond the practical necessity of an approach that is not strictly imitative, identification has theoretical purchase as a philosophical and even spiritual *good.* "All this is true," Pound says with finality of the old woman's valorization of becoming, and of course he means not just that the anecdote must be believed as a true story but that it extols a belief with truth value. In turn, Pound's belief in the positive value of identification leads him to attempt it as a translator of Nō drama. Just as the actor in drag must, through identification, overcome material impediments to portray a woman like Komachi, so, too, must Pound hurdle a major obstacle—his lack of knowledge of Japanese, and his consequently total reliance on Fenollosa's notes—in order to render Komachi's language in English that is "felt as a whole, from the inside."

As he translates the Zeamian method of becoming from the medium of acting to the medium of translation, Pound also approximates something like the Bergsonian process of becoming, articulated in such texts as *The Creative Mind* and guided by the principle that "each object is more than itself, contains within itself the material potential to be otherwise and to link and create a continuity with the durational whole that marks each living being."[20] More recently, Deleuze and Guattari, influenced strongly by Bergson's philosophy, have viewed such becoming as the province par excellence of the writer—and specifically of the modernist writer. In this regard, they provide another useful angle from which to understand the radical implications of Pound's identificatory strategies as a translator; as they explain:

> When Virginia Woolf was questioned about a specifically women's writing, she was appalled at the idea of writing "as a woman." Rather, writing should produce a becoming-woman as atoms of womanhood capable of crossing and impregnating an entire social field, and of contaminating men, of sweeping them up in that becoming. . . . The rise of women in English . . . writing has spared no man: even those who pass for the most virile, the most phallocratic, such as Lawrence and Miller, in their turn continually tap into and emit particles that enter the proximity or zone of indiscernibility of women. In writing, they become-women.[21]

Though Deleuze and Guattari are thinking here principally of novelists, we might easily add Pound to their Anglo-American list of "those who pass for the most virile, the most phallocratic" among modernist writers. And even though no one resisted the "contaminating" influence of women in the "social field" as strenuously as Pound did at times, we find him positively embracing the principle of "becoming-woman" in his *"Noh" Plays.*

Reading the translations, we get a sense of Pound's identifications with female figures not just from the passionate language in which he renders their stories but from the formal structure of the book as a slow unfolding of plays bracketed by lengthy essays and notes. Consider the first play in the volume, *Sotoba Komachi,* in which two priests "meet with what appears to be an old woman sitting on a roadside shrine—though she is really the wraith of Ono [no Komachi], long dead" (223). Immediately before and after his translation of the text, Pound speaks in his own voice. First he announces that "[a] play very often represents someone going on a journey" (222); then he pre-

sents the text, following which he offers the historical detail, "Umewaka Minoru acted Ono in this play on March 8, 1899. It is quite usual for an old
actor, wearing a mask, to take the part of a young woman" (225). The text
itself is incredibly short; thus we slip so quickly from Pound's voice into Ono's
(the dominant one in the play) and back into Pound's again that the two
become conflated. Indeed, if the "play represents someone going on a journey," then it is difficult not to read the journey, on a metatextual level, as
Pound's journey of identification with Ono; and if it is "usual for an old actor
to take the part of a young woman," then we also come to understand Pound,
and not just Umèwaka, as an older man donning Ono's mask as he delivers
into English her highly emotional and sexually charged monologue:

ONO

Daft! Will you hear him? In my own young days I had a hundred
letters from men a sight better than he is. They came like rain-drops in
May. And I had a high head, may be, that time. And I sent out no answer. You think because you see me alone now that I was in want of a
handsome man in the old days, when Shocho came with the others—
Shii no Shocho of Fukakusa . . . that came to me in the moonlight and
in the dark night and in the nights flooded with rain, and in the black
face of the wind and in the wild swish of the snow. He came as often as
the melting drops fall from the eaves, ninety-nine times, and he died.
And his ghost is about me, driving me on with the madness. (224–25)

The madness of which Ono—and Pound—speak here is the fury of a sexual longing that has been unleashed but can no longer be quenched. In
Pound's rendering, Shii no Shocho's nocturnal visits to Ono shade into the
language of seminal eruption, when "he [comes] as often as the melting
drops fall from the eaves, ninety-nine times, and he die[s]." The violence
of their passionate encounters commingles with the violence of the elements
—flooding rain, black wind, wild snow—as Pound imagines himself, with
Ono, in the grip of a powerful desire for the "handsome man." It is no doubt
surprising to think of Pound identifying with such an overtly feminine sexuality, but he makes patently clear that such identification, though difficult,
is the necessary prerequisite for the pleasure he derives from the translations. Later in the book, he offers a kind of reimagining of Keatsian negative capability, or the "capability of being in uncertainties, Mysteries, doubts,
without any irritable reaching after fact and reason,"[22] as the more specific
capability to venture uncertainly and perhaps irrationally into sympathetic
identifications; as he explains, "I do not say that this sympathy [with the

characters] is easily acquired. It is too unusual a frame of mind for us to fall into it without conscious effort. But if one can once get over the feeling of hostility, if one can once let himself into the world of the Noh, there is undoubtedly a new beauty before him. I have found it well worth the trial" (237). Is Pound's insistence here on the "unusual" nature of these sympathetic identifications, his "hostility" to which he must struggle to overcome, a case of the lady (or the translator in lady's clothes) protesting too much? Is his emphasis on the radical alterity and exteriority of the characters in Nō drama a defense against what David Savran calls the "extraordinary anxiety produced by a man's confrontation with the [feminine] Other" that he internalizes?[23]

Pound's translation of the play *Awoi no Uye* suggests that the difficulty of his source material—and his consequent "trial" to identify with it—is perhaps just camouflage to cover his desire to plunge himself into sexually overwrought, feminine states of mind. In the headnote to the translation, Pound says, "I give the next two plays, Awoi no Uye and Kakitsubata, with very considerable diffidence. I am not sure that they are clear; Japanese with whom I have discussed them do not seem able to give me much help" (323). Indeed, from a strictly literal point of view, *Awoi no Uye* is one of Pound's least accurate (and therefore least "successful") translations. Nobuko Tsukui, whose book *Ezra Pound and Japanese Noh Plays* assesses just such inaccuracies, explains the plot of the original play and weighs it against the major errors of Pound's version:

> The play is based on Book 9, "Aoi no Ue," of the *Tale of Genji.* The story of the play is as follows. Aoi no Ue is very ill, apparently possessed by some evil spirit. Efforts to cure her have been in vain. Then a witch (Tsure: Teruhi no miko) is called in and asked to find out by her craft who or what the evil spirit is. When the witch begins to chant her spells, Shite (the spirit of Rokujo) appears and through her complaints shows the deep-rooted hatred she has for Aoi no Ue. Because Rokujo is disappointed, distressed, envious and jealous, she strikes Aoi no Ue and disappears. Then Waki (an exorcist named Yokawa no Kohijiri) appears at the request of the court to cure Aoi no Ue. The exorcist begins his powerful prayer, causing the spirit of Rokujo to reappear in the form of a female demon. Now the contest between the exorcist and Rokujo begins. The exorcist finally wins by reciting the Buddhist scripture called Hannya Kyo, which frightens Rokujo away. . . .
>
> The subject of the play is the love and jealousy of a lady of noble

birth. It is important to note that although the title of the play is "Aoi no Ue," Aoi no Ue herself does not really appear in the play. She is symbolized by a sleeve on the stage. Instead, the chief character of the play, or the Shite, is the phantom of Rokujo. At the end the jealousy and anger of the spirit of Rokujo are defeated by the exorcist's recitation of the Buddhist prayers. . . .

The most serious problem with Pound's version of *Aoi no Ue* is the fact that he completely misunderstands the play—he fails to realize that the title of the play does not represent its chief character—and believes . . . that Princess Rokujo is actually Aoi no Ue in disguise. Pound fails to see that the subject matter of the play is the jealousy of Princess Rokujo which causes the illness of Aoi no Ue. This misunderstanding accounts for some passages and some remarks in Pound's version which are inaccurate or completely erroneous.[24]

To remark, with no apparent irony, that "the most serious problem with Pound's [*Aoi no Ue*] is [his complete misunderstanding of] the play" is to level quite a serious charge, albeit a fair one. Whereas the original play concerns one woman (Rokujo) jealous of another (Aoi no Ue), Pound writes a lengthy introduction to the play in which he takes great pains to develop his more complex theory that the play represents only one woman "tormented by her own passion, and this passion obsesses her first in the form of a personal apparition of Rokujo, then in demonic form" (324). For emphasis, he states the proposition twice: "And again we cannot make it too clear that the ghost is not actually a separate soul, but only a manifestation made possible through Awoi and her passion of jealousy." The most significant obsession delineated here is not the actual, sexual obsession of Aoi no Ue but Pound's insistence on his idée fixe that the woman suffers from such a sexual obsession.

Tsukui assumes, along with Arthur Waley, that Pound's mistranslation results from "ambiguities he found in the Fenollosa notes" (47), but a more careful look at a page from Fenollosa's notes—previously undiscussed by these scholars or others—reveals that he is fairly unambiguous in his summary of the play's chief features:

Outline of Aoi No Uye.
(Legal wife of Genji)
Genji was like a butterfly, with many women. He didn't love his wife.
So Aoi became a type of envy or jealousy. (Shitto = jealousy.)
She is in great sickness, for jealousy.

She struggles in her bed.
A spirit haunts her. (Mononoke = spirit, "blesser of things")
Really that spirit is the ghost of the Princess of Rokujo—she hates Genji,
    also haunts his wife.
The scene opens at the deathbed of Aoi.[25]

Fenollosa explains accurately that Aoi, as presented in *The Tale of Genji*, is
the legal wife of Genji, and she represents "a type of envy or jealousy"; as the
novel states, she and her family are "even unhappier [than Genji's own fam-
ily] about his infidelities, but, perhaps because he did not lie to them, they
for the most part [keep] their displeasure to themselves."[26] Fenollosa also
explains, again accurately, that Aoi is disturbed by "the ghost of the Princess
of Rokujo," who "hates Genji" and "haunts his wife." Though Fenollosa
does (rightly) attribute jealousy to Aoi, he also emphasizes that the ghost
who haunts her is a manifestation of *another* jealous woman's spirit. There
can be no doubt that he delineates Aoi and Rokujo as two separate, if similarly envious, characters, and any effort to read Rokujo as an external manifestation of Aoi's internal state is entirely Pound's interpolation.

Given Pound's claim that he has struggled to decipher the play, and
given the relative straightforwardness of Fenollosa's notes, we must attribute Pound's aggressive misunderstanding of Aoi, which has no basis
in the text, to his own desire to identify with the feelings that he attributes to her. Tellingly, his description of the sexual psychology that he supposes—wishes?—her to embody refers to Western ideas that interest or
preoccupy him, not to the play, Fenollosa's notes, or source texts such
as *Genji:* "This play was written before Ibsen declared that life is a 'contest with the phantoms of the mind.' The difficulties of the translator have
lain in separating what belongs to Awoi herself from the things belong-
ing to the ghost of Rokujo, very much as modern psychologists might
have difficulty in detaching the personality of an obsessed person from
the personal memories of the obsession. Baldly: an obsessed person thinks
he is Napoleon; an image of his own thought would be confused with
scraps relating perhaps to St. Helena, Corsica, and Waterloo" (324). This
elaboration of a sexual neurotic in the mold of Ibsen's drama or modern psychology is purely Pound's invention. He claims that this back story
is the only one that allows a "moderately coherent and lucid" interpretation of the play, but it would be more accurate to say that this back story
is the only one that allows him to feel and render lines that he considers
"as beautiful as anything [he has] found" in Fenollosa's notes (323–24),

as he, like the "obsessed person [who] thinks he is Napoleon," thinks that he is the Aoi whom he invents: "When I was still in the world, spring was there with me. I feasted upon the cloud with the Sennin, they shared in my feast of flowers. And on the Evening of Maple Leaves I had the moon for a mirror. I was drunk with colour and perfume. And for all my gay flare at that time I am now like a shut Morning-glory, awaiting the sunshine" (327). More completely than his identification with Ono no Komachi, Pound's projection into being of Aoi no Ue allows him to fantasize from the position of a young woman "drunk with [the] colour and perfume" of her eventually spurned attachment to a faithless man. He describes the "gay flare" of her excessive passion with an immediacy that we might not be too cheeky to attribute to his own "gay flair."

The ghost of Pound's Aoi reappears, somewhat surprisingly, in *The Pisan Cantos,* as Pound lies sleepless beneath the glare of electric light in the detention center's cage:

> *As Arcturus passes over my smoke-hole*
>   *the excess electric illumination*
>   *is now focused*
> *on the bloke who stole a safe he cdn't open . . .*
>   *and Awoi's* hennia *plays hob in the tent flaps*
>   *k-lakk . . . . . thuuuuuu*
>   *making rain*
>   *uuuh (485)*

So strong was Pound's identification with Aoi—and so divorced was she in his rendering from her Nō forebear, so wholly a figment of his own imagination—that her "*hennia,*" or the demonic manifestation of her jealousy, could symbolize his feelings a full thirty years after he completed his Nō translations. In an interpretation of this passage, Daniel Albright, following Pound's inaccurate version of the Nō play, corroborates the idea that Aoi serves in *The Cantos* as a figure of identification for Pound: "In the Noh play *Awoi No Uye* the Lady Awoi is exorcised of her pathological jealousy when the exorcist manages to embody, to incarnate that jealousy as an evil spirit, a *hannya,* which is then susceptible to dismissal. Pound therefore imagines that he is justly persecuted by his own ill will, his own spitefulness."[27] Here, then, Aoi is subject to a reversal: in her first appearance, she provided Pound with an alibi to fantasize emotions that would otherwise remain alien to his experience; but in her encore, she allows him to externalize, or make alien to himself by way of a purge, emotions that he has experienced all too intimately and painfully. A similarly double-hinged identification propels Pound's version of *Electra,* as he travels from Italian prison to American hospital ward.

"AS PER NOH"

In early 1959 Pound wrote to his friend the Japanese poet Kitasono Katue to tell him of the success of his *Women of Trachis,* a translation of Sophocles' *Trachiniae* first published in English in 1957: "Both the german and italian versions of TRAXINIAI are in process of production (stage) as well as print. BUT it will need the Minoru or japanese technique to get any result near to what I or Sophokles could get much pleasure from."[28] Here and elsewhere, Pound makes clear the strong affinities that he finds between ancient Greek and Japanese theater (both, significantly, all-male theaters), and his postwar experiments in Sophoclean translation are best understood as a continuation of his earlier interest in Nō. A decade before *The Women of Trachis* brought his attention to Athenian drama out of the closet, he wrote the following stage direction in his unpublished *Elektra:* "(ELEKTRA *masked, at first not even looking at* CHRYSOTHEMIS *but boredly into distance, gradually grows attentive. Slowness in turning of head, as per Noh*)."[29] This remark is one of Pound's only observations in the text that gives an indication of how he envisioned the performance of his *Elektra:* masked, "as per Noh" and as per the conventions of the Dionysiac festivals. The modernity and Americanness of Pound's idiom in *Elektra* may seem like a strange way to honor theatrical tradition, but some of his "pleasure," as he described it much later to Katue, clearly derived from his supposition that his brash and edgy language could be compatible with the techniques of the classical stage.

Also "as per Noh," or at least as per Pound's orientation toward Nō in his 1916 translations, another aspect of the pleasure he took from Sophocles must be attributed to his strong identification with Electra. As Christine Syros observes, "Elektra was a *persona,* but not just any one in a long succession of *personae* that the poet had held to his face for the wink of a poem, and then dropped for still another one. His *Elektra* was a highly intimate piece of evidence, a metaphor of his personal tragedy."[30] The parallels between Pound's life and Electra's story are immediately discernible: Electra is sequestered in her house, denied physical mobility, and stripped of her personal freedoms for speaking out against her father's murder, just as Pound was sequestered in St. Elizabeths, denied physical mobility, and stripped of his personal freedoms for speaking out against capitalism and the American government in favor of fascism. Pound insinuates most clearly the links to be drawn between their situations in his translation of one of Chrysothemis's warnings to Elektra:

> *I certainly will [bring Elektra's gift to Agamemnon's grave], it's what ought*
> *   to be done*
> *and no point disputing it.*
> *But keep quiet about it for gods' sake,*
> *don't let mother get wind of it,*
> *if she does the old usurer will*
> *make me pay extra for the risk. (21)*

Throughout his *Elektra*, Pound uses many words and phrases that are deliberately anachronistic, but to call Aegisthus "the old usurer" strikes a note that is not only stridently modern but also deeply personal, as usury is Pound's catch-all everywhere in his writings for the enemies of righteous thinking and conduct. No mere money lenders in the philosophy that he espouses and the mythology that he devises, usurers are to blame, at least indirectly, for all the ills of the world—including, in the 1940s, Pound's incarceration. If Pound's tormentors are usurers, and Aegisthus is one of them, then Pound *is* Electra in some profoundly felt way.

Yet just as Pound imbues Electra's tragedy with shades of his own, so, too, does his identification with her allow him some escape from his daily reality in St. Elizabeths, as he dives headlong into the aspects of her world that are not reducible to or commensurate with his experience. To be sure, Pound, ever aware of the weight of history and keen to the complex interrelatedness of different texts, is not only or simply translating Sophocles when he translates Sophocles. As Batya Casper Laks (whose book-length study of the Electra myth devotes a chapter to Pound's play) rightfully reminds us, each new version of *Electra* encompasses all the previous versions, their interpretations, and the social and historical contexts into which those versions and interpretations radiate outward.[31] Thus when Pound writes of Orestes and his "dear friend Mr. P[y]lades, stranger in these parts" (3), he evokes the dear friendship between Orestes and Pylades as described in various sources, not just its incarnation in Sophocles. Lucian's *Amores* gives a good sense of how this friendship was generally construed both in the classical period and in early modern interpretations:

> Phocis preserves from early times the memory of the union between
> Orestes and Pylades, who taking a god as witness of the passion between

them, sailed through life together as though in one boat. Both together put to death Klytemnestra, as though both were sons of Agamemnon; and Aegisthus was slain by both. Pylades suffered more than his friend by the punishment which pursued Orestes. He stood by him when condemned, nor did they limit their tender friendship by the bounds of Greece, but sailed to the furthest boundaries of the Scythians—the one sick, the other ministering to him. When they had come into the Tauric land straightway they were met by the matricidal fury; and while the barbarians were standing round in a circle Orestes fell down and lay on the ground, seized by his usual mania, while Pylades "wiped away the foam, tended his body, and covered him with his well-woven cloak," acting not only like a lover but like a father. . . .

Such love is always like that; for when from boyhood a serious love has grown up and it becomes adult at the age of reason, the long-loved object returns reciprocal affection, and it is hard to determine which is the lover of which, for—as from a mirror—the affection of the lover is reflected from the beloved.[32]

Pound subtly preserves the homoerotic dimensions of Orestes' and Pylades' friendship, as described by Lucian and others, in his version of *Electra*. When he chooses to call the Phocian prince "Mr. Pylades," I cannot help but hear an echo of "Mr. Eugenides, the Smyrna merchant," another homosexually inclined and perambulatory Greek.[33] Though Pylades is entirely silent in Sophocles' text, Pound gives Orestes a voice that intimates, like his companion's moniker, a queer bent. Thoroughly Americanized, Pound's Orestes walks with the swagger and talks with the drawl of a wrangler who has traversed the Wild West—but with just enough of an effeminate touch to suggest the rich homosocial and homoerotic legacy of the cowboy's world. Consider his opening address to the Tutor who has guided him and Mr. Pylades back to Mycenae:

All right, Old Handy,
you sure have stuck with us
like a good ole horse . . .
This is what we're agoin' to do,
listen sharp and check up if
I miss any bullseyes.
. . . We'll go to Dad's tomb as ordered
with libations an' all my pretty curls. (4)

Simultaneously rugged and "pretty," Orestes conjures the queer cowboy ethos as represented in nineteenth-century visual and literary culture and as described more recently by the critic Chris Packard: "A cowboy's partner . . . is his one emotional attachment, aside from his horse, and he will die to preserve the attachment. Affection for women destroys the cowboy *communitas* and produces children, and both are unwanted hindrances to those who wish to ride the range freely."[34]

Of course, as *Elektra* opens, Orestes is pulled back precisely from the *communitas* of the open range into a world of familial duty and domestic obligation, particularly to his sister. Various versions of the Electra myth inform us that, following the murder of Clytemnestra and Aegisthus, Orestes weds Electra to Pylades and ends her long lament that her youth has been wasted "without a man and unmarried, . . . unbedded, unchambered" (41).[35] Following the early work of Eve Sedgwick, we might read the union of Electra and Pylades, proleptically implied but unaccomplished in Sophocles, as a mediation, substitution, or compromise-formation of Orestes' own desire for his friend.[36] But in the knotty triangulation among these characters, it would also be valid to invert the equation and to understand Orestes' queer love for Pylades as a transmuted version of the equally queer love between him and his sister. Recall Lucian's description of the men's bond: Pylades acts "not only like a lover but like a father," and "when from boyhood a serious love has grown up . . . it is hard to determine which is the lover of which, for—as from a mirror—the affection of the lover is reflected from the beloved." This account of a sexual love tinged with the filial, which involves an intimate identification between the two parties, could apply equally well to the relationship between Elektra and Orestes. Elektra's first mention of Orestes conflates her maternal and erotic investments in him: "Whom I keep on expecting, / childless, wretched, / unwed" (9–10). When Pound writes that Elektra is "expecting" Orestes, he mines a pun to suggest that she is not simply waiting for him to come home but that she has, in some sense, borne him and that it is *his* absence that leaves her "childless": indeed, we learn later that she "as mother and sister both" was his "nurse also ere [he] hadst [his] growth" (51). But it is not simply the case that Elektra is a surrogate mother for Orestes; the juxtaposition of her "expectancy" with her "childlessness" and "unweddedness" implies that Orestes, her metaphorical son, must also return to marry her and sire new children for her. Klytemnestra understands well the imbrication of Elektra's parental and sexual feelings for her brother when she calls Elektra a "slut" and accuses her of "[cheating] me out of

Orestes, you sneak" (13). And Elektra herself understands that her already overdetermined relationship to Orestes also includes the identificatory mirror described by Lucian. A version of both son and lover, her brother is also a version of herself: "What you like, I like," she tells him, "and my / pleasure's from you not me" (61).

If, as readers of *Elektra* have generally agreed, a strong identification yokes translator to his heroine, then these words redound to Pound, too: what Elektra likes, he likes, and his pleasure comes from an engagement with the complex erotic dimensions of her characterization. "As per Noh," he speaks with and through her ecstasy when she realizes that the strange visitor bearing her "brother's" ashes is none other than Orestes himself: "Heart, heart, heart, thou art come" (57). Feeling her speech from the inside, he distills four lines of Greek to the economy of six taut, charged words. The stark repetition of the word *heart,* coupled with the excision of all verbs from the speech save *come,* results in a powerful line that is—to borrow Pound's own words from a stage direction for the Chorus—*"emphatic and explicit with meaning to ram it in"* (8). Less explicit but equally emphatic is the dialogue that follows this scene of recognition. Elektra is so overwrought that she can't stop her outpouring of words, despite the danger to her brother's enterprise if they are heard inside the palace. Orestes admonishes her several times over and with increasing intensity ("And you damn well keep [your mouth] free . . . by not talking too much at the wrong time," "lay off the talk," "HUSH") and even, according to Pound's stage directions, covers her mouth—first gently, then with a forceful hand (58–62). For most of the play, Elektra, physically helpless against her enemies, has no recourse but to talk, but here the talking takes on a different meaning. No longer a survival instinct or form of self-preservation—indeed, a direct threat to her safety —her speech here becomes a displaced erotic manifestation of her reunion with Orestes. Repeatedly, both she and Orestes refer to her words as the medium of her "enjoyment," "pleasure," "joy," "delight" (59–60). Her mouth overflows with a passion that can only be dammed by force, akin to the sexual logorrhea that Roland Barthes describes in *A Lover's Discourse;* Elektra typifies what Barthes calls "the amorous subject's propensity to talk copiously, with repressed feeling, to the loved being, about his love for that being, for himself, for them: the declaration does not bear upon the avowal of love, but upon the endlessly glossed form of the amorous relation."[37] Just as Barthes postulates, Elektra's talk, which represses its own erotism, is not a declaration of love for Orestes but a self-referential declaration *about* declaring her love for him:

Oh dearest friends
if now's to ear
a voice I ne'er
had hoped to hear

If joy shall not
burst forth at this
then ever dumb in wretchedness
should one live on in deep distress.

Now thou art here
  in full daylight
  I shall not pour
  forth my delight,
who ne'er in deepest woe
  had forgot thee. (60)

Even as Elektra claims that she "shall not pour / forth [her] delight," she nevertheless continues to pour forth—and could keep doing it endlessly were she not forcibly stopped. As Barthes says, "To speak amorously is to expend without an end in sight, without a *crisis;* it is to practice a relation without orgasm" (73).

But the crisis—Orestes' murder of Klytemnestra—does come quickly on the heels of Elektra's "blasted roaring exuberance," as the Tutor calls it (73); and with that crisis comes at last her coded orgasmic fulfillment. As Orestes and Pylades enter the palace, Orestes prays, "May the gods of the door be with us" (64), and Elektra, "*emerging from the door, or slowly turning as part of a pivoted door,*" opens her body to him figuratively just as the door opens literally onto the space of the throne room. "Let the gods show their god head," she prays in her turn, sustaining the metaphor of arousal and penetration; and as she senses that Orestes will deliver the fatal blow to their mother, she speaks to the Chorus as though she approaches sexual climax: "Oh my dears, my dears . . . / It's coming . . . / sh hh hhh" (65). At the very beginning of the play, Orestes describes his task of vengeance as a "kinky course, clean in the kill" (4), and though he refers explicitly to his roundabout arrival in Mycenae and his indirect preparation for the murder, his words finally resonate, too, with the indirect expression of Elektra's sensual gratification. More simply, the word *kinky* is lent retrospectively its other connotation of sexual twistedness as Elektra gets off on her brother's matricidal fury, which no longer seems like such a "clean" kill.

When Elektra calls out "Hit her again" after the penultimate stroke of Orestes' axe, we can't be sure whether she refers manifestly to Klytemnestra or euphemistically to herself (66).

As Orestes follows Elektra's command and strikes again, Klytemnestra shouts from offstage in her death throes, "Twice / twice / always twice" (67). Indeed, she departs a world (among other things, the world of *performance*, which Richard Schechner defines as "twice-behaved behavior")[38] in which the principle "always twice" generates a series of doubles: the double murder of her and her lover; the doubling of Elektra's incestuous love, which alights first on the father "neath" whose bed she is "housed" (10) and then on the brother with whom her "fortune" is "equal" (52); the doubling of sisterly deprivation, against which Elektra rails and to which Chrysothemis submits compliantly; and—perhaps most interesting—the doubling of Elektra and Pylades, whose intractable silence complements her almost equally intractable loquacity. As if to underscore this last doubling, Orestes says to Pylades before they enter the palace, "Come on, Pylades, cut the cackle," a joke that associates Elektra's cackling with Pylades' muteness and suggests that his modus operandi—all action, no talk—is, as the inverse of hers, also a mode of love for Orestes (64). If, in Barthes's words, Elektra's "language is a skin," and she has "words instead of fingers, or fingers at the tip of [her] words" (73), then skin is a language for Pylades, who can communicate his devotion to his friend only by putting his fingers to work and letting them speak in the service of homicide. These counterpoised orientations merge earlier in the play when Elektra "[*clutches*] *at the urn which Pylades is carrying*," supposed to contain Orestes' ashes, and "[*sings*] *to* [*it*]" a lament for her brother (50–52). Yoked together by the urn, Elektra and Pylades enter into a symbolic union that prefigures their eventual marriage —but here it is a marriage of utter negation, as Elektra wishes to become, like the silent Pylades, a cipher: "Take me in with you," she sings to the urn, "I now am nothing, make place beside thee / naught into naught, zero to zero" (52). Whatever normativity the pairing of Elektra and Pylades implies is undercut completely by their symmetrically matched, libidinal investments in Orestes. Without their respectively incestuous and homoerotic loves, they are "naught," "zero."

At the end of *Elektra*, the play itself can feel as though it's come to naught. No catharsis releases the heirs of the house of Atreus from the bonds of their righteous anger; instead, as Orestes drags Aegisthus offstage to meet his bloody end, the Chorus brings the play to a huddled close in five breakneck lines:

My god, it's come with a rush!

DELIVERED, DELIVERED

SWIFT END

so soon

te nun teleoothen. (73)

But is anyone really "delivered, delivered"? Or is it simply death that is delivered twice (always twice)? Elektra's own last line, "and let me forget it," is unsettlingly ambiguous (72). There is no assurance that her plea can be answered, and the obsessive weight of her memory, with which the play is so heavily suffused, suggests rather that the curtain closes on a woman haunted further, not released, by Orestes' avenging acts. Certainly Pound himself remained haunted by his time in St. Elizabeths, whatever compensatory function his identification with Electra may have briefly provided. A few more bursts of productivity followed this translation, but as his life drew to a close he was increasingly withdrawn, to the point in his final years of a silence almost as total as Pylades'. The force that he channeled into *Elektra* would remain for other, later enthusiasts to harness and bring to life.

"FRONTAL ATTACK"

In her introduction to *Elektra,* Carey Perloff says of her 1987 production of the play for the Classic Stage Company, "The performance style sprang from the kinetic, energetic, frontal attack of the language. . . . The actors were made acutely aware of changes in rhythm from line to line, and of the need to use the language as an active tool" (xxii–xxiii). Just as Perloff's *Elektra* was a "frontal attack" that worked in concert with the intonations of Pound's translation, so, too, was it a frontal attack *on* Pound, an assault on certain notions that he had about the play's performance. As indicated earlier, Pound hoped for an *Elektra* in the style of Nō theater; and not only did he imagine the title character as a masked tragic heroine, but he may also have conceived that the part, à la Nō and ancient Greek practice, would be played by a male actor. When Pound renders Elektra's request to Chrysothemis to make an offering of her hair at their father's grave, he directs that Elektra "*(jerks out a lock of her own (wig) violently)*" (20). To be sure, a wig might be required for the accomplishment of "jerking out a lock" onstage whether Elektra is played by man or woman, but the explicit mention of this pragmatically obvious point underscores the artifice of Elektra's femininity, as construed by Pound, and his envisioning of her as an actor in drag —indeed, on some level, as a version of himself. Not so CSC's Elektra, brought to life by Pamela Reed with no wig but, in Perloff's words, "her bleached blonde hair flashing in the white light." The cross-gender role assignment hinted by Pound gives way in Perloff's hands to multiracial casting; in a play that she views as crucially concerned with "dark/light imagery," Reed's ultrawhiteness figured in stark and pointed contrast to the blackness of Orestes, as "played by African-American actor Joe Morton in cowboy boots and blue jeans" (xxii).

Racially dissonant casting has become a commonplace of contemporary theater and film, and how we are meant to read such cues is by no means unilaterally clear. In the case of a play like Caryl Churchill's *Cloud Nine*, the first act of which "takes place in a British colony in Africa in Victorian times," the fact that colonial administrator Clive's "black servant," Joshua, is "played by a white" has overtly thematic implications.[39] At the other end of the spectrum, the appearance of Denzel Washington (Don Pedro) as the brother of Keanu Reeves (Don John) in Kenneth Branagh's *Much Ado about Nothing* has arguably less to do with meditations on race than with the desirable feature-status of a celebrity of Washington's magnitude in a generally star-studded cast. Somewhere between these two extremes, Perloff's casting decisions in *Elektra* beg us to consider with some complexity the category of race and how it might operate in the various contexts of Sophoclean tragedy, Poundian translation, and Manhattanite theater of the late 1980s. Concerning the last, J. Ellen Gainor notes that Reed's "bleached, short hair . . . could as easily have been found right outside the theatre" on the streets of the East Village,[40] and Batya Caspar Laks enlarges upon this point when she observes of the set, "a large, fenced area reminiscent . . . of a [downtown] basketball court," that Orestes' presence in such an evocative space renders him "a black avenging hero and deliverer of the victims of city-squalor." Laks is quick to add of this conceit that it "play[s] upon the concept of vitality which is . . . a cliché associated in Western literature with dark skin." She implies, nevertheless, that the cliché is used effectively, as "Electra's [sic] diminutive figure, her white hair and her rasping voice which is at times drained of all energy stand in sharp dramatic contrast to the strong, dark vitality, the new-blood, the fresh perspective of her brother" (137).

Laks's use of the neologism *new-blood* is telling, because Elektra and Orestes are supposed, of course, to be bound in duty to each other and to their Atrean lineage by the oldest of blood ties. On the face of it—quite literally—the idea that Reed and Morton could share identical parents may strike a viewer as absurd, and Perloff's choice to cast them as siblings certainly rings in time with the "absurdism" of "tragedy turned into black comedy" that she finds so pervasive in Pound's translation (xxiv). But to convey that black comedy, in part, through the tragicomic misfit of Orestes' blackness in a white family raises a host of questions about Elektra, her brother, and their relationship to racial constructions—and other constructions of identity—that extend beyond mere absurdism. Does the pairing of Reed and Morton as brother and sister force a shift in our assumptions and perceptions of who "can" and "can't" share a blood tie and serve, consequently, as a powerful reminder that race is always a matter of shifting assumption and perception, not a universal category? Indeed, does the casting highlight the contingency of race in such a way that it also calls attention to the contingency of family, another naturalized but culturally determined institution? Or does the stark contrast between Reed's and Morton's respective appearances simply reify the idea of racial difference?

Imbricated in and ultimately inseparable from these questions of race is the question of sexuality. Perloff didn't shy away from the incestuous attachment between Elektra and Orestes but rather foregrounded the erotic aspects of their relationship in her direction. As she says of Reed's heavily sexualized response to Morton when she realizes that he is her brother, "We examined dozens of Greek vase paintings of Maenads in ecstacy while choreographing the recognition scene between Elektra and Orestes" (xxiii). Elektra's love for Orestes, as embodied by Reed and Morton, is potentially open to inverse interpretations. On the one hand, the interracial love between Elektra and Orestes could be seen as a suspension or displacement—a whitewashing, so to speak—of the troubling question of incest, as so-called miscegenation opposes incest diametrically as a kind of transgression (the latter being an instance of a relationship that is "too close," the former a straying "too far" from one's "kind"). On the other hand, the transgression of interracial love could stand in precisely, albeit metaphorically, for the transgression of the incest taboo, as both erotic choices have been subject to the prohibition that certain parties (black and white, brother and sister) "don't mix." The second interpretation seems to me the far more likely reading of Perloff's project—chiefly because her description of *Elektra* as a "frontal attack" suggests that she has no desire to assuage her audience, by easing their confrontation with incest or with any other uncomfortable subject—and this interpretation has far more radical implications. American historical injunctions against interracial love had slackened—if not, regrettably, disappeared entirely—by 1987, and whatever offense such a love might be supposed to embody certainly pales in comparison to the offense of incestuous love, which is still strongly taboo, if not as forbidden now as it was for Pound and even for Sophocles. By yoking interracial love to incestuous love, and likening each to the other, Perloff's *Elektra* suggests a loosening of the incest taboo and opens a space for the positive, if qualified, valuation of Elektra's attachment to her brother. Though Perloff chose to abandon Pound's idea that his *Elektra* should be performed as a masked drama, the actors' gendered, familial, and racial assignments— "white sister," "black brother"—*become* the masks that they wear; and if these masks can't be taken off so easily as the literal ones of the ancient Greek and Japanese stage, then they are at least understood as profoundly shaped and shaping personae that gain their currency performatively rather than constatively.

In this regard, Perloff's production radicalizes *Elektra* to a far greater extent than even the linguistically innovative and provocative Pound, whose attitudes about race, for instance, were far more conservative. In his repeated descriptions of African-Americans as "niggers" and "coons," he is undeniably racist, and even his commendatory depictions in *The Pisan Cantos* of the black soldiers and inmates at the U.S. Disciplinary Training Center are at best partial and problematic.[41] Pound celebrates such black soldiers as "Mr. Edwards," who defied regulations to supply him with a packing crate that he could use as a desk and thereby exemplified "charity," the "greatest" manifestation of love; but he immediately undercuts this tender picture by juxtaposing it with an allusion to the primitivizing and racialist work of the anthropologist Leo Frobenius (539). Mr. Edwards's face may appear to Pound as "a mask as fine as any in Frankfurt," but could he imagine, as Perloff did, a man like Edwards wearing the mask of his Orestes? As Clive Wilmer rightly notes, Pound's praise for Edwards evaporates into the most idealized vision of whiteness, as "the dark 'ground' [of the detention center] is characteristically transcended with the appearance in the tent of the white goddess Aphrodite."[42] More generally, Pound's retreat from the racially complicated terrain of *The Pisan Cantos,* published in 1948, to the dynastic Greek world of Sophocles' *Electra* marks a similar move. While Pound inarguably makes his *Elektra* "American" in the kinds of vernacular and colloquial speech that he sometimes assigns to his characters, his notion of America in the play is a mythological one that exorcises the racial heterogeneity of the United States, just as he may have used the project in translation to exorcise painful memories of Pisa.

On quite different grounds, some critics have attacked Pound's idiom in the translation for a perceived lack of reverence for and deference to his source text. In a review of Perloff's production of the play for CSC, Michael

Feingold of the *Village Voice* took Pound to task for an approach to the "lucid beauty and gravity of [Sophocles'] diction" that approximated the work of a "team" composed of "Dashiell Hammett, Algernon Swinburne, Will Rogers, a fifth-rate pop lyricist, and a drunk prep-school Classics prof."[43] In a slightly less scathing account, Mel Gussow of the *New York Times* claimed that "Pound deconstructs the dialogue from the sublime to the Ridiculous,"[44] but in her own earlier piece for the *Times,* Perloff, trained as a classicist at Stanford and far more sensitive to the humor of the original Greek, lauded Pound for his translation's likeness in places to the "film slang" of the 1940s, which "somehow . . . embraces both our own humor and the hugeness of Greek tragedy."[45] All of these accounts hover around but fail to name the play's *camp* sensibility as the quality that either rankles or delights audiences of *Elektra*. Campiness is not an attribute that we would usually associate with Pound, but it is, finally, of a piece with the other queer dimensions of his poses as a translator. In her introduction to the New Directions edition of *Elektra,* Perloff recalls a moment from her production of the play that corroborates perfectly Pound's occasional detours into camp, even as she resists such a reading: "The best that Pound's Orestes can promise Elektra after the murder of Klytemnestra is that, 'You won't have any more trouble with mother.' This line caused immediate laughter in the audiences that saw the production in New York: a laughter of horror, granted, but laughter nonetheless" (xxiv). Must we attribute this laughter, as Perloff does, to horror? Or is it possible to hear in that laughter's echoes a recognition of a "private code," a "badge of identity" between the "small urban cliques" in the East Village theater and a translator whose style could display his "love of the exaggerated, the 'off,' of things-being-what-they-are-not"?[46]

Of course, Susan Sontag's description, which I quote here, is by no means the final word on camp. Indeed, a more recent generation of scholarship has concerned itself precisely with a complication of—if not radical distancing from—Sontag's formulation.[47] Among these various, related critical perspectives, I find most useful, in my understanding of Pound, a theorization of camp articulated by Jane Feuer in a study of the 1980s serial *Dynasty* and audience responses to it: "Very early on [*Dynasty*'s] producers were aware of camp decodings and intended to encode them in the text by devising 'outrageous plots' and 'walk(ing) a fine line, just this side of camp.' . . . It is important to stress that the camp attitude toward *Dynasty* in both gay and mainstream culture does not preclude emotional identification; rather, it embraces both identification and parody—attitudes normally viewed as mutually exclusive—at the same time and as part of the same sensibility."[48] Just so Pound. His translatorial approach to *Electra* is a carefully calibrated balancing act that allows him to accommodate "both identification and parody"—and that allows us, in turn, to answer with an equally ambivalent and complex mixture of affect. Such an understanding of *Elektra* might also redound to the more familiar Pound of *The Cantos*, who may not be as dissimilar to this other, queerer Pound as first supposed. To be sure, a simultaneous identification with his subjects and parodic ease in their handling manifests itself in such famous passages as the opening of Canto II:

> *Hang it all, Robert Browning,*
> *there can be but the one "Sordello."*
> *But Sordello, and my Sordello? (6)*

Whether or not Pound intends it—and it would seem that he does not when he is at his most (offensively) dogmatic—his work may invite a similar response from us. If we are at all disposed to camp, we can choose to greet him with transformative laughter rather than programmatic outrage. Hang it all, there can be but the one "Pound." But queer Pound, and *my* Pound? Of further interest, my Pound, queer Pound, seems also at times to be his protégé Zukofsky's Pound, as indicated by the early correspondence between them to which I will turn at the beginning of the next chapter. In turning to Zukofsky, we also turn to a poet and dramatist who, if not necessarily more comfortable with such queer postures as camp, much more regularly and consistently inhabited them.

2

bottoming zukofsky

"DON'T GET GAY"

At the outset of his correspondence with Ezra Pound, Louis Zukofsky seems to have been anxiously aware of the homoerotic potential in exchanges between men of letters. Zukofsky began the correspondence when he submitted his "Poem Beginning 'The'" to Pound for publication in *The Exile,* and his third letter to Pound, dated December 23, 1927, registers his excitement over Pound's enthusiastic response to this work:

> Dear Mr. Pound:
> The 18 Aug. you wrote me a very kind letter on my ms., Poem Beginning "The." I answered to Rapallo with an enthusiasm that maybe deserved a "don't get gay"; also with emendations. These, probably, never reached you. If you are still interested, I can forward corrected copy.
> Tho' what with the passport nuisance you have enough on your hands without me. And yet I should be grateful, if—and am anyway,
> Yours,
> Louis Zukofsky.[1]

Zukofsky's pregnant dash suggests so many potential gestures that might have earned his gratitude: publication, to be sure, but also criticism, advice, tutelage, filiation. And love? Following strictly, if perversely, the semantic logic of the letter's final paragraph, in which Zukofsky recognizes that Pound "[has] enough on [his] hands without me," I am tempted to fill in the blank, "And yet I should be grateful, if I, too, could be on your hands"—or rather, "your hands could be on me"? Surely this inference

constitutes a willfully provocative misreading. Yet it may also be a productive misreading, for the letter is, in fact, sexually charged, if only delicately and implicitly so. What's more, Zukofsky recognizes the erotic
subtext of his supplication to Pound: "I answered to Rapallo with an enthusiasm that maybe deserved a 'don't get gay.'" Ironically, the very gesture by which Zukofsky seeks to banish (or at least to repress further) his
letter's latent eroticism only serves to make it manifest. Because he names
his desire not to get gay, his letter gets gayer than it otherwise would have
been.

And what of the other letter that Zukofsky sent to Pound and of which
he makes mention with a fear that it "never reached" the elder poet? This
letter of September 1927 did indeed reach Pound, was preserved, and offers a glimpse of Zukofsky's early thoughts on his "Poem Beginning 'The'":
"I was at the time of writing too pleased, however shyly, with Peter Out."[2]
Given this confession, it is perhaps premature to read Zukofsky's concern
about "getting gay" as an expression of worry, when it may just be "shyness"
—or even coyness—about the homoerotics of his letters and poems; for
Peter Out is the figure about whom Zukofsky's speaker reveals an intimate
companionship in "Poem Beginning 'The'":

> 61. *This is the aftermath*
> 62. *When Peter Out and I discuss the theatre.*
> 63. *Evenings, our constitutional.*
> 64. *We both strike matches, both in unison,*
> 65.   *to light one pipe, my own.*
> 66. *'Tis, 'tis love, that makes the world go*
>   *round, and love is what I dream.*[3]

Peter Out is a name that means, quite simply, "exposed dick." Given the
crudity of this joke, it is difficult not to read into the loving men's pipe-light-
ing either a coded gay gesture for each other's benefit, or an instance of
quasi-Freudian symbolism for the reader's benefit, or both.[4]

But what exactly would the word *gay* have meant in 1927 to Zukofsky,
a then-bachelor born and bred in Manhattan and living at that time on the
Upper East Side? As George Chauncey observes in *Gay New York,* the word
gay had already, by the late 1920s and early 1930s, acquired a very specific
slang meaning. Originally a self-attribution of "fairies" meant to denote
their flamboyance, the word was adopted by "queers" who did not identify
as effeminate but who nevertheless sought male sexual partners: "A properly intoned reference or two to a 'gay bar' or to 'having a gay time' served

to alert the listener familiar with homosexual culture" (18). To what extent might Zukofsky have been such a familiar listener? Whatever direct experience he may or may not have had of gay bars and times, I imagine that an ear as finely attuned as his own to the nuances of American English could have, in the New York of his young adulthood, fastened rather easily onto such a camp usage.

Even Pound, all those transatlantic miles away in Rapallo, seems finally to have wondered, after a few years of correspondence, what kind of contacts Zukofsky might be making in New York; and we might conclude that his curiosity was piqued by the tone and affect of Zukofsky's letters. When Zukofsky made such overwrought declarations as "You see-saw my heart ups and downs,"[5] perhaps Pound, who happily played "papa" to Zukofsky's "sonny" or "junior," suspected that he was being interpellated less as a traditional father figure than as a gay daddy.[6] At any rate, Pound made a typically circuitous inquiry about Zukofsky's predilections and behaviors in a letter of April 1933:

> Can jewish gentlemen meet sodomitical gentlemen in New York without the irritations of interactive prejudice, or do ONLY jewish sodolitical [sic] gentlemen meet sodomitical gentlemen of other reeligious persuasions???
>
> If unable to make a general an objective statement of local custums, you are at lib. to send personal, if an[y], view.
> Alien to this queery[7]

Though Pound was cocksure of his alien relationship to the "queery" and to queerness in general, he betrays here some provocative doubt and circumspection about the planet on which Zukofsky was living. In his response, Zukofsky, who accuses Pound of vagueness, proves equally evasive in his language:

> Yr. question as to Jewish gentlemen & sodomitical too vague to make me feel sure of my answer. However, will attempt it: (This is not a personal view, since you can consider me out of the picture for which I have only a "to-hell-with-it")
> 1. Jewish gentlemen meet sodomitical gentlemen in N.Y. without the irritations of interactive prejudice when the sodomitical gentlemen fall for Jewish gentlemen who are sodomitical, which happens I believe only in literary cases.[8]

On the one hand, Zukofsky seems to deny here any firsthand knowledge of urban gay life, or at any rate sodomy: "This is not a personal view." On the other, his language is just elliptical enough to warrant some skepticism about the denial. If he is, in 1933, "out of the picture" of gay life, was he, at some earlier point, ever in it? Does he "have only a 'to-hell-with-it'" now because "it" proved less than heavenly in his former experience?

And the rest is silence, at least where Zukofsky's willingness to address this issue is concerned—and thus where biographical speculation may and perhaps ought to be concerned. Not that such speculation is always so chaste: in an exemplary case of mining Zukofsky's life for juicier ends, the gay poet, novelist, and critic Kevin Killian, in collaboration with Brian Kim Stefans, recently produced a short play, "The American Objectivists," which parodies Zukofsky's marriage to the composer Celia Thaew. Belying its bland title, the play is a frothy romp that imagines the hijinks that ensue when the Zukofskys are visited at their Brooklyn apartment by John Ashbery and gal pal Bunny Lang (and later by George and Mary Oppen and Lorine Niedecker). Trading in crude, if highly amusing, stereotypes and unverifiable gossip, Killian and Stefans depict Celia—played on two occasions by a male actor— as a sex-starved harridan who throws herself at every man in sight and Louis as a cold fish oblivious to Ashbery's gay innuendo.[9] The cumulative effect of these characterizations is to suggest of Zukofsky that he is a closet case— and, worse, a clueless one. In so doing, the play elevates to the level of textual legibility issues that seem to hover beneath the surface (and perhaps only for the perversely disposed viewer motivated to find them there) in another, documentary representation of the Zukofskys in their domestic interior: a short film featuring a 1966 interview with and reading by Zukofsky.[10] The film is arguably most striking for the scene in which Zukofsky, smoking in his living room and surprisingly effeminate in voice and manner, makes pronouncements about literature that are somewhat undermined by Celia, who seems to be angling for attention by clanking pots or plates in the off-screen kitchen, then walking "accidentally" (and barely perceptibly) into and out of a shot of her husband. It is tempting, as Killian and Stefans seem to do, to explode suggestive moments like this one into full-blown narratives of homosexually inflected marital dysfunction; far harder—but more penetrating, and thus the subject of this chapter—is the task of apprehending the much more complexly queer moments negotiated in Zukofsky's texts (and, sometimes, in Celia's compositional responses to them).

In short, Zukofsky is no doubt wrong when he supposes that sodomites, Jewish or otherwise, can have truck only with other confirmed members of their species. In his joking assertion to Pound that such interactions occur "only in literary cases," I hear an embedded invitation to "meet" Zukofsky "sodomitically" on the surfaces of his writing, however irrecoverable the details of his private life. Just a few letters to Pound alone prove that the writing, full of every queer specimen from homoerotic longing to homosexual panic, rewards such an investment. What's more, the queer textures of Zukofsky's writing are not limited to his personal correspondence. To date, Libbie Rifkin, adapting critical terminology from Lee Edelman, is the only Zukofsky scholar to investigate his "homographesis"—or his "putting into writing" of "a strategic resistance to [the] reification of sexual difference"[11] —which she explores in exemplary readings of some early movements of his long poem "A" (88–89). While I applaud Rifkin for breaking this ground, and while I concur with her view that we need not finally "out" Zukofsky in order to trace "the broad range of desire" in his work, I deviate strongly from her further contention that this broad range of desire manifests itself only in the limited range of his early work (91). More specifically, I want to challenge her assertion that Zukofsky's *Bottom: On Shakespeare* "poses marriage as a vessel for containing excesses of subjectivity, desire, and mutability within the bounds of artistic mastery" and therefore provides a lens through which to understand what Rifkin takes to be the generally conservative impulses of Zukofsky's later work (98). In a radical alternative to this point of view, I will argue that a queer interpretation of *Bottom,* which can be read as the first of Zukofsky's "closet dramas," offers a blueprint not for a confirmation of Zukofsky's growing conservatism but for an illumination of the devious and deviant energies that continue to animate his later work. In particular, I will offer readings of the late dramatic experiments in his long poem "A," *Rudens* ("A"-21) and *L.Z. Masque* ("A"-24), to demonstrate how Zukofsky's turn from normative dramatic conventions entails a concomitant turn from normative sexuality. Specifically, Zukofsky's representations posit alternative sexualities as dark, aggressive—and thereby alluring—in ways that oppose directly his imagination of heterosexual domesticity as placid and static. As a final excursus, I will consider the ways in which several 1978 San Francisco Bay area performances of the *L.Z. Masque* animated onstage the queer dynamics of Zukofsky's writing —and the potential for aggression implicit in those dynamics.

BOTTOMS UP

To identify *Bottom: On Shakespeare* (nominally a work of Shakespeare criticism) as a closet drama is not an obvious move, but then to propose any stable(r) classification for a text as hybrid and heterogeneous as *Bottom* would prove equally problematic and necessarily provisional. In an excellent introduction to Wesleyan University Press's recent reissue of *Bottom,* which was originally published by Ark Press in 1963, Bob Perelman highlights well "the knottedness of *Bottom*'s arguments and structure" and its obstinate "resistance to summary."[12] Perelman is right that both the argument and the structure of *Bottom* defy simple description, but the claim is more demonstrably clear where structure is concerned: long quotations, a poem, a letter, a dialogue, and a musical score are just some of the multifarious elements in *Bottom*'s maddening zigzag, which propels the book from one generic pose to another without apparent reason or discernible motivation for the generic changes. The book's longest and most prominent section, "An Alphabet of Subjects," cedes organizational logic to the arbitrariness of abecedarian order (a passage on "Continents" is preceded by one on "Birthplace" and followed by one on "Definition," and so forth); and this affirmation of the letter as a guiding principle is matched by the book's careful attention to typography. As with its letters, the book's fonts, italics, intricate spacings and indentations, illustrative adornments (such as swords and donkeys), and related features of print and design seem to have been given as much attention as, or more than, how the book will be organized into units and how those units will relate to one another. Available for interpretation as a parody of early- and mid-twentieth-century practices of (and theories for) editing Shakespeare —but a parody firmly invested, nonetheless, in the complexities and contingencies of print—*Bottom* models, in a hyperbolic way that contributes to its potential status as a closet drama, the general demand of modern dramatic texts to be seen, in W. B. Worthen's compelling formulation, *as texts* with a rich materiality.[13]

However demanding readers may find the intricacies of the book's structure and design, its argument is, at least superficially, quite clear. As a cursory glance at almost any page of the book makes apparent, *Bottom* is ostensibly all about eyes: Zukofsky proposes that all of Shakespeare's writing can be reduced to the claim that *love sees,* then attempts "to consider the forty-four items of the canon as one work" that affirms continually and consistently a "definition of love" in which *love:reason::eyes:mind.*[14] According to this definition, Shakespeare's "characters are happy only when their eyes judge for equable equals. Then because they look with their eyes they love reasonably. The text says so—over and over—explicitly" (266). Whether or not Shakespeare's text says so explicitly, Zukofsky's text certainly says so over and over, and it would consequently be easy to read this "thematic loop," as Libby Rifkin does, as *Bottom*'s "main end" (92).

But should we really take anything at *face* value in a book entitled *Bottom*? As Zukofsky might say, many thanks to the dictionary, which, in at least one of its incarnations, reminds us of meanings of the word *bottom* available to him in the "U.S., mid 1900s":

> **bottom 1.** the buttocks. [British and U.S. colloquial euphemism since the 1700s] . . . **bottoms** a nickname for a catamite. For synonyms see BRONCO. [U.S. slang, mid 1900s–pres.][15]

Surely Zukofsky, a great lover of all things paronomastic and homophonic, knew the usages he risked when he named his book on Shakespeare after *A Midsummer Night's Dream*'s weaver. Following his claim in his *Autobiography* that "the work says all there needs to be said of one's life,"[16] I want in turn to risk the assertion, in the absence of biographical proof or even psychobiographical speculation, that bottoms play a significant role in Zukofsky's conception of love in *Bottom*, though less obviously than the eyes that recur so insistently. For bottoms recur with an equally palpable insistence—at least to the reader who answers the book's call to *see* what she reads, and at least in two ways:

1   Puns on bottoms appear and sully the philosophical language of the text, as if Zukofsky wanted to make his lavishly quoted sources (and "his own" words) say what "the philosopher blessed with a body might say," or, more particularly, what the philosopher blessed with a bottom might say (297). Thus actors on the stage are "incontinent" (66); spontaneity is "posterior" to nature and intelligence (82); Bacon explains Americans' lack of contributions to "posterity" (159); art that is "unretentive" is deemed wanting (182); one must see with one's own eyes in order to "*ass*ent" (208); metaphysics' "*ass*urance" is only I, not Eye (215), "a good coate with rich trappings gets a *gay asse*, entraunce in at a great Gate" (330); and "the mind should see bottom" (392)—all of which makes me want to ask, with Zukofsky, of the Lucretius whom he quotes: if the human is "the proper . . . species to which accidents happen" (118), do those accidents include the ones that even the best potty training cannot always prevent?[17] In almost any other text, I would call these puns themselves accidental, or at any rate viral, but here the infection seems to be invited, if not courted.

2 Many passages that are ostensibly quoted for their references to seeing
   eyes also happen to mention bottoms: Gaudier Brzeska on what he sees
   in statuary—and simultaneously on "solid excrements" and "whistling
   gases" (178); Chekhov's characters speaking in the same breath of looking and "buttocks" (219); Aristophanes' recognition that you can scratch
   both your eyes and your arse (372); and a confusion (or coincidence)
   in *Love's Labour's Lost* of "backs" and "eyes," in relation to the narrative context of which Zukofsky cannot help punning that "the end is in
   sight" (281–82). While there is no reason, in the service of the analogy
   love:reason::eyes:mind, and with so many passages on eyes at his disposal,
   that Zukofsky *had* to invoke bottoms alongside eyes, there may nevertheless be a reason that he often does. In other words, I may be able to
   demonstrate more or less convincingly that *Bottom* is obsessed with bottoms, but (like, Zukofsky, I cannot resist the pun) if so, to what *end*?

I do not want to suggest that buttocks are as important to Zukofsky as
eyes, but at the same time I do not think that this accretion of bums in *Bottom* is a simple case of "ass for ass's sake." Rather, I would claim that all these
bottoms serve as signposts, if you will, pointing to another, less dispensa-
ble meaning of *bottom* (as in the catamites of the second dictionary entry):
the submissive partner in an erotic encounter. In order to appreciate the
nuances of Zukofsky's notion of love, I want to deemphasize the rigor with
which he promotes the analogy *love:reason::eyes:mind* and consider instead
the ways in which he advocates the lover's role as "bottom." Such a role is,
after all, the one played by Nick Bottom in *A Midsummer Night's Dream.*
In contradistinction to Zukofsky's emphasis on eyes, Bottom, the central
figure of his book, is himself blinded, blindfolded, or sightless throughout
almost all of Shakespeare's play. He is also the eager capitulant to Titania's
domination—and, further, the dupe of Oberon, who seems to take a deli-
cious, perverse thrill in unleashing the weaver on his estranged wife.

     As for *Bottom,* at many turns in the book, Zukofsky undercuts and dis-
tances himself from both the single-minded vehemence of his definition
and its "correctness" or superiority to other ways of reading Shakespeare.
Most notably, he suggests early in the text that his definition of love, like the
products of spontaneity and chance in Aristotle's *Physics,* is "incidental"
(39). What seems to be fundamental (a word that echoes the bottom) and
necessarily prior to the definition is the claim that, in Spinoza's words, the
love object is one "of which we may never seize the mastery, . . . of which
no one is truly master" (16). For Zukofsky's definition of love, the loss of

mastery is a prerequisite. The "cure" to this problem (for Zukofsky, following Spinoza, conceives it as a problem) would be to reduce the passions to as little a part of mental life as possible (24). Barring such an extremity, the lover's proper posture or attitude toward love requires submission and even self-abnegation: the posture or attitude, in other words, of the bottom.[18]

The necessity and even desirability of bottoming extends, in Zukofsky's view, from erotic behavior to aesthetic and critical practice. When Zukofsky observes that "Ovid had exercised his mastery over Europe a long time," he does not bemoan the lack of so-called originality entailed by early modern writers' acquiescence to this mastery. Rather, he seems to delight in the ways in which Ovid's "thought . . . penetrates the smallest joints of words" written by Marlowe, Wyatt, and, of course, Shakespeare (28). Nor is it "incidental" that the thought of which Zukofsky writes is Ovid's thought about love. Bottoming as a lover and bottoming as an artist are inextricably linked and perhaps mutually constitutive goods, so that we are left to wonder, when Zukofsky describes Shakespeare as a man with "a reputation for satisfying all comers," whether he refers to the page, stage, or bedroom (28).

Given the content of *Bottom,* which is largely a string of quotations, Zukofsky himself clearly enjoys the pleasure of penetration by other voices that he identifies and approves in earlier writers. We should also recall that Zukofsky's contribution to *Bottom* is, after all, only one of two volumes, that the second volume is his wife Celia's score for *Pericles,* and that the long second part of his volume is entitled "*Music's master:* notes to Her music for *Pericles* and for a graph of culture" (33). Described as "notes to" Celia's score, and thereby made subordinate to it, Zukofsky's essay valorizes uppercase Her and deemphasizes his lowercase graph of culture, a graph that he never in fact completes. And, as a further reminder that he is the bottom to Celia's top—that she is the master not only of music but also of him—he adds in a footnote, "Celia Thaew's *Pericles* an opera to all the words of the play by William Shakespeare—the one excuse for all that follows in this part" (37). What better place to find Zukofsky ceding mastery than in a footnote, whose appearance at the bottom of the page must call conspicuous attention to itself in a work called *Bottom*?[19]

As a score for performance that has, to my knowledge, never been publicly performed, Celia's companion volume to Zukofsky's *Bottom* also points back to my earlier contention that *Bottom* is best described less as an effort of literary criticism than as a sort of closet drama. The likely section of Zukofsky's volume to cite as evidence for this claim is its "Definition," presented as a dialogue between "Son" and fatherly "I," but the rest of the work also reads strangely, if less explicitly, like a play. Passages from many different sources are not just quoted but juxtaposed (and often abridged) in such a way that they are put in sensible and meaningful dialogue with one another. Consider, as one brief illustration of this curious effect, a passage from "Continents" in *Bottom*'s third part, "An Alphabet of Subjects," in which Zukofsky discusses—and uses other voices to discuss—the role of boy actors on the Elizabethan stage:

> "If I were to have a play put on in which women had roles, I would demand that these roles be performed by adolescent boys, and I would bring this to the attention of the spectators by means of a placard which would remain nailed to the right or left of the sets during the entire performance."
>
> —Jean Genet, *Notre-Dame des Fleurs*, 1942
>
> On Shakespeare's stage there was a placard for *place;* the boy actor's casual history was his "face valenc'd since I saw thee last . . . nearer heaven by the altitude of a chopine." As for the play: *Boy . . . And all those swearings keep as true . . . As doth that orbed continent the fire / That severs day from night*—the sun more reassuring of love than Sartre's whirligig comment on *The Maids*—
>
> "Translated into the Language of Evil: Good is only an illusion; Evil is a Nothingness which arises upon the ruins of Good."
>
> Genet, *Journal du Voleur*, 1948:
>
> "Unless there should befall me an event of such gravity that my literary art, in the face of it, would be imbecilic and I should need a new language to master this new misery, this is my last book."
>
> "The wonder is he hath endur'd so long."
>
> —K.L., V,iii,316 (236)

If I am right to claim that Zukofsky takes pleasure from the penetration of other voices, then how telling that he allows Genet's penetration to utter a desire for the spectacle of boy actors in drag—a desire that couldn't otherwise be authorized? Boy actors aside, this passage is of equal, if less prurient, interest, for the way in which Zukofsky plucks one of Kent's lines from *King Lear* and uses it, without comment of his own, to answer Genet's claim in *Journal du Voleur* that "this is my last book." No longer a character in *Lear* speaking of the king's death, Kent is now a character in a different play —call it *Bottom: On Shakespeare*—in which he muses about the character

"Genet" as though in aside to yet a third character (Zukofsky? the reader?). Suddenly, Zukofsky's assertion that Shakespeare wrote one long play to prove that *love sees* seems less like a claim that he really wants us to take seriously than like a cheeky, even campy, projection of his own desire in *Bottom* to *re*write Shakespeare as one long closet drama, in which all the Bard's characters, plus a few sexy supporting players like Genet, interact in a theater of the imagination. Even more perversely, Zukofsky seems to find a precursor for his method in Spinoza, who, as he claims, "'demonstrated' geometrically but asserted dramatically" (94). Whatever drama is latent in Spinoza Zukofsky makes manifest not only as a manner of argumentation but also as a matter of form.

Insofar as *Bottom* may be read as a closet drama, it remains "closeted" or armchair bound by its status as one man's meditation, however much he ventriloquizes. In other words, the pleasure of penetration by other voices is coupled by the pleasure of speaking all the parts. When we read the father-son dialogue of the "Definition," we might do well to remember Zukofsky's quotation of Joyce much earlier in *Bottom*: "the Father was Himself His Own Son" (22). Even if we do not, we must still recognize the extent to which the "son," who anticipates the father's arguments and rehearses them in a voice that draws ever nearer in tone and diction to that of the "I," is simply a rhetorical prop, not an actual interlocutor.

The desire to play all the parts is, of course, Bottom's desire in *A Midsummer Night's Dream,* and the one for which David Román and Tim Miller cite him as a quintessentially queer performer.[20] If multiple, contradictory, and transgressive identifications are queer, then who could be queerer than the author of *Bottom,* who wants to speak not only as Wittgenstein and Julius Caesar, but also as Gertrude Stein and Julia? As Zukofsky says of Shakespeare's variations on his (Zukofsky's) definition of love, "As words and lines they are an after-persistence of a thought that sometimes borrows a fool's heart and a woman's eyes so that naked men may see it better" (216). So too in *Bottom* does Zukofsky sometimes borrow a fool's heart or woman's eyes—that is, identify with and speak through marginal figures (and for the benefit, no less, of "naked men")—and more often than we would notice if we became preoccupied with his ventriloquism of, say, Aristotle. Take, for instance, his entry in "An Alphabet of Subjects" for *J:* "Julia's Wild," a twenty-line poem in which, as though modeling a fugue in miniature, he offers a series of modulations on Julia's line from *The Two Gentlemen of Verona,* "Come, shadow, come, and take this shadow up" (393). In this treatment, Julia has indeed gone wild—or rather, Zukofsky has gone wild in his identification with her and his obsessive handling of the sexually charged words *come, take,* and *up,* which appear in such erotic recombinations as, "And up, come, come" and "come and take this up."

In short, "Julia's Wild" is a love poem, more specifically a valentine, and not, as is usually the case with the poems Zukofsky calls valentines, one for Celia or his son Paul but for his friend the poet and magazine publisher Cid Corman. As Zukofsky explains in an addendum-cum-dedication to the poem, "For Cid Corman who after reading *The Two Gentlemen of Verona* wrote: 'Apart from the Sylvia Song, I like best the line—*Come, shadow, come, and take this shadow up.* Ring a change on that for me? A dark valentine.'" Corman, pleased with his friend's dark valentine, responds via letter with a poetic coda, one stanza of which reads,

> *There we may not waver nor hesitate*
> *But move within each other like the tides*
> *Confronted always by the shores that rest*
> *Under and over us releasing us. (394)*

In obvious appreciation of the gesture, Zukofsky reprints the poem in *Bottom,* as well as the rest of Corman's letter, in which he adds, "Needless to say, this is written for you." If it is "needless to say" that Corman's desire to "move within each other like the tides" is directed toward Zukofsky, then why does Zukofsky need to say it explicitly for his readers' benefit? And if, as Rifkin contends, *Bottom* is (after eyes) all about marriage, then why does an exchange of love letters between two married men enjoy this pride of place in the book?

Though Zukofsky states early in *Bottom* that "Shakespeare handles [the passions] time and time again in the essentially same prescription for a 'marriage' or a 'sleep'" (24), his repeated emphasis on *friendship*—and specifically friendship between men—belies his averred interest in Shakespearean wedding rites. After all, in almost the same breath that he speaks of Shakespeare's prescription for marriage, Zukofsky cites Falstaff's friendship for Hal (and not, as we might expect, Romeo's love for Juliet or even Othello's for Desdemona) as the Shakespearean example par excellence of Love as tragic hero. Indeed, as he teases out his definition of love, Zukofsky often refers to such male friends as Antonio and Mercutio when we would think it likely for him to invoke the great lovers of the plays; and some of his most enthusiastic writing (or quoting) about love foregrounds love between men. It is difficult, then, not to call to mind Zukofsky's passionate exchange of words with Corman when rereading a passage earlier in *Bottom* in which Zukofsky declares, "One, after all, loves the child, the tree, or loves another's words, or life, as one colloquially speaking 'has' religion, piety, or honesty" (90).

Piety and *honesty* (if not *religion*) are crucial terms for Zukofsky, at least in part for their centrality to Spinoza, whose definitions of these very words Zukofsky proceeds to cite. These Spinozan concepts appear with equal weight in the second half of "*A*"-9, written contemporaneously with parts of *Bottom*:[21]

> *A wise man pledging piety unguarded*
> *Lives good not error. By love's heir are asserted*
> *Song, light obverted to mind, joy enjoined to*
> *Least death, act edging patience, envy discarded;*
> *Difficult rare excellence, love's heir, averted*
> *Loss seize the hurt head Apollo's eyes point to:*
> *Ai, Ai! Hyacinthus, the petals in vision—*
> *The scission living acquiescence, coded*
> *Tempers decoded for friendship, evaded*
> *Image recurring to vigilance, raided*
> *By falsehood burning it clear to the vision,*
> *Derision transmuted by laughter, goaded*
> *Voice holding the node at heart, song, unfaded*
> *Understanding whereby action is aided. (110)*

Bottom and the second half of "*A*"-9 clearly speak to and with each other. Even the tiniest details corroborate their consonance, as, for instance, the striking phrase "act edging patience" rings in time with Zukofsky's comment on Thisby's speech in *Midsummer,* "These words edge pleasure, innocence, and terror" (34). More striking still, the latter half of "*A*"-9, which is typically supposed to turn away from the Marxist politics of Zukofsky's youth toward a celebration of domestic tranquility, inscribes at the heart of its marital project—much like *Bottom*—a dark figure of homoerotic love.[22] The paradigmatic lovers whom Zukofsky chooses to enlist in his discussion of "piety unguarded" are Apollo and Hyacinthus, a Spartan youth who is killed by an errant discus and of whom Apollo says as he "seize[s] the hurt head" of his dying lover, "I am the author of your death. / And yet, what crime is mine? Can play, can sport / be blamed? Can having loved be called a fault?"[23] To paraphrase "*A*"-9's own rhetoric, what we might expect to be an evaded image of loving men recurs to the vigilant reader who is willing to burn clear to vision Zukofsky's investment in coded friendship.

Such coded friendships—and the codes that regulate them—become an even more obsessive theme in Zukofsky's translation of the Latin play *Rudens.*

INCOMPRESSIBLE LOVE

Before leaving *Bottom* behind (so to speak), I want to puzzle through one of the book's most obsessive—and curious—repetitions. Zukofsky opens "Music's Master," the first long part of *Bottom,* with a quotation of Scarus's lines from *Antony and Cleopatra,* "I had a wound here that was like a T, / But now 'tis made an H" (33). After several more allusions to the lines or references to Scarus's wound scattered throughout the book, Zukofsky again quotes the passage in "Z (*signature*)," the last entry in "An Alphabet of Subjects," which concludes his volume of *Bottom* (442). If *Bottom* (almost) begins and (almost) ends with Scarus's wound, then surely that wound has some special significance to Zukofsky and to *Bottom*'s project, but where exactly does that significance inhere? In "Music's Master," in which Zukofsky promises (but never delivers) a graph of culture, he elaborates, "Scarus had a wound that an added stroke to a T, turned either clockwise or counterclockwise by its head, made an upright visible H —and all invention headed off by thought in late cultures has this wound" (33). Like many of Zukofsky's gnomic glosses in *Bottom,* this so-called explanation of Scarus's wound verges toward the incomprehensible, or at least raises more questions than it answers: How exactly does Zukofsky read Scarus's wound? What is "invention headed off by thought"? What relation does thought bear to the wound? And why do all "late cultures" (which cultures?) have it?

I want to suggest, in the spirit of my earlier interpretations of *Bottom,* that to read Zukofsky's musings about Scarus's wound at face value would be to fall for a red herring. Late cultures and their immaterialized graphs aside, what about the loving and careful language in which Zukofsky describes the wound? The T, "turned . . . by its head," is "made upright"—as if the shifting letter were a flaccid penis suddenly become erect. As tangible things, letters are certainly as real (and sometimes more real) to the materialist in Zukofsky as bodies, so why not read this letter—which is, after all, inscribed on Scarus's flesh—as a body part? (Remember his mention of the "smallest joints of words.") And if the letter is a genuine body part, then perhaps it is a mistake to read it too hastily as penile. A new opening on Scarus's body, the T is more like a second mouth (as a letter, it "speaks"); and when the added stroke makes it an H, the insistence on its status as gash

or tear make its more like a second anus. Finally, this restless, mutable orifice cannot be metaphorically reduced to anything other than itself—a restless, mutable orifice—and it seems to me that precisely this sexually pro-
tean quality of the letter provides Zukofsky with so much renewable pleasure
and fascination.[24] Tellingly, Zukofsky "crammes" his final quotation of
Scarus in "Z (*signature*)" between two passages that speak of O's:

> "*Or may we cramme*
> *Within this wooden O*"
> —*Folio:* The Life of Henry the Fift. *Prologue*

> "Scar *[us]*, *I had a wound here that was like a T*,
> *But now 'tis made an H.*

> *The little o'th'earth.'*
> *Folio:* THE TRAGEDIE OF / Anthonie, and Cleopatra., IV,vii,8; V, ii,81

Later texts of Antony *(sic) and* Cleopatra *letter (* verb*):*

> "*The little O, the earth.*"
> *And there is a tone and an earth of difference . . . (442)*

Like two eyes looking straight at Scarus, the two O's remind us that we might
think of Scarus's differently lettered wound as a sort of O, or hole, in its own
right; and in turn, Scarus's wound reminds us that the O's themselves may
afford a not merely ocular pleasure. Indeed, the O's may finally make less
an earth than a m*oo*n of difference.

With the erotic valence of Zukofsky's wordplay (or, more accurately,
letter-play) in mind, I want in addition to link Scarus's wound, "turned either clockwise or counterclockwise," to another passage in Zukofsky, the
final line of his *Rudens:*

> Sweet   turn on your side. (507)

With no precedent or referent in the Plautus play that Zukofsky has translated, this line, like several other interludes scattered throughout the text,
is described as a "*Voice off* "—and this last voice off should be intoned, we
are told, "*as the audience is already moving out*" (507). Bracketing for a moment all the problematics of what a production of Zukofsky's *Rudens* would
look and sound like, we can at the very least observe that the pregnant space
(a pause for breath?) between "Sweet" and "turn" suggests that *Sweet* is a
term of endearment for the person to whom the imperative *turn on your
side* is addressed. But who is this dear addressee, and who's making the ad-

dress—and, for that matter, what does the statement have to do with the action of *Rudens*? In *Zukofsky's "A": An Introduction,* Barry Ahearn suggests one interpretation:

> The myth [about the recovery of things lost] that *"A"*-21 adopts treats dreams as truthful oracles. In *Rudens* a dream shows Daemones a cryptic vision of his daughter's plight. The importance of sleep and dreams in *The Tempest* [echoed, as is *Pericles,* in the movement] needs no elaboration, and *Pericles,* too, invests dreams with deep significance. In his only play, *Arise, Arise,* Zukofsky specifies that much of the action takes place behind a "dream curtain." The final words of *"A"*-21 suggest that his *Rudens,* like *Finnegans Wake,* has all been a dream; we hear someone asking his (or her) spouse to make more room in the bed. (179–80)

While I assent to Ahearn's reading of *Rudens* as no mere closet drama but a sort of dream play, I question the certainty with which he reads the translation's final, "waking" line as "someone asking his (or her) spouse to make more room in the bed." Implicit in this reading is a reliance on and reference to the biographical Zukofsky; no doubt the spouse in question is Louis or Celia—and more likely Louis, complaining in one of his hypochondriacal distempers that he hasn't been sleeping comfortably. But if we unfetter the line from what we know about the Zukofskys' marriage, and if we remember the lessons taught by Scarus's turning wound, then it should be apparent that this other turning is equally susceptible to an erotic reading. Rather than a request to make room in the bed, might not the imperative express a desire for easier access to or entry of an orifice? And who's to say definitively to what sort of gendered body that orifice might belong? While Ahearn's heterosexual couple is certainly one possible configuration of bodies in a bed, Sweet and partner might equally well be two women—or two men.

Given the homosocial ethos of *Rudens,* an address (and a suggested sexual act) between two men is a more probable conclusion to the play than any other potential scenario. This homosocial ethos has, nevertheless, been entirely neglected by critics of Zukofsky's translation. Because of his interest in the theme of "the recovery of things lost" (177), Ahearn, for instance, emphasizes in his interpretation of *Rudens* the reunion of father Daemones (in Zukofsky's translation, "Dads") with his daughter Palaestra ("Polly"), who was kidnapped and enslaved by a pimp ("Leno") but who is ultimately restored to her parents en route to a marriage with Plesidippus ("Placey"). As Zukofsky has it in his version of the prologue's argument:

Plot

fisheRman's sea   net dragged Up a leathery wicker
rattling the baby's charms of his master's Daughter
a leno had kidnapped for his slave brothEl.
unknown to her father she was his little ward
after her shipwreck: later they fouNd out—
she married her Sweetheart   a young man. (438)

On the basis of this synopsis, we might assume that Polly plays a central role in the action of *Rudens,* but in fact she hardly ever appears onstage. With the exception of a couple of brief scenes, her subjectivity fades from view as her exchange among the play's men serves as an alibi for their various verbal and physical exchanges with each other, which occupy nearly all of the play's five acts.

In advancing such a reading of *Rudens,* I take a cue from David Wray, a classicist who proposes a similar approach to the poems of Catullus in *Catullus and the Poetics of Roman Manhood* (which includes an excellent chapter on Zukofsky's Catullan translations). Wray advocates a decentering in Catullan criticism of the figure of Lesbia and underscores the fact that most of Catullus's poems are not, in fact, love poems about Lesbia but narratives about or exchanges with men—and that even the poems addressed to Lesbia are often written for the benefit of other men or as oblique addresses to men in their own right.[25] Drawing on the work of the cultural anthropologist Michael Herzfeld, Wray finds "not only present but pervasive through the Catullan corpus" this "central feature": "a prioritizing of the performative over the ethical, so that there is less focus on 'being a good man' than on 'being good at being a man'" (67). As Catullan speakers and their interlocutors perform their manhood for each other, they vacillate between aggressive speech acts, which usually take the form of sexual insults or threats, and paradoxically effeminizing displays of tender affects toward other men.

Though Plautus (250?–184? B.C.E.) and Catullus (84–54 B.C.E.) are separated by a span of historical context and change that should not be underestimated or discounted, I want nevertheless to suggest that a similar spectacle of exclusively male performance animates Plautus's *Rudens*—and that Zukofsky is not simply sensitive to this spectacle but renders it with exuberant translatorial pleasure. Moreover, that pleasure is intimately bound to Zukofsky's perverse method of translation. Often quickly glossed by commentators as a homophonic translation, like passages of "*A*"-23 and

Catullus, Zukofsky's *Rudens* is in fact a much more mixed bag of transla-tor's tricks, which include but are not limited to homophony.[26] As Barry Ahearn says of Zukofsky's heterogeneous approach to the translation of Plautus:

> To call it a translation expands that term beyond its recognizable bounds. . . . Zukofsky . . . [manufactures] variations, arabesques, jokes, and strained readings not present in the Latin—but extractable from it. Zukofsky relied on a particular edition (the Loeb) but "relied" in a strange fashion. He treated the text as a frozen language on which he could play variations. . . . Even while treating the Latin with apparent abandon, Zukofsky sticks so close to the Loeb edition that the number of lines in his *Rudens* and Plautus's *Rudens* are equal. It seems that Zukofsky has deliberately flouted the cardinal rule of good translation; he has tortured the spirit of the original on the rack of the letter. (177)

Nor is Zukofsky's "torture" limited to the constraint "that the number of lines in his *Rudens* and Plautus's *Rudens* [be] equal"; for most of the trans-lation, he also operates at the level of each discrete line under a quincunc-tial constraint—that is, he writes lines of exactly five words. Ahearn observes of the effect of this game, "[Since] the Latin has no such cramping in its line length, '*A*'-21 has to pack its meaning into fewer words. As a result, we often have trouble following the action. Again and again we are forced to consult the Loeb text to discover what is 'going on.'" Of course, Zukofsky did not produce a translation whose narrative is often opaque simply in order to confound his readers and send the enterprising ones back to Plau-tus; the ingenuity into which his self-imposed constraints forces him also allows him to heighten the effect of the homoerotically charged perfor-mances of manhood that so dominate the action of *Rudens*.

This heightened effect is especially conspicuous in Zukofsky's render-ings of the sexually aggressive or threatening language that men unleash on each other. Consider the following exchange in I 2 between Placey, Dads, and Dads' slave Scape:

PL: Salvé daddy—'lo too.
SC: Who're you, boy or girl
"dad-dée"?
PL: He-man.
SC: Bore your own.
DA: I had a daughter. Lost.

No sons.

PL: God may yet—

SC: Give *you* Hercules' club for

         piddling here while *we're* working. (442–43)

In order to see just how much expansion of meaning Zukofsky's conden-
sation entails, it might be helpful to compare these lines with the English
translation provided by Paul Nixon in the Loeb edition on which Zukofsky relied:

PLES.:   (coming up) *Good-day to you, father—to both of you, in fact.*

DAEM.:   (brusquely) *And to yourself.*

SCEP.:   (looking up from his digging with a growl) *See here, are you male or female, calling him "father"?*

PLES.:   *I'm a man, of course.*

SCEP.:   (digging again) *Look for your father further, man.*

DAEM.:   (with a scowl at Sceparnio) *I did have one little daughter, sir. But I lost her, my only one. I never had a son.*

PLES.:   (with hasty encouragement) *Oh, well, the gods will give you one.*

SCEP.:   *Yes, and they'll give you one, by Jove—a blistering big one, whoever you are, bothering us busy men with your babble.*[27]

Sceparnio/Scape's initial insult of Plesidippus/Placey loses much of its force
in the limp and overly formal rendering, "See here, are you male or female,
calling him father?" Conversely, Zukofsky's line, "Who're you boy or girl
'dad-dée'?" packs considerably more punch. In this version, Scape impugns
Placey's masculinity not only semantically but also sonically: we can hear
the effeminizing jab in his fey, mocking repetition of the word *daddy*, pro-
nounced with jeering flair "dad-dée." In Scape's next line, Zukofsky even
manages to add a meaning that wasn't present in the original Latin. "Bore
your own," as a variant on the phrase *bear your own*, preserves, albeit in a
very strained way, something of the meaning, "Look for your father further,
man." But in another register, it also acts as a response to Placey's terse assertion that he is a "He-man." Capitalizing on a meaning of *bore* not as the
past tense of *bear*, but as a present tense verb, namely "to pierce or penetrate,"[28] the line means additionally *penetrate your own He-man*, or *fuck another man, if you're so manly*. The implicit suggestion is that Placey could
not rise to such an occasion because, as Scape's first insult proposed, he is
effeminate or submissive; and Scape proposes as much a second time when
he says, "Give *you* Hercules' club," a more learned variant of the all-too-

familiar *take it up the ass.* Again, Zukofsky adorns his translation with a meaning absent from (or less explicit in) Plautus: Hercules' tumescent club is a loosely homophonic approximation of the Latin *hercle,* an oath meaning *by Hercules* or, as in Nixon's less literal translation, "by Jove."

Zukofsky performs a similar feat of embellishment when, in III 4, he writes Dads' threat to Leno as, "Rap'n I'll reap your face!" (467), a line for which Nixon offers, "You touch that door and, by the Lord, I'll make hay in your face the next minute—with a fist for a fork!" (359). *Reap* echoes the *hay* and *fork* of Nixon's version, but it goes far beyond that imagery in brutality. We cannot help but hear in *I'll reap your face* the phrase *I'll rape your face,* both because the words are juxtaposed with Zukofsky's *rap* and because the threat is almost immediately preceded and followed in Zukofsky's translation by explicit mentions of *rape* (465, 469). Here, Zukofsky, who by the time he embarked on *Rudens* had already spent years working on Catullus, makes his Plautus veritably Catullan. To his ear, the line *I'll reap your face* must have recalled the various threats of irrumation scattered throughout Catullus's corpus; and in the context of *Rudens'* third act, full of aggressive acts and gestures, the interpolation of even further sexual hostility must have seemed warranted. After all, Dads' threat to Leno comes right on the heels of a challenge made to the pimp by Placey's slave, Track:

> *Tripes, strip!*
> *If your back hasn't more*
> *stripes than nails'n a fo'c's'le*
> *I'm top liar. After you—*
> *inspect mine: if it isn't*
> *guarantee tight leather wine-flask, absolutely*
> *all of one piece, why*
> *shouldn't I whip you sick? (467)*

In the world of *Rudens,* a man stays on top by proving he's not a "top liar," and sometimes the proof is less in the pudding than on his own naked body, which Track describes here with the lush, erotic phrase, "guarantee tight leather wine-flask." Paradoxically, Track must sexualize himself—and potentially even expose himself to other men—to assert his masculine superiority.

Of course, sometimes men's displays for each other are not aggressive at all, but genuinely affectionate. After Polly's identity as Dads' long-lost daughter is established and her betrothal to Placey secured, we never see an onstage reunion between the lovers. Rather, it is Track who, in IV 8, bears the good news to Placey—and to whom Placey expresses his amorous enthusiasm: "Ditto my love, my Track / my libertine, sponsor, almost father—" (497). In Zukofsky's intensification, Track's interpellations by Placey as *anime* and *liberte*, rendered by Nixon as *darling* and *freedman* (415), become *love* and *libertine*. In abandoning *freedman* as a translation of *liberte* for the more homophonic *libertine*, Zukofsky forgoes one meaning of the line, namely that Placey is so thrilled by Track's news that he will grant the messenger his freedom. What he gains in this loss, however, is the ability to render explicit through the use of the word *libertine* the implicit sexual connotations of Placey's effeminizing prostration before his own slave; indeed, the cost of emasculating abjection before one's inferior may be equivalent to an elevation in the inferior's status. Sure enough, as the scene continues, Placey is no longer in a position to give orders but only, in Zukofsky's idiom, to get Track's "consent." Track, now love and libertine, tellingly grants his consent in all matters save Placey's request to "kiss my— / girl?" or embrace her parents, and Placey submits without complaint: "Tuck my sponsor" (498). In Plautus (and Nixon's translation), Plesidippus *does* complain, "Now I want him to [consent], he [consents] not," before following his slave to Daemones' house with the scene's final line, "Lead me where thou likest, patron mine!" (417–19). In Zukofsky's version, not only the omission of Placey's resistance to Track's orders but also his rendering of the last line, "Tuck my sponsor," corroborates Placey's erotically tinged enthrallment to Track. A homophone of the Latin *duc, tuck* distorts the sense of leading necessary for the line's literal comprehensibility, but offers at least the following meanings in its place: "to compass; stuff; cram . . . to cover snugly with wrappings, as with bedclothes or rugs . . . to put into one's stomach; eat."[29] If Placey's desire to be stuffed, eaten, or covered snugly with bedclothes by his slave-cum-sponsor ever did come to pass, perhaps Track would be the likely candidate to tell his unmanned master to "turn on his side."

Whether men's performances yoke them together in aggression or affection, they are, finally, in *Rudens* always yoked together—or, if you like, *roped* together. *Rudens* is, of course, Latin for *rope* (and also *sheet*), and Zukofsky says of the play's rope motif in one of his voice offs,

> As rope braided
> rude deigns, not
> to hang by,
> to tug and bind. (476)

A homophonic transliteration of *Rudens*, "rude deigns" suggests the dual aspects of male performance in the play: sexually aggressive acts of aggrandizement (*rude*) "braid" with effeminizing acts of capitulation or debasement (*deigns*) to "tug and bind" men to one another. Though the rope that binds men in certain configurations may not "hang" them, the "tug" that pulls them closer may nevertheless involve a degree of violence, which Zukofsky highlights through his play on the consonance of *rope* and *rape*. After he's been "lassoed" by Placey in III 6, Leno complains to his indifferent friend Chum,

> *Sacred cow this rope's strangling*
> *me—Chum!*
> . . . .
> This *is rape!* (472)

Rope also serves as a euphemism for the male member, as when Track says to the fisherman Greave in IV 3, "*I'll* pull your rope!" (481). In this scene, the metaphorical meaning of rope as a sexually charged binding mechanism is bodied forth with particular vividness. Greave has dragged from the ocean a valuable chest (in Zukofsky's idiom, a "wicker"), which Track recognizes as Polly's and wants to take from the truculent fisherman. As they play at tug of war on the rope with which Greave hauls his booty, their struggle over the absent woman's property images the more abstract ways in which men in the play struggle over the exchange of absent women *as* property. Finally, Track, like Placey in III 6, lassoes his combatant with an exultant taunt:

> TR: I've roped
> *You!* dock ya now!
> GR: I'm helmsman
> drop the rope!
> TR: Wicker first!
> GR: Today Hercules can't ram me! (484)

As we must by now expect, the agon over the wicker is quickly translated into a sexual power play. "I've roped *you!*" echoes obviously with *I've raped you*, and Greave, attuned to this subtext, replies to the suggestion that he has been in some sense sodomized, "Today Hercules can't ram me," recalling the mention of "Hercules' club" in I 2. As in that scene, Zukofsky's overtly sexual language is his own adornment. "Today Hercules can't ram me" combines homophony with pure invention to approximate the Latin, *Numquam hercle hinc hodie ramenta fies fortunatior*, which Nixon translates more faithfully, "You'll never be a blessed bit the richer for this find, confound you!" (387). Unlike Track, the reader who patiently works through Zukofsky's confounding language is blessed for finding the ways in which this *Rudens* is richer—and queerer—than a more straightforward translation would be.

These observations raise a further question about compositional practice: if the results of Zukofsky's method of translation are queer, then is there something queer about the method itself? Perhaps. In an early version of an essay on Zukofsky's translations of Plautus and Catullus, David Wray makes the following observation about one of Zukofsky's Catullan quirks, a substitution of the word *care* for the Latin *quare* ("wherefore"): "'Care' is a mighty 'quare' way of englishing the Latin *quare*. And the almost excrementally horrible silliness of that observation literalizes, perhaps, the sense in which translating Catullus like this . . . brings us into (befouling? taboo?) contact with an alien tongue, and of course also a dead one."[30] In this case, neither the Latin *quare* nor the English *care* is, in any semantic way, queer —so why is it that Wray cannot resist describing the translation not only as queer but also and more explicitly as excremental, befouling, and taboo? What is it about Zukofsky's translations—and not just of Catullus, but of Plautus, too—that makes them cross the line between perversity and *perversion*? By way of beginning to answer this question, I want to consider a bit of dialogue among Dads, Greave, and Track in IV 4. Dads, Greave's master, has been elected to arbitrate the dispute between Greave and Track over the "wicker," and Greave is aggrieved that Dads has consented to hear Track's side of the story first:

> DA: Quiet
> Greave!
> GR: And let him peach?!
> DA: You'll wait your turn.
> GR: You'll
> hear th'alien preach first?
> TR: Incompressible! (487)

Surely it is no accident that Zukofsky substitutes *incompressible* for the more likely (if we can reliably expect anything to be likely in this *Rudens*) *irrepressible*. In part, this word choice must be Zukofsky's self-conscious joke about his own translation, in which he has demonstrated that Plautus's play, far from incompressible, can be compressed to exactly five words per line. But the word also echoes deliberately the Latin *comprimere*, a verb that, in some contexts, means *to rape;* thus, it is almost as if Zukofsky were tacitly acknowledging that his translation has, in the process of compression (and other forms of distortion), done some sort of sexual violence to Plautus's *Rudens.* Indeed, whether or not sexual violence—or sex at all—comprises the content of Zukofsky's writing, his consistent formal decision, like Dads, to "hear th'alien preach first," or to let the abnormal and aberrant meaning take priority over the applicable and appropriate one, may be understood as a queer practice.

Of course, it is finally impossible, or at least fallacious, to try to separate form from content, nor do I wish to do so. In the spirit of considering the two inseparably, I want to turn finally to another description, much tamer than Wray's, of Zukofsky's approach to translation. Considering Zukofsky's mention in his first voice off of "*nine/ men's/ morris*" (at least in part an allusion to *A Midsummer Night's Dream,* II.i.98), Barry Ahearn writes:

> Nine men's morris, a game for two that is older than human memory, could be an analog for the myth that powers *Rudens* and *"A"*-21. Both are millennia old, and both have survived variation—perhaps because of variation. The game's rules are also applicable to *"A"*-21. Pieces are moved one at a time, on a small grid. This conforms to the reduction in *"A"'*s line length and the consequently corseted style. The game ends when one of the three players no longer has enough counters to arrange three in a row, a termination fit for the lessening number of movements that remain to *"A."* (Only three are left after *"A"*-21.) (178)

Zukofsky was certainly preoccupied with numerology in a way that invites such a reading, and Ahearn provides a useful lens through which to consider the importance of nine men's morris to *"A"*-21 and to the project of *"A"* as a whole. But might the game, as a figure for the translation, have other, equally compelling interpretations? We should remember that the game is called nine *men*'s morris because the pieces, or counters, used to play are themselves called "men." If *Rudens* is in some sense a game of nine men's morris, then perhaps Zukofsky's nine men are the eight major male characters in the play (Arcturus, Scape, Placey, Dads, Track, Leno, Chum, Greave) plus *himself,* in the various personae of his voice offs (sometimes authorial, sometimes ventriloquisms of other men's voices, such as Bach). Moreover, as Zukofsky "moves" these men through an elaborate choreography of aggressive and affectionate performances, he may also have had in mind that other old morris that has "survived variation": the morris dance. He may even, in this play concerned with shipwrecks and fishermen on the one hand and (in)compressibility on the other, have meant to invoke yet a third morris, "a curious fish, allied to the eels . . . [whose] body is so *compressed* as to resemble tape."[31] Indeed, Zukofsky invites such speculation about the incompressible love of language compressed in his lines. As Guy Davenport relates in a review of the 1972 edition of *"A"*-24, "I once asked Zukofsky what the 'mg. dancer' is who dances in *"A"*-21, a milligram sprite, a magnesium elf, a margin dancer, or Aurora, as the dictionary allows for all of these meanings. 'All,' he replied" (19).

"HIS WORDS MADE QUEER THOUGHT"

Zukofsky's *Rudens* has been publicly performed only once—at a 2004 academic conference and before an audience composed largely of Zukofsky scholars who, despite their knowledge of his work, found the play hard to follow.[32] Its linguistic convolutions, which at times approach incomprehensibility, pose enough difficulty for the hard-working reader, let alone the audience member who strains (and probably fails) to catch its meanings. In this sense, the work announces its deliberate "unperformability"; as Barry Ahearn says, "This movement [of *"A"*] has all the trappings of a play, but it is clearly not intended for the stage. It is, rather, one of those dramas— such as *Prometheus Unbound* and *Pippa Passes*—meant to be read" (176). Never published under separate cover but only poised between other movements of a work that bills itself as a long poem, *Rudens* can certainly be said to invite primarily readers, not theater practitioners, to enter its world. But who's to say that some of those readers, like those who mounted the 2004 production, will not also be theater practitioners who will wonder how a staging of *Rudens* might be pulled off—and attempt it? And if *Rudens* is only "meant to be read," then why does Zukofsky bother to furnish it with "all the trappings of a play" and invite speculation about its potential staging? What purchase do voice offs and stage directions have if the play is not "really" a play but a poem in play's clothing?

I raise these questions not because I think they can be neatly resolved but rather in order to demonstrate that the author of *Rudens* is not so much averse to as ambivalent about the theater—and that ambivalence haunts *"A"* from start to finish. After all, the poem begins with an ill-received performance, and I would characterize the rest of the work as the artist's sprawling, often wayward attempt to overcome his "performance anxiety." *"A"*-1 chronicles an evening on which a young, solipsistic "Zukofsky" (or his proximate persona) leaves a concert of Bach's *St. Matthew Passion* in a hostile and alienated mood—an attitude, as Ahearn observes, that Zukofsky immediately satirizes in *"A"*-1 and from which he already begins to distance himself in *"A"*-2 (39–49). Some eight hundred pages later, the poem ends with *"A"*-24, or *L.Z. Masque*, Celia's score for an arrangement of different excerpts from Zukofsky's work. Between its opening suspicion and dismissal of performance and its culmination in a masque, *"A"* charts Zukofsky's progress as he learns to embrace collaboration and dramatic polyvocality, to move from *Rudens*'s homophony to *L.Z. Masque*'s polyphony.[33]

This move may also be understood as a belated but powerful reckoning with the associations between the Jewish body and overt theatricality. While the speaker of *"A"*-1 feels a keen alienation from the performance of explicitly Christian music that he has tried to embrace, his turn toward that performance is also a turn away from another set of prior performances: the staging of plays by Shakespeare, Ibsen, Strindberg and others, translated into Yiddish, at New York's Yiddish Theatre, where Zukofsky was a frequent spectator in his childhood. Dedicating *Rudens* to his brother Morris, with whom he often attended these productions, Zukofsky begins a partial rapprochement with Jewish theatricality—and the possibility for that theatricality to be associated with queerness, since the Jew's relationship to gentile culture has been routinely allegorized as sexual.[34] This tentative and gradual peacemaking is also felt in Zukofsky's veiled references to the other major site of Jewish (and queer) theatricality in the United States in the twentieth century—Broadway musical theater—and is epitomized perhaps by the ways in which his "dark valentine" for Cid Corman "rings a change" not only on *The Two Gentlemen of Verona* but also evasively on the title of the queer lyricist Lorenz Hart's "My Funny Valentine."[35]

Far from this kind of evasiveness and ambivalence—about Jewishness and its relationship to queer theatricality, or otherwise motivated—*L.Z. Masque* makes clear from the start that it is a prompt for live, embodied performance. In a headnote to the text, completed in 1968, Celia Zukofsky provides not only an explanation of the piece's composition but also very explicit instructions (if not demands) for its execution:

> *L.Z. Masque* is a five-part score—music, thought, drama, story, poem. Handel's "Harpsichord Pieces" are one voice. The other four voices are arrangements of Louis Zukofsky's writings as follows:
>
> Thought (T)—Prepositions
> Drama (D)—Arise, Arise
> Story (S)—It was
> Poem (P)—"A"

The Masque is centrally motivated by the drama. Each character *speaks* in monologue, acting the complete sequence of the assigned role in *Arise, Arise.*

The metronome markings for the music determine the duration of each page for all the voices on each page. The speed at which each voice speaks is correlated to the time-space factor of the music. The words are NEVER SUNG to the music. Dynamics are indicated by type point size—(14 pt = loud; 12 pt = moderate; 10 pt = soft). Each voice should come through clearly. Performance time: approximately seventy minutes.[36]

Though this introductory matter leaves no doubt that *"A"*-24 wants to be *heard,* not read, the masque does share with *Rudens* a history of being known only to readers of Zukofsky's poetry and not by a larger theatergoing or musical community. Indeed, most readers of *"A"* have never seen a performance or heard a recording of the masque; and those who have must, as Bob Perelman asserts, bring to it a fairly extensive working knowledge of Zukofsky's writing—prose, poetry, *and* drama—in order to appreciate fully (or at least *more* partially, in both senses of the word) the nuances of the piece: "Clearly, everybody hears all the *sound* of the piece. But Zukofsky is trying to hook up the physical instantaneous unconscious undistortable act of hearing with the fullest possible range of thought (all of a life). Performing and hearing 'A'-24 presupposes a thorough knowledge of Z's work, an ecstatically dilated time sense in which every syllable continues sounding until they all have resolved each other, and an eternity in which the whole work is present in any of its sounds. A properly ambitious conclusion to 'A.'"[37] To be sure, the masque is not a closet drama like the *Rudens* of Ahearn's description, only "meant to be read." But insofar as the piece is inaccessible or even hostile to initiates who do not know Zukofsky's writing inside and out, it may be said to exemplify another definition of closet drama as drama intended chiefly or exclusively for a coterie audience. Before proceeding to examine just such a set of coterie performances of *L.Z. Masque,* I want to linger for a moment with those readers—the majority—who know the piece only on the page, as "a properly ambitious conclusion to 'A.'" The implied or potential meanings of *"A"*-24 as a written text differ radically from its effects in performance; and those meanings are worth considering in their own right, particularly because some of the queer dimensions of the masque are accessible only from a close examination of the written document as document. As one of Zukofsky's lines quoted in the masque attests, "His words made queer thought" (209). Celia's graphic rearrangement of Zukofsky's words makes his queer thought visible and, more radically, makes his thought visibly queer in ways that the words never disclosed in their previous written configurations.

The most important difference between the "look" of "A"-24 and the rest of the poem results from its generic qualities as a score, in which the four lines of text that accompany the music are overlaid on any given page. Such overlaying could prompt the reader to move "horizontally" through one line of thought, drama, story, or poem for discursive meaning; but she could also move "vertically" down the page and try to absorb all four lines more or less at once. In an excellent essay on "A"-24, Marnie Parsons discusses some of the possible effects of a vertical reading strategy: "Reading [the masque] vertically emphasizes its polyphonic nature, its simultaneity, and saves a lot of frantic flipping back and forth. While resonance of word and theme might continue (it's hard for a meaning-seeking mind not to strike up some connection, ironic or not, when [for example] the phrases 'picking a pocket' and 'profit-sharing' are overlaid . . .), vertical reading allows the words to exist as phonic representations, moves them toward expressions of a moment and away from constructions over time."[38] Parsons emphasizes the "exist[ence of the words] as phonic representations" in order to suggest the ways in which the masque is "suspend[ed] . . . between performance and print." While I don't dispute the idea that the masque begs us to think of its performative—specifically, sonic—dimensions even when we encounter it on the page, I find it telling that Parsons cannot resist, in parenthetical aside, engaging in precisely the sort of vertical "meaning-seeking" away from which she wants to move. Indeed, I would argue that vertical meaning-seeking is at least as valid and in fact a more likely response to the score than an imaginative appreciation of the words as phonic representations. Such an appreciation can be abstract only so long as the words are seen rather than heard simultaneously; and, moreover, the reader who pauses long enough to consider the thematic coincidence of "picking a pocket" and "profit-sharing" is really looking at the words not simultaneously but consecutively, after all.

Consequently, I advocate vertical reading of "A"-24 precisely as a meaning-seeking strategy that can reveal the dissonances that often animate the movement at the expense of any consonance among its voices. Consider the following fragment from the section of the masque entitled "Son: Fugues" (act II, scene 4):

> terror   of   the   blow
> *going to a wedding.*
> of   a   naval   battle,
>   *Variants/13 Pomes (232)*

In performance, the phrase "going to a wedding" would be the loudest voiced part of this moment; it is also, in twelve-point type, the most visually conspicuous element on the page and the one on whose meaning the other parts seem to comment as (in the movement's own idiom) some sort of "Variants." But what strange variants they make. Hardly the celebration of marriage that we might expect from Celia's "marriage" of Louis's words to each other and to music, the idea of going to a wedding is implicitly equated here to the "terror of the blow" and likened by juxtaposition to "a naval battle." In short, the passage suggests that a wedding, whether of words and music or husband and wife, is less a perfect union than a violent conflict. In a complication of the trend that we have located elsewhere in Zukofsky's writing, Celia proposes not the alternatives to nuptial love, but that love itself, as more martial than marital.

This passage's challenge to heteronormativity points to other moments in the masque whose troubled and troubling contiguities are more explicitly queer. In "Girl: Fantasia" (act I, scene 4), an excerpt from Zukofsky's essay on e. e. cummings's play *Him,* in which the main characters are Him and his female lover Me, collides with the Girl's dialogue from *Arise, Arise* and passages from *"A"*-3 and the short story "Thanks to the Dictionary" to blur with dizzying confusion boundaries of gender identification. The fragmentary phrases "play solely thru her relation with Him," "When I look at it, I begin to wonder if my body is my," "her elbow gently," and "This is my form" overlap provocatively, so that the confidence of the male speaker's assertion *this is my form* is entirely undermined (49). Indeed, we might begin to wonder whether his body is no longer his body but her elbow. Similarly, in "Son: Fugues," we find run together the phrases "sex was strength," "weren't on the other side in the first place," "pace and the characters," and "in revolution are the same!" (200). In this moment of sexual revolution, the idea that there is strength in the classification of sexed bodies is put under pressure, with the result that bodies on the other side of the gender binarism turn out to be the same. Or, in another possible interpretation, strength comes in revolution from alliance with same-sex oriented subjects, who weren't on the other side in the first place. The related possibility of celebratory same-sex desire also flourishes in the movement, as when the phrases "a passion with him," "beautiful, gather them," and "butt, butt" merge (186). Here the masque approaches, albeit in a much more formally challenging idiom, something of Zukofsky's erotic expression of love for the fellow smoker Peter Out in "Poem Beginning 'The.'" The beginnings of Zukofsky's work come full circle in the ending of "A," and this circularity illuminates his dedication to Celia's L.Z. Masque:

> the gift—
> she hears
> the work
> in its recurrence. (unpaginated)

Part of the gift's power comes from his wife's willingness, even eagerness, to let queer energies recur with as much force as, or more than, wedded love.

INSIDE OTHER VOICES

Of course, the energies that recur in performance diverge from those available to the close reader of L.Z. Masque. When four human voices and an instrument overlap in real time, the listener hearing what Guy Davenport has described as "a grand Jewish family affair, with everybody cheerfully talking at once" cannot possibly attend to the minutiae of resonances among the different lines that I have outlined above (24). Nevertheless, I want to argue that the different effects of L.Z. Masque in performance are still, if differently, queer—and much of that queerness depends specifically on which "family" members participate in the "affair." Though L.Z. Masque enjoyed its first public performances in New York on June 14–23, 1973,[39] I want to focus here on three performances of the masque organized by Bob Perelman and staged at various locations in the San Francisco Bay area between April and November 1978.[40] I investigate these particular performances not only because they best illuminate the dynamics (and especially the queer dynamics) of Zukofsky's work in performance, but also because these performances, properly contextualized and situated alongside contemporaneous public events in the Bay Area, occupy a special place in American literary history quite apart from—but perhaps best understood in relation to—Zukofsky's life and career.

As he relates in his short essay on "A"-24, Perelman, at "piano, should have been harpsichord," was joined in performances of the masque by his fellow poets Kit Robinson (Thought), Steve Benson and Carla Harryman (Drama), Lyn Hejinian (Story), and Barrett Watten (Poem) (292). Alongside numerous other writers of their generation, this small group of poets and friends have sometimes self-identified, sometimes resisted the identification, and at any rate often been identified by others as "language poets." Whether or not a coherent "school" of language poetry could be responsibly defined and who its "members" would be is beyond the scope of my present argument, but I do want to stress the importance of the personal and professional associations and collaborations among these six poets and other peers. Their performances of *L.Z. Masque* indicate just a fraction of the public events through which avant-garde writers in late-seventies San Francisco articulated their scholarly interests, political investments, and aesthetic visions (as if these concerns could be neatly separated). In *The Marginalization of Poetry*, Perelman recounts: "A coffee house in the Haight-Ashbery district of San Francisco, The Grand Piano, was the site of a long-running series of readings; a performance of Zukofsky's *'A'-24;* and a production of Frank O'Hara's play, *Try! Try!* The Talk Series that I curated would include a presentation of Shklovsky and Russian Formalism, a meditation of open versus closed forms, or an improvised performance piece."[41] Carla Harryman, who performed in the production of *Try! Try!* that Perelman cites, recalls playing "to a packed audience that seemed to be spilling out into the street. I remember performing a lot on a table so I could be seen in the deep narrow space."[42] This particular performance led to further collaborations under the rubric of "Poet's Theatre," in which she, Nick Robinson (Kit's brother), Eileen Corder, and others wrote, directed, and acted in a number of different plays.

I emphasize this diverse, public activity not only to provide a context of performance history for *L.Z. Masque* but also to challenge the received notion of language poets as predominantly "writerly" writers. Performance was just as important a means of artistic definition to Perelman, Harryman, and others as "the formation of self-managed literary venues" and "the development of presses," which Perelman also mentions. Perhaps more important, the centrality of performance to language writing also problematizes the assumption that language poets have sought simply or programmatically to refuse the concept of identity. If, as De Villo Sloan claims, "the SELF is implicated [by language poets] as [a] false reality construction [that] must therefore be eradicated," then how to account for the embodied spectacles, especially authorial readings, in which these poets' selves, far from eradicated or even eradicable, were announced and foregrounded?[43] In an interview that I conducted with him, Perelman highlighted both the importance of performance to the development of a new American avant-garde aesthetics and the complicated role of identity in this aesthetic formation:

All of these [performances] felt like—I don't mean in the ponderous sense of "we are making HISTORY" with turgid capital letters—but there was a sense of, we're taking this really seriously, it's really fun, and it's easy to be really interested in making a new poetics. It's not a kind of monastic, kind of algebraic, tedious study. It was very pragmatic and active. [Though many performances were improvisational and driven by impulse,] there was very little sense of displaying our charismatic persons. So it wasn't like the display of impulse you get on talk shows. . . . The antipersonal cast of all the aesthetics at the time—I certainly participated in it. . . . There was so much cape-wielding, dull charisma-flaunting in poetry at the time. It was pretty grim, so it was good not to buy into that.[44]

Perelman suggests here that he and others were not necessarily interested in abolishing identity or the self but, through collaborative work such as performance, were emphasizing a social, collective, and relational self in opposition to "charismatic" or "cape-flaunting" exhibitions of personality. Specifically, the 1978 performances of *L.Z. Masque* provided an exemplary occasion for precisely this sort of "antipersonal" personal display. A video recording of the November 15 performance at San Francisco State University testifies to the masque's ability to accommodate the paradoxical evacuation of personality within a personal performance.[45] Tom Mandel (then director of SFSU's Poetry Center) introduced the five performers by name and with brief descriptions of their published work, and each wore plain, everyday clothes; hardly were the performers in "character" for the staged reading, yet neither were they flaunting their personalities. Standing at microphones, the members of the ensemble maintained very sober expressions, almost entirely devoid of affect, until the first note was struck on the piano; then, as they breathed life into Zukofsky's work over the course of the masque's various scenes, they came to life, so to speak, and even smiled as they read passages in which they clearly delighted, as though inhabiting Zukofsky's words allowed them to inhabit their public roles as poets more easily and freely.

At this historical moment, animating Zukofsky's words must also be understood as reanimating Zukofsky, who had died in March 1978, a month before the language poets' first performance of the masque. If *"A"* is, as it has been so frequently described, Zukofsky's "poem of a life," then what better way to memorialize his life and death than to perform the long poem's last movement? Given the performances' status as a series of celebratory memorial services, I want to link them to another memorial of Zukofsky, a meditation on his work also sponsored by SFSU's Poetry Center and held on December 8, less than a month after the SFSU performance of *L.Z. Masque*. Indeed, Tom Mandel announced this later event in his introductory remarks for the masque, a mention that corroborates the idea that they should be understood as related phenomena. As planned, the program would feature the rare 1966 filmed interview with Zukofsky in his New York apartment (mentioned at the beginning of this chapter), following which Barrett Watten (the masque's "Poem") and the poet Robert Duncan were each to give a brief presentation on Zukofsky's work and lead, in Mandel's words, "what I hope will be a lively discussion from the floor." The course of events that December afternoon took a turn somewhat livelier than Mandel anticipated, and the day's "performances" have enjoyed a much livelier and more legendary afterlife in the memories of the participants and in the annals of literary history than anyone could have predicted. Carla Harryman, who was present for the proceedings, recalls the event with intensity:

> Barrett started talking and Duncan became hysterical, jumped up and went over to the speaker's area, and started jumping up and down in this histrionic manner, which some people loved and other people were irritated by. Then he read from [Zukofsky's last book, *80 Flowers*]. Barrett tried to retake the floor, I think rather adamantly, but I'm not sure about this part: my account of this could be unreliable. At the time, it just seemed unbelievably cruel and small-minded and my feelings get in the way of some of my recollections. Also, Duncan's performance values were silly. The fact that he could be cruel, small-minded and uncompelling as a performer and still get a chunk of the audience to cheer him lowered my esteem for the world I lived in. . . . Duncan was focused on trying to humiliate Barrett through his hieratic public voice. Of course, he wanted to keep his power in a manner consistent with the vicious m.o. of his scene. It was ugly. At the same time, Barrett was no mere victim: he was approaching Zukofsky on his own terms. And, I suppose, it's these terms, either way, that are finally of interest. (interview)

The dispute that broke out on this particular occasion—and that cannot help but recall, uncannily, the aggressive masculine displays of *Rudens*—developed over time into something of a literary feud. In an interview for the Winter 1985 issue of the journal *Sagetrieb*, Robert Duncan said of "the language people," "They're like a crowd of mosquitos off there in somebody else's swamp." In the same issue of *Sagetrieb,* De Villo Sloan documents the "poetry war" that "erupted" on the pages of *Poetry Flash,* a small San Francisco–based literary magazine, the previous summer: recalling the events of December 1978 in a review of a documentary film of Duncan and Zukofsky, David Levi Strauss ignited a series of heated editorial debates between the language poets and their detractors (241, 243–54). In Sloan's interpretation, the basis of this poetry war was fundamentally theoretical: "The central issue of the poetry war relates directly to other political and social events in the Bay Area that summer: a definition of SELF" (241). For the Duncan camp, according to Sloan, "there is still an objective/subjective world defined in terms of the self," whereas for the language poets, "transformative power does not come from SELF, which is illusory, but from the process of language" (243). As I have already attempted to demonstrate, this reductive argument does not adequately account for the language poets' ideas about identity. More important, the lens through which Sloan reads these literary skirmishes fails also to consider the central role that Zukofsky plays in the disagreements between the language poets and Duncan and his followers.

In contrast to Sloan, I would argue that the central ideological issue at stake in this literary feud was not a theory of self but an attitude toward literary tradition and filiation. Corroborating Harryman's claim that Duncan "wanted to keep his power in a manner consistent with the vicious m.o. of his scene," Perelman opines, "He definitely wanted followers, in the sense that he was the authority, and we basically weren't buying into that." Among the language poets, according to Perelman, "Nobody had much of an oedipal relation with earlier scenes. . . . It was much more of a self-made, somehow pragmatic avant-garde, and nobody was hoping for the approval of Robert Duncan, or hoping for the approval of whoever. We didn't get it, but it wasn't required in a way" (interview). I want here to underscore Perelman's description of Duncan's orientation toward literary tradition as oedipal. If Duncan wanted literary sons and daughters, then he also wanted literary mothers and fathers, and Zukofsky was one of these father figures. His outburst in 1978 over Barrett Watten's remarks did not happen in a theoretical vacuum but was specifically motivated by Watten's approach—not sufficiently or obediently oedipal?—to Zukofsky; as Harryman puts it, Watten "was approaching Zukofsky on his own terms." Indeed, when Duncan described the language poets several years later as "mosquitos . . . in somebody else's swamp," the swamp he had in mind was again Zukofsky's: "[They] were usurping [Zukofsky's work]," he asserted to his interviewers, "so the beauty of Zukofsky is lost in the transaction." In a war over the proper mode of literary initiation, agon, and ascent, Zukofsky's corpse and corpus became the literal battleground.

As an alternative to Duncan's oedipal tendency, I would characterize the language poets' approach to the past as a mode of surrogation. In *Cities of the Dead*, Joseph Roach defines surrogation as follows: "Culture reproduces and recreates itself by a process that can be best described by the word *surrogation*. In the life of a community, the process of surrogation does not begin or end but continues as actual or perceived vacancies occur in the network of relations that constitutes the social fabric. Into the cavities created by loss through death or other forms of departure, I hypothesize, survivors attempt to fit satisfactory alternates."[46] Rather than worshiping Zukofsky as a dead father (and Duncan as a living one), the language poets sought to fill the void created by Zukofsky's death with their own work, both written and performative. Their performances of *L.Z. Masque* provide an apt figure for the larger process of surrogation that their "self-made, somehow pragmatic avant-garde" accomplished: in the absence of the living, breathing Zukofsky, they spoke words in his place. Because such acts of surrogation, according to Roach, will likely "provoke many unbidden emotions, ranging from mildly incontinent sentimentalism to raging paranoia," Duncan's reaction to the language poets is not surprising (2). His sentimental nostalgia for "the beauty of Zukofsky . . . lost in the transaction" of the language poets' interpretation of Zukofsky's work, coupled with his paranoid suspicion that their interest in Zukofsky constituted a "usurpation," fits perfectly the model of responses to surrogation hypothesized by Roach and borne out in a variety of historical scenes of performance (and performative scenes of history). Yet far from usurpation or theft, the language poets' surrogation of Zukofsky constituted a gift: their attention to Zukofsky's work prompted the attention of others in a way that enabled them simultaneously to vault themselves *and* Zukofsky into the canon—or at least certain canons—of American literary history. As Guy Davenport observed as late as the early 1970s, "Zukofsky's work has been published for forty years and the reviewers and scholars, except for a few, have been silent and indifferent. . . . Our greatest living poet is usually a man as unknown to the professariat [*sic*] as to the corps of reviewers and the deaf custodians of the laurels. It was true of Whitman in 1873, and it is true of Zukofsky in 1973" (23). As the language poets began to be read in universities and, in some cases, became part of the "professariat" themselves, they brought Zukofsky with them—and to a much larger audience than he ever enjoyed in his (or Duncan's) lifetime.

In their performances of *L.Z. Masque,* a handful of these poets also brought a sensitivity to the queer resonances of Zukofsky's work. It would be tempting, but ultimately facile, to interpret the language poets' divergence from Duncan as a straight insurrection against an openly gay combatant, with a concomitant wresting of Zukofsky from a queer tradition of twentieth-century writing into which he might otherwise have been figured. This crudely identitarian version of the story would seriously misrepresent the motivations of the different parties concerned. As Perelman has observed, the service into which Duncan sought to enlist Zukofsky was entirely normative, even nationalistic: "There was a kind of contest. Duncan certainly wanted his version of Zukofsky, this echt American Zukofsky, which is kind of amusing in a way because Zukofsky is such an immigrant linguist. [In a very different way,] Zukofsky was a major figure—Zukofsky and Stein —to all of us at the time" (interview). Perelman's association of Zukofsky with Stein, a more patently queer figure, points perhaps to an aesthetics common to Zukofsky, Stein, and Perelman himself, as articulated in his introduction to the 1999 edition of his selected poems, *Ten to One.* The immediate referent for Perelman's remarks is his poem "Fake Dream: The Library," in which an unidentified graffitist draws arrows to change the words *Finger my asshole, cunt!,* scrawled on a men's room wall, to *Finger my cunt, asshole!,* thereby demonstrating that

> *syntax was not mere*
>
> *vanity and that bodies could use*
> *it to resist the tyranny of*
>
> *elemental words.*[47]

In his subsequent exegesis, Perelman draws larger artistic and political conclusions from these lines of the poem:

> For living poets writing is closer to a graffiti situation than to inscribing the canonized pages of Wordsworth. Our pages are not pristine, they're scrawled over with prior social postings, threats, blandishments. From the vantage of the men's room, the particular snarl of shame, rage, and threatened violence is all too familiar. Despite the poem's humor and its messing around with narrative probabilities, I'm quite serious about the need to resist the tyranny of elemental words. Which are what? Jew? Serb? Woman? God? Cunt? Nature? Poetry? They're words that brook no argument, that are intended to be outside of syntax and thus

outside of history. I try to resist these when I write. So I'm all for that third graffitist—a woman? a man? gay? straight?—who drew the arrows and critiqued the male threat, mocked it, began to undo it. Elemental words are always a threat, to whoever's outside their slanted beneficence. Resisting elemental words is a prerequisite to the pleasures that poetry can offer. (xvi)

Like the author of that other line that "mess[es] around with narrative probabilities," "Sweet turn on your side," Perelman seeks to challenge and complicate the boundaries of sex, gender, and desire in order to arrive at certain "pleasures that poetry can offer"—pleasures that I would identify as queer. These queer pleasures also inform, to borrow Harryman's phrase, the "performance values" with which the language poets sought to infuse their stagings of *L.Z. Masque.* In contrast to the "hieratic public voice" that Duncan used to try to silence Watten, the language poets used voice to more radical ends in their performances. As Harryman says of performing the masque, "Listening is everything and so is the placement of language. Ideally the experience is for each performer to be inside the voices of the other performers, but that only happened some of the time: I feel like I never knew the piece well enough to get there" (interview). To be inside the voices of others: is this not another way of saying that bodies can use language to resist certain elemental tyrannies? In the performance of the masque, the inhabitant of others' voices would speak not only Drama, for instance, but also Thought, Story, and Poem. She would experience the bewildering, pleasurable simultaneity of being Carla Harryman, Steve Benson, Lyn Hejinian, Barrett Watten, Louis Zukofsky—and who knows how many others? Harryman says that she "never knew the piece well enough to get there," but recordings of the performance belie her modesty. When I watch the tape of the November 15 masque, I look at close shots of a single performer— and it seems, sometimes, that several voices emerge at once from one mouth. At other times, the sound seems to exist in the spaces between bodies, as if no one person were speaking at all. To an ungenerous listener, the performance might seem like a silly cacophony. But it is also a queer polyphony: that is, a profusion of voices whose resonances and consonances, as well as their dissonances, destabilize the boundaries—gendered, sexual, and otherwise—of and between bodies. Such a queer polyphony also complements, and perhaps suggests an advance on, the tendency epitomized in *Bottom,* where one central figure, Zukofsky, wants to play all the parts; here, that central figure has submitted to a decentering, projected into a perpetual future, in which all the other parts (Thought, Drama, Story, Poem), once voiced, will play *him,* variously and elastically. The bottom's penetration by other voices gives way to his even more radical dispersal into other voices.

This decentering or dispersal is not wholly new to *"A"* in its final movement. Though I have suggested a progressive trajectory in Zukofsky's long poem from homophony to polyphony, the final, most fully polyphonic moment embodied by *L.Z. Masque*—both in text and in performance—is an homage to principles that Zukofksy may have been slow to adopt dramatically, but that were already manifested in embryo in his poetic praxis. Throughout the pages of *"A,"* a multitude of competing voices, gesturing in their crowdedness toward an eventual polyphony, constitutes the fabric of the poem, often in the form of quotation. One voice quoted by Zukofsky on three separate occasions belongs to Gertrude Stein, who was as much a guiding figure for him as he and she would come to be, together, for the language poets; and one of these quotations, figured in the poem's central movement, *"A"*-12, is particularly worthy of attention here:

> *G.S. as an old woman spoke to GI's:*
> *(—It is natural to speak of one's roof*
> *Between four walls, under a roof,*
> *And here was a whole city*
> *Spread without a roof)*
> *You will be flattered to death,*
> > *to death*
> *Because*
> *You will have to fight again.*
> > (One of them)
> *—After all we are on top.*
> *—Is there any spot on earth*
> *More dangerous than on top?*
> *And there it was.*
> *South Ferry almost erased*
> *By the wind in the slip.*
> *Horse ran there.*
> *Desire. (223–24)*

Here Zukofsky adapts a passage from a piece of Stein's reportage ("Off We All Went to See Germany," published in the *New York Times Magazine* in August 1945) and turns her conversation with the American G.I.s into a mini–closet drama, replete with the quasi-stage direction "*(One of them).*"[48]

As telling in his omissions and condensations as in his citations, Zukofsky leaves out of his dramatized version of the passage Stein's description of her "bitter[ness]" as she "got very angry" with the soldiers and called them "big babies." Stein cannot help but try to "top" the macho soldiers even as she warns them that there is no "spot . . . more dangerous than on top." Zukofsky, the perennial bottom, seems to want to soften Stein's tone—to make her "Desire," the word with which he concludes the stanza, conform to his own?—but as we shall see in turning to Stein's closet drama, her appetite for topping others is irrepressible.

3

topping stein

"NOT LITERARY SEX"

In a 1935 interview with the young novelist John Hyde Preston, Gertrude Stein speaks with unusual frankness about the role of sex in literature: "Sex and death are the springs of the most valid of human emotions. But they are not all; they are not even all emotion. . . . Literature—creative literature —unconcerned with sex is inconceivable. But not literary sex, because sex is a part of something of which the other parts are not sex at all. No, Preston, it is really a matter of tone. You can tell, if you can tell anything, by the way a man talks about sex whether he is impotent or not, and if he talks about nothing else you can be quite sure that he is impotent—physically and as an artist too."[1] The immediate referent for Stein's remarks about impotence is Ernest Hemingway, a former friend and protégé whose relationship with Stein had deteriorated and toward whom Stein's measured and indirect cattiness is not especially surprising. What does surprise a longtime reader of Stein (or this longtime reader of Stein, anyway) is the detail, eloquence, and candor—the almost philosophical systematicity—with which she talks here about sex. From Melanctha's "wandering" in *Three Lives* to the tender buttons of *Tender Buttons*, Stein's typical approach toward sex is the suggestive phrase, the knowing wink—never a posture of prudishness or avoidance, but never a frontal assault or dissection of sex, either. To find Stein talking directly about sex, then, is to find an unfamiliar Stein whose directness deserves attention.

Of course, Stein's directness here is precisely about the importance of indirection—or at least multidirectionality. When Stein insists as an aesthetic article, "not literary sex," she means at least in part that realistic depictions of sex—the sort of sex scenes that we find in D. H. Lawrence, for instance—are finally trivial and fail, in her view, to achieve the level of artistic inventiveness with which she is so obsessively concerned. Though initially shocking and perhaps even titillating, graphic sex scenes typify for Stein merely the inevitable, if extreme, limit of a Victorian logic and sensibility with which she seeks to break entirely; such scenes are not modern, and they are certainly not modernist. Indebted to cubism and other radical innovations in the visual arts, Stein must confront sex obliquely, abstractly, and from many different angles. Though her experimental province as a writer is not the image but "a matter of tone," she must, as she puts it, treat sex as "part of something of which the other parts are not sex at all." Sex must be subject to fragmentation, manipulation, and juxtaposition with other subjects if its role in literature is to serve anything other than, and more interesting than, a strictly representational purpose.

But even if this interpretation of Stein's remarks provides us with something like her theory of (writing) sex, it is nevertheless a theory that can be subsumed under and derived from the more general ideas about style and technique that we find in her essays and lectures. Yet in her further remarks to Preston, Stein does not make recourse to the sort of formal conjecture that we might expect of her; rather, she elaborates her ideas about sex from a more affective perspective: "'One thing which I have tried to tell Americans,' she went on, 'is that there can be no truly great creation without passion, but I'm not sure that I have been able to tell them at all. If they have not understood it is because they have had to think of sex first, and they can think of sex as passion more easily than they can think of passion as the whole force of man. Always they try to label it, and that is a mistake'"(191). It would seem that passion, then, and not sex or even formal innovation, is the real bee in Stein's bonnet. Indeed, when Preston goes on to ask her, "What has passion got to do with choosing an art form?" she replies, "Everything. There is nothing else that determines form" (193). Independent of its object or aim, passion as passion is, in Stein's calculus, the real prime mover behind creative expression and artistic genius. As she explains to Preston, passion—sexual or otherwise—is fruitfully harnessed not when it is merely "described" but rather when it is "transferred" from the artist to her creation (192).

How might this account of passion affect our understanding of what Stein means by her dictum, "not literary sex"? Though Stein takes great pains not to reduce simply to sex the passion that she heralds, she nevertheless claims too that writing "unconcerned with sex is inconceivable." So when

Stein does in fact conceive of sex in her work, how does she do it passion-ately? I want to suggest that the "passion" of which Stein speaks constitutes an insistence, relentlessness, and even ruthlessness in writing—an almost destructive impulse inherent in the creative one—that can also be under-stood as a kind of *violence;* and I would further contend that this violence manifests itself most apparently in Stein's writing where sex, sexuality, and so-called sexual deviance are concerned. We should not be surprised to find that violence, power, and at times outright sadism appear as preoccupations in Stein's work; consider not just her biographical reputation as something of a bully to the artists and friends who surrounded her, but more impor-tant, her by-and-large positive depictions of soldiers and sovereigns, such as Napoleon and Grant. And though such depictions can be found through-out the various phases of her career, I would argue that in the period of Stein's interview with Preston, her sadism surfaces chiefly in her late, vio-lent playwriting.[2]

I don't invoke lightly the word *sadism,* with all of its psychoanalytic and popular connotations, for there is a particularly sexual charge to Stein's re-lentless writing that owes largely (though not exclusively) to her relentless—and notorious—repetitions. Indeed, I would liken those repetitions, which evoke conflicting affective responses ranging from wonder and plea-sure to boredom and disgust, to the repetitions of pornography. Through-out her vast body of work, Stein often tackles the subjects of sex and so-called sexual deviance, but, like at least some pornographic films, her plays constitute an assault on the senses less because of the acts depicted or sug-gested than because of the style and manner of their representation.

Imagine the following cinematic scene: In the middle of the woods, a woman holds one end of a rope, the other end of which is tied around an-other woman. The first woman, anchored on one spot of muddy ground, whips the second woman and forces the bound woman to run in circles around her. Because of the way in which the shots are framed, we never see the whip touch the skin of the second woman. Rather, the camera cuts back and forth, repetitively, between dizzying shots of the woman running in cir-cles and equally dizzying shots of the trees and the sky, also whirring by in a series of circles. The viewer identifies with the woman's torture not be-cause the torture is imaged directly but because the cinematography makes him or her feel as disoriented as the victim of the whipping. Similarly, in Stein's 1938 play *Doctor Faustus Lights the Lights,* a reader understands the heroine's pain and confusion when she is stung by a viper not because the viper sting is graphically depicted but because the heroine's repetitive and

obsessive language in the aftermath of the sting makes the wound unfor-
gettable, invests the sting with indelible importance, and, in effect, *stings* the
reader.

Like the scene from Stein's *Doctor Faustus,* the cinematic scene that I
have just described is neither imaginary nor incidental. Indeed, it is the
penultimate scene of *Olga's House of Shame,* a 1964 film that the Wooster
Group juxtaposed with Stein's *Doctor Faustus* in its 1999 adaptation of the
play, *House/Lights.* In finding an innovative way to perform one of Stein's
performatively challenging closet dramas, the Wooster Group has also highlighted the very theme of repetition as sadism that I have sketched here.

To call Stein's plays (late or otherwise) closet dramas requires some
qualification, justification, and situation among various critical perspectives. In the most recent book-length study of Stein's drama, *Mama Dada:
Gertrude Stein's Avant-Garde Theatre,* Sarah Bay-Cheng rejects the idea that
Stein's plays ought to be construed as closet dramas. Bay-Cheng, who wants
to tell a developmental narrative about Stein's dramatic writing and who is
interested in the connections between experimental writing and the cinematic revolution, proposes that "the cinema made a profound impression
on [Stein's] dramatic writing after 1929" and "helped her to understand
how to manipulate time and meaning on stage." As a consequence of Stein's
confrontation with film, Bay-Cheng argues, "Stein's best dramatic writing
emerges only after her second, more adventurous film experiment [a screen-
play] in 1929." Though "the methods of making movies and staging plays
are obviously different," Bay-Cheng suggests that Stein eventually wrote
with an eye to performance precisely because of her exposure to cinematic
methods of representation.[3]

Several significant issues call into question the validity of Bay-Cheng's
account. Chiefly, the strength of her argument rests on the credibility of
the idea that cinema made, in Bay-Cheng's words, "a profound impression"
on Stein, but there is scant evidence to support this claim and, in fact, no
compelling reason to distrust Stein's own claim in the essay "Plays" that "I
myself never go to the cinema or hardly ever practically never and the cinema has never read my work or hardly ever."[4] Moreover, Bay-Cheng's interest in the relationship between cinema and Stein's drama motivates her
to ignore the many writings that Stein labeled "plays" before 1929, as though
these dramatic efforts do not count as such because they do not serve her
argument. A closer look than Bay-Cheng allows at the similarities between
Stein's early and late plays suggests that an uncomplicated story of Stein's
so-called growth and maturity as a dramatist is untenable. Many of Stein's

late plays, entirely unmentioned by Bay-Cheng, continue to resemble early efforts in their lack of discernible plot, character, and dialogue. And even the late plays that do rouse her attention—what she calls "Stein's best dramatic writing"—disrupt dramaturgical conventions in ways that Bay-Cheng fails to consider out of a desire, it would seem, to uphold a notion of Stein as a dramatist who ultimately learned how to write a "good" play. I finally view with suspicion Bay-Cheng's preservation of traditional notions of theatricality and the recourse that she makes to taste to camouflage (or at least to suspend contention with) the conservatism of her point of view. Though she applauds, early in her book, Stein's movement away from Freytag's schema of dramatic structure (19), Stein goes far beyond a dismissal of rising and falling action in the most radical of her dramatic experiments. Indeed, I would cite her extreme radicality—the at-times complete abandonment of theatrical method and principle in her plays—as the signal factor that makes Stein such a compelling figure in the history of modern drama.

I would also cite this extreme radicality as the basis on which to understand Stein as a closet dramatist. We need not suppose that Stein intended her plays only to be read—or indeed suppose any programmatic intention at all—to call the work "closet drama." Rather, the term *closet drama* may be assigned to Stein's work simply because of her refusal to follow the rules —anyone's rules—of how to write a play. As an essay such as "Plays" makes clear, Stein was hardly ignorant of the mechanics of staging a play. Far from it, she had thought deeply about—and was dissatisfied and frustrated with —the disjunction between what she called one's "emotional time as an audience" and "the emotional time of the play" (xxix). At the same time, her plays do not, in any obvious or immediate way, propose an alternative mechanics to compensate for the "syncopated time" of the theater (xxix); they simply do away with the mechanics altogether by blurring beyond recognition the distinctions among dialogue, didascalia, and other diegetic language that seems to belong to the province of neither dialogue nor didascalia. Martin Puchner, who also views Stein as a closet dramatist, attributes such perverse playwriting strategies to Stein's "conflicted form of resistance [to the theater], a resistance that entails a simultaneous attachment to the theatre" (111). While I appreciate the finesse with which Puchner identifies Stein's ambivalence toward the theater, I would finally characterize the form that this ambivalence takes less as a resistance to theatricality than as a taunting provocation to theater practitioners. Stein's plays so aggressively—so *passionately,* to return to her word of choice—violate theatrical norms that they constitute an implicit challenge. "Stage *this*," they seem egotistically to dare, beckoning an ingenious director to top Stein's own ingenuity. Yet Stein's ego was finally more gratified by being topped than by topping others. She may have stopped going to the theater, but she was nevertheless thrilled at the prospect that anyone would stage or see one of her plays staged, so hungry was she for any attention to be paid to her work.[5]

Given this violent passion for recognition and the seeming ease with which it was appeased, I cannot help but wonder what Stein would have made of *House/Lights*. (I suspect she would have adored it.) As I offer an interpretation of Stein's play and an account of the Wooster Group's adaptation, I will also consider two of Stein's other plays of the 1930s, *Byron A Play* and *A Play Called Not and Now,* which are likewise intimately concerned with the issues of recognition and celebrity. In all of these readings, I will also stay attuned to the queer dynamics of Stein's drama, which have been all but ignored by critics of her plays (a surprisingly small concentric loop within the otherwise large circle of Stein scholars).[6] Though the "queerness" of Stein's writing is evident everywhere throughout her corpus, I find in the particular nexus of sex, violence, and dramatic experimentation that I have outlined here one of the most fruitful areas for a queer inquiry of her work. To return to the conversation between Stein and Preston with which I began, Stein says, as she ruminates on passion and its meaning to the artist, "I think of Byron. Now Byron had a passion" (191). Stein also had a passion, and her play *Byron,* written almost contemporaneously with this interview, betrays it in all of its rich and strange contours.

"BABY AND BYRON"

Scholars have paid little attention to *Byron,* which is not surprising given the difficulty of the text and its continued place "in the closet" (no professional production of the play has ever been attempted). This critical oversight constitutes a major omission, because *Byron* is the locus of some of Stein's most extended meditations on playmaking, which ought to be of interest not only to Stein enthusiasts but also and more generally to theorists and historians of modern theater. With a curiously obsessive fixity of focus, discussions of Stein's ideas about the theater settle almost invariably on her essay "Plays," in which her likening of the play to a landscape has led critics to describe her drama—and her theory of drama—with the term *landscape play*. Though Stein herself never uses this precise phrase, it is easily derived from a much-cited passage in the essay:

The only one [of my plays] that has been played is Four Saints. In Four Saints I made the Saints the landscape. . . . These attendant saints were the landscape and it the play really is a landscape.

A landscape does not move nothing really moves in a landscape but things are there, and I put into the play the things that were there.

. . . All these things might have been a story but as a landscape they were just there and a play is just there. That is at least the way I feel about it.

. . . Anyway the play as I see it is exciting and it moves and it also stays and that is as I said in the beginning might be what a play should do. (li–lii)

The tension between movement and stasis, unyoked from narrative obligation, that Stein describes here certainly captures well the guiding principle that animates *Four Saints in Three Acts*. And it is also true that a similar interest in the manipulation of objects and bodies, in a series of repetitions with minor modulations and variations, shapes others of her plays as well. As Bonnie Marranca, who sees the landscape as the central prism through which to view Stein's drama, summarizes of the landscape play, "Pictorial composition replaces dramatic action, emphasizing frontality and the frame, flatness and absence of perspective. The play is just there. It has no center. . . . Stein was not concerned with creating a drama but an image."[7]

But is that all she wrote? While I agree that "Plays" is an important essay and that Stein's landscape metaphor provides one useful angle from which to approach her drama, an overemphasis on the importance of the landscape obscures the other theoretical observations that Stein makes about plays—and their helpfulness in interpreting her drama. Consider *Byron*, in which Stein asks insistently and repeatedly, "What is a play."[8] Here are some of the more direct answers to the question that the play posits:

This which I think is a play is a play. (335)

A play is this. They manage to stage this. (336)

As beautiful as it is a play is not but a play is. (337)

Anything can be a play if they stand or sit to-day (338)

I wish to say everything I know about a play a play can proceed not to widen. (339)

A play they know a play.
But not if they dovetail a play.
Five ducks leaning all make six.
This is a play. Byron is a play.
When will they come is in a play.
Imagine is a play.
A play is used to eat used it.
How can hours be a play but naturally it is
                    A Play Byron a play (340)

A play is a day or nor to say so I wish to make a play not a day or even not
what happened but only not what is seen. (342)

A play may be in speed indeed. (345)

        A play is spelled spacious . . .
What is a play a play is pause or loss. (347)

Could he look and see. In this is the essential of a play. (351)

Many of Stein's dicta about what makes a play are designed deliberately to
contradict one another. A play "can proceed *not* to widen," but a play is also
"spelled spacious"; it "may be in speed indeed," but it is also a "pause";
"the essential of a play" is the requirement that someone can "look and see,"
but Stein also wishes "to make a play . . . only *not* what is seen." Even more
patently, some of Stein's statements about playmaking are baldly self-con-
tradictory: "As beautiful as it is a play is not but a play is." Her notion of
what a play can be is finally so capacious that merely a short phrase ("Five
ducks leaning all make six") or a single word ("Imagine") can constitute a
play—and yet even language is not a definite or absolute criterion: as she
says elsewhere in *Byron,* "A play then may be a day without words" (348).
Anything, it would seem, can be a play, so long as some presiding consciousness deems it so and as a near-tautology makes clear: "This which I
think is a play is a play." Yet the authorial voice is not all; some other consciousness must also construe the play *as* a play: "Anything can be a play *if*
they stand or sit to-day." The receiver of the communication could be a
reader, but ideally the play would be staged for an audience, sitting (or standing—Stein is not picky about the details) at a performance. Indeed, when
Stein says, "A play is this. They manage to stage this," I cannot help but hear
in the pause between sentences, "A play is this *if* they manage to stage this."
And if they don't manage to stage this to an audience's satisfaction, the play

may very well cease to exist as such; as Stein declares late in the text, "If the one seated rises Byron falls" (371).

Certainly Stein was right to wonder, as she does throughout *Byron,* whether anyone else would acknowledge her drama's dramaticity. Such aphoristic statements as I have quoted above, not all of which are strictly concerned with playmaking, are typical of the text as a whole. Whether they are meant to be spoken, provide stage directions, or occupy some even less well defined category of theatrical language is never clear. Most of the sentences are headed with the title "Act I," a smaller number with "Act II," and a still smaller group are designated as "Scenes" (usually "Scene I"). As "Act I" and "Scene I" are announced over and over, one gets the sense that Stein, dissatisfied with the way that her play has started, attempts to begin it again and again.⁹ Yet if this is the case, she never discards the "false starts" but instead allows them to accumulate and to comment upon each other, so that the final result is an accretion of jerks and halts that can be taken together to make a plausible, if disjointed, whole.

It is equally plausible, however, that "Act I" is a character, or at least a voice of some sort that speaks to itself and, occasionally, to and with "Act II." The play opens as follows:

BYRON A PLAY
But Which They Say Byron A Play
Act I

Byron
Yes Byron
Act II
Will she need me if they go too.
Act I and II
I think so. Byron came himself to ask if he were not satisfied but believe me.
Act I
Byron is a queen
Act II
Indeed but two (333)

As the subtitle makes clear, *Byron A Play* is not only the title of the play but also its first intoned line, which "they" say: "Byron A Play." If "they" can be taken to designate some voices in unison, which may or may not include "Act I" and "Act II," then Act I would deliver singularly the play's second line, "Byron / Yes Byron." The idea that a dialogue ensues is encouraged by the question and answer that follow. Act II asks, "Will she need me if they go too," and Act I responds, "I think so." But even this simple proposition cannot be advanced without complication, because Act I does not respond *alone* to Act II's question. Indeed, he is joined in his response by Act II. If Act II would provide precisely the same answer to his own question as Act I, then why ask Act I in the first place? Moreover, the very content of the questions indicates the characters' reluctance to contribute to the play at all and their uncertainty about whether they have to do it. Act II wants to know whether "she"—the playwright?—will "need" him if other voices, the once again nebulously identified "they," participate in the play. Neither he nor Act I knows the answer to the question for sure (they "think" they are needed), and the only thing asserted with confidence is their utter *lack* of confidence in the play and their role in it, amplified by their doubled voices. In short, only four terse lines into the play, Stein has already concocted the most absurd brew of metatheatricality and made it the stuff of a vigorous comedy of errors.

Yet even my identification of Stein's opening gambit as a "comedy of errors" betrays a desire to understand the play in somewhat familiar terms. It would be comforting to think of Act I and Act II as two fools who inaugurate the play in much the same way that a pair of soldiers, servants, or slaves ushers in a Shakespearean comedy, but there is no guarantee that this is the case.[10] In another reading, we might conclude that the whole text is a monologue, in which every word, including the mentions of "them" and the phrases "Act I" and "Act II," are spoken aloud as if in soliloquy. This idea would have to be considered, however, alongside Stein's mocking and dismissive references to soliloquies throughout the text. Equally possible is the notion that "Act I" and "Act II" really do designate the first two acts of the play, whatever their spoken or unspoken content. But then what would we make of the simultaneity suggested by the yoking together of "Act I and Act II"? How could two acts be staged at the same time? And if this impasse forces us to revert to the idea that the play is one long monologue, why would Stein subject an audience to such an exercise, which, at fifty-odd pages, would grow intolerably tedious? Every generous impulse to make sense of *Byron* is stymied by some new set of problems. Whatever our various attempts at interpretation, we can only consistently describe the play as a violent attack on our sensibilities and expectations.

In the midst of this assault, we are circuitously introduced to Byron, the ostensible subject of the play. Act I says (perhaps), "Byron is a queen," to which Act II responds (potentially), "Indeed but two." These lines present us with another interpretive challenge, though one less grievous than the confusion engendered by the structure of the play as a whole. Byron may never even appear onstage (indeed, Marc Robinson describes the play as so preoccupied with "lengthy disquisitions" on playwriting that it never reaches its subject),[11] but wherever he is, he is "two." As a "queen," one of the Byrons in question is undoubtedly Lord Byron, whose flamboyant dress, arch witticisms, and bisexual exploits certainly qualify him for this slang attribution. Though less immediately discernible to readers unfamiliar with Stein's life and her other writings, the other "queen" is her spoiled and temperamental Chihuahua puppy Byron,[12] whom she describes at some length in *Everybody's Autobiography:*

> So they [Francis Picabia and his wife] called the two little Mexican dogs Monsieur and Madame and Byron was a son and a grandson. We called him Byron because he was to have as a wife his sister or his mother and so we called him Byron. Poor little Byron his name gave him a strange and feverish nature, he was very fierce and tender and he danced strange little war dances and frightened [the poodle] Basket. Basket was always frightened of Byron. And then Byron died suddenly one night of typhus.
>
> Picabia was in Paris and he said we should have another one immediately have another one, and Basket was happy that Byron was dead and gone and then we had Pépé and as he had feared and dreaded Byron Basket loved Pépé.[13]

Hovering in the background of this play, then, are two sudden and violent deaths: the highly publicized end of a larger-than-life poet and the intensely private end of a little dog. What's more, poet and dog are not just intimately related by name and nature but are ultimately, in the play's idiom, indistinguishable. Whether or not Byron—or Byron—appears onstage, Stein can insist through a kind of incantatory language on drama's potential, if never necessarily actualized, to reanimate both subjects. From her doubt at the beginning of the play, "Byron will you come" (340), Stein moves to the assurance,

> *He will come again*
> *If he can come again*
> *Thursday he can come again*
> *And be one of one*
> *And then the play will come again*
> *To be a play of come again Byron. (358–59)*

When Stein announces that Byron will "be one of one" and not, as we might expect, "one of *two*," the conflation of man and dog is complete; and in this conflation, the sexual life of the man and the daily routine of the dog intertwine almost farcically. Mining a crude pun, Stein, who was never too shy to write about orgasms, has Byron "come" again and again—at once the dog obeying a familiar command and the poet obeying an urge that he satisfied with women and men alike. As Michael Trask has observed, "In both her early and late writing, Stein exploits the customary proximity of loyal domestic pets and disloyal, shifty, or undomesticated persons,"[14] and *Byron* is no exception. Here the proximity may result from no more than a shared name, but Stein takes full advantage of this nominal coincidence to imbue *Byron*'s repeated mentions of coming, playing, lying, and resting with overtones of both (human) sexual spontaneity and (canine) ritualized domesticity.

At least one effect of this imbrication—and the one that protects Stein's obsessive punning, finally, from farce (though not, perhaps, from camp) —is the suggestion that sexual spontaneity can *inhere* in ritualized domesticity. Having implicitly posited this idea through linguistic play, and as a logical development of it, Stein shifts focus to explore, primarily, the sexual side of domestic life in the latter part of *Byron*. Indeed, about halfway through the play, there is an abrupt shift in method and tone; syntax is subject to less disruption, and acts and scenes proceed regularly and are numbered accordingly. In its final version, the text reads as follows at the moment of its turn:

Scene I

Byron I request you not to be fastidious in coming again fortunately.
It is very fortunate that you have found such a happy home.
Byron a play two months later (364)

In the manuscript notebook in which Stein originally drafted *Byron,* a break in the page precedes the line "Byron a play two months later," which is written in ink (as is the rest of the play), whereas Stein previously composed the play entirely in pencil.[15] This document encourages a pedestrian explanation for Stein's altered approach to the play: she simply put *Byron* aside and began working on it again two months later, at which point her stylistic and thematic concerns were different than they had been before. But the document encourages, too, a more theoretical speculation about the materiality of dramatic texts. If, as W. B. Worthen claims convincingly, "Stein sees the page as a unified field of writing, where ink and white space, dialogue and its accessories all identify—and are identified with—the play,"[16] then is something crucial to the play(s) lost in the transformation from manuscript to published text, in the latter of which the uniformity of the ink on the page fails to measure as palpably the passage of time (and, with it, the flux of meaning and perception)?

However we may situate or muse about the evidence from the manuscript notebook, Stein chose to suture together the two parts of the play not only in the notebook but also in the published version of the text—and to let that suture show *linguistically.* Just as she yoked together Byron the poet and Byron the dog as "one of one," so too did she decide to yoke together "Byron a play" and "Byron a play two months later" as one (of one) drama. In order to make sense of this decision and to read the play's disparate halves as a coherent whole, we might consider the lines that anticipate the play's second half: "Byron I request you not to be fastidious in coming again fortunately. / It is very fortunate that you have found such a happy home." The repetition of the word *fortunate,* linked both to Byron's coming and to Stein's happy home, suggests that the happiness of the home depends upon Stein's ability to make Toklas, like the poet and the dog, come again and again.[17]

The surviving erotic notes between Stein and Toklas, preserved in the Yale Collection of American Literature, indicate that the couple had no trouble meeting this criterion for happiness. The sheer magnitude of the notes from Stein to Toklas, not to mention the repetitiveness of the language in those notes over a period of many years, is staggering. For brevity's sake, I will allow two short notes to figure here for the many scraps of paper on which Stein scribbled her impulsive desires to Toklas:

> When all is told lovely baby precious does not mind the cold, when little hubby surrounds her warm, the cold can't do her harm, bless the baby yes she says it is it is indeed warm and I will be bold and I will not be cold and little baby will do what he is told by little wifey who is not cold, who knows the cold is warm and will do her no harm bless her X.O.

> Little daisy dot sat behind a trot a trotting horsey and where is husband here he is sadly waiting for little bossy and what will she say when they kiss today she will say he is a good little boysy. Sweetest tender meat I love you to your feet. Sweet little mosey which is short for morsel. X.O.[18]

Two features of these notes deserve particularly to be underscored. First, Stein conceives of "his" relationship with Toklas as simultaneously transgendered, marital, and parental; Stein is the "hubby," "husband," and "boysy" to Toklas's "wifey" and "baby."[19] Second, both food and heat serve as governing metaphors for sex: Toklas is a "morsel" and "tender meat" to be eaten (literally and figuratively) by Stein, who will "surround[] her warm." All of these attributes of the love notes work their way into a more or less autobiographical scene of domestic bliss (or, more accurately, *jouissance*) in the second half of *Byron:*

> Act I Scene I
>
> In the room she is sitting by a new lamp reading a book and holding Byron.
>
> He is not holding a basket he is sitting beside a table writing and if he sneezes he covers his shoulders with a shawl knitted for him as a new years present by a dear friend.
>
> When all this has happened it has fairly begun. And no one has been not only not famished but indeed have determined durably have determined not only more which but not at all that without an obligation to an error. Think lightly while they meet.
>
> Byron cannot be punished for the sins of commission and omission because partly and happily he earns nothing for any one. He can by contact impart so it would seem or would they mean that they like what they ate or eat.
>
> Should they prepare. (365)

"He" wrapped in his shawl for warmth and "she" by the lamp are unmistakable versions of Stein and Toklas, who are "not only not famished" but happily "meet" and "eat"—perhaps as a result of an erotic fervor "imparted" by "contact" with the lusty revenant of Byron, or perhaps simply because Stein slips an erotic invitation between the pages of Toklas's book. The scene of writing described here ("When all this has happened it has fairly begun") blurs beyond distinction the act of composing a play and the act of composing a love note. Likewise, Stein may equally well be turning the pages of her notebook or exchanging notes with Toklas when, later in the text, "paper is moving":

> *Byron. I love not cold nor freezing.*
> *I love not following when a sound is coming*
> *I do not love whether I love or whether paper is moving*
> *I love and do not gather crumbs for birds which have been*
> *Birds which have not been there*
> *Once more I hear paper moving.*
> *But whether which have more Byron. (372)*

Again, "cold" and "freezing" are contrasted with the (implicit) warmth of physical contact, and "crumbs" are gathered, we presume, not for birds but from "sweet little mosey which is short for morsel." Finally, it does not matter "whether which"—whether the suggestion of sexual congress is real or imagined, and whether the "paper moving" marks the progress of play-writing or the initiation of an erotic encounter. In either event, Stein will "have more Byron," because *Byron* has evolved into a closet drama whose existence is fueled by—and in turn fuels—the drama of another "closet," Stein's boudoir.

As we contemplate the latter drama and its place in Stein's writing, we should not suppose, on the basis of a received notion of Stein and Toklas as two sedate ladies, that there was necessarily anything sedate or ladylike about their shared sexuality. Consider a passage in a love note from Toklas to Stein (one of the few in her hand preserved among Stein's papers), which intimates of their life together all the terror and violence—as well as the affection and tenderness—that sex can signify:

> *Baby is hot.*
> *A hot little sacrifice.*
> *For a husband who was chilly.*
> *But is now warm and frilly.*
> *Frilly as to temper is he*
> *But his wifey oh his wifey is good*
> *And she is wooed.*
> *By hubby as food and indeed*
> *As everything. God bless baby.*[20]

Suddenly the "warm and frilly" side of hubby's nature is eclipsed by a recognition of the devouring impulse inherent in his approach to wifey "as food." Self-identified as "a hot little sacrifice," Baby seems less like a sweet morsel than a slaughtered lamb, and the deity from whom she seeks a benediction is perhaps no benevolent protector but a wrathful and hungry god. Thus, when *Byron* ends with the following tableau—

Scene IX

Baby and Byron

Finis

—we are left with a conflicted image. "Baby and Byron" may portray either a housewife and her little lap dog or two dying animals, falling prey to coitus and typhus, respectively. Or, as Lord Byron's specter also haunts the scene palpably, they may be a pair of sexual adventurers on a hunt of their own.

"LORD BERNERS HAD NOT PRONOUNCED THAT NAME"

It is difficult to read a canine-themed play like *Byron* without calling to mind Stein's oft-quoted line, "I am I because my little dog knows me."[21] Taken out of its various contexts (Stein herself quoted or alluded to the line many times and with a variety of discursive glosses), this aphoristic statement may seem like a paean to the comfort and assurance of domestic attachments, but the identity conferred by the little dog's recognition is finally, for Stein, a mixed blessing—and perhaps even a sinister curse. Identity is a necessary condition of being in the world, but it is the world, as William H. Gass puts it in his introduction to Stein's *Geographical History of America*, of "neighbors, relatives, husbands, and wives. . . . Identities [are] the persons hired, the books and buildings bought and sold, the famous 'things,' the stars."[22] Most important, identity—to which Stein also refers as "human nature"—is the aspect of human subjectivity most antithetical to creative expression, which is a product of the "human mind" contemplating its object in detachment from worldly obligations. Indeed, when Stein herself became an almost overnight "star" (if not a "famous thing") as a result of the blockbuster success of *The Autobiography of Alice B. Toklas,* she learned first-hand what an impediment such stardom could be to artistic endeavor. In an early passage of *Everybody's Autobiography*, Stein begins obliquely to discuss the anxiety—ultimately a severe case of writer's block—that resulted from her sudden celebrity:

> Well anyway my success did begin.
> And so Mr. Bradley [Stein's literary agent] telephoned every morning and they gradually decided about everything and slowly everything changed inside me. Yes of course it did because suddenly it was all different, what I did had a value that made people ready to pay, up to that time everything I did had a value because nobody was ready to pay. It is funny about money. And it is funny about identity. You are you because your little dog knows you, but when your public knows you and does not want to pay for you and when your public knows you and does want to pay for you, you are not the same you. (45–46)

If Stein's little dog knowing her could handicap and even arrest her creative impulse, then how much worse to have a public whose thousands of little dogs *also* knew her. Though Ulla Dydo describes *Byron* as a piece in which "Stein has regained her voice" after a period of intense frustration and creative aridity (560), something of Stein's dilemma about identity nevertheless percolates into the play. On its penultimate page, Stein offers the following rapid-fire scenes:

Scene II

Byron. May be we are Byron.

Scene III

May be we have Byron

Scene IV

May be we do

Scene V

But may be you

Scene VI

Know Byron by Byron. (385)

With the conjecture, "May be we are Byron," Stein plunges more deeply into her fear of identity than do her usual articulations on the subject. What if she is not simply she because her little dog knows her; what if she *is* her little dog? As Gass describes this nightmarish sort of existence, "There were people who were no more than their poodles. . . . Like mirrors they reflected what fell into them, and when the room was empty, when the walls were removed and the stars pinched back in the sky, they were nothing, not even glass" (40). Stein preempts this particularly nasty fate, however, through a series of linguistic modulations and variations—and it is the prospect of a continued facility with language, despite a bout with writer's block, that can save her from identity's worst perils. "May be we are Byron," but "may be we *have* Byron," firmly on his leash and in his place. What's more, maybe Byron is not the one doing the threatening, canine knowing at all. "May be you / Know Byron by Byron": maybe you—the audience for this drama—can know Byron the dog, a guarantor of human nature, by *Byron A Play,* a product of human mind, in which case creative entity will have trumped identity for one round, at least.

Despite such wariness of identity, and particularly of identification as a "star," Stein seems also to have enjoyed certain perks of recognition and celebrity. Like Lord Byron's relationship to fame, and perhaps too like her attitude toward the theater, Stein's navigation of her own success was marked by a profound ambivalence. As she says at the outset of *Everybody's Autobiography,* "It is very nice being a celebrity a real celebrity who can decide who they want to meet and say so and they come or do not come as you want them. I never imagined that would happen to me to be a celebrity like that but it did and when it did I liked it" (2). On one especially memorable occasion, Stein banked on her newfound celebrity to make just such a demand to meet other stars, and it worked. In April 1935, during Stein and Toklas's visit to Los Angeles, Lillian May Ehrman received the two women at her Hollywood home for a dinner party whose other guests included Charlie Chaplin, Dashiell Hammett (at Stein's personal request), and Lillian Hellman. Though Stein admits in *Everybody's Autobiography* to "liking" the cachet to summon other luminaries, the moment of liking it was also a moment of disappointment. Alice B. Toklas recalls the party in her memoir, *What Is Remembered:* "Conversation at dinner was fairly lively. Mr. Chaplin had brought with him Paulette Goddard, who was an enfant terrible. There was also a Spanish diplomat and our hostess' brother, who was a film director. After dinner there were some guests who came, amongst them Anita Loos, to whom I took an immediate fancy. The film directors gathered around Miss Stein and said, We would like to know how you came to have your enormous popularity, and she said, By having a small audience, whereupon they shoved their chairs away from her, discouraged with what she had to advise."[23] Stein describes the party in nearly similar terms in *Everybody's Autobiography* and concludes, with tongue half in cheek, "it had been an amusing evening" (292). Stein may have somewhat amused herself at her interlocutors' expense with her barbed advice, but she also alienated herself from the company in the process. Indeed, Stein's feeling of social alienation may have touched on some deeper sense of exile—from herself and from the human mind—in Hollywood, an environment hostile to the "realest poetry" that she cited to the other guests as the initial and ultimate source of her "biggest publicity" (292).

Certainly such a darker sense of self-alienation becomes the obsessive theme of Stein's looser rendering of the dinner party, *A Play Called Not and Now.* The text begins with a list of characters called "A man who looks like Dashiell Hammett," "A man who looks like Picasso," "A man who looks like Charlie Chaplin," "A man who looks like Lord Berners," and so forth. On the heels of this list, Stein offers the following explanation of the simulacral characters that she has posited: "The difference between not and now. That is what makes any one look like some one." The difference between not and now is a variation on the difference we have already encountered between identity and entity, or human nature and human mind. "Now" signifies for Stein the immanence of a person fully present in the present moment; these people are "not" because they are playing at being themselves, with a distracting and falsifying consciousness of their identities. "A man who looks like Dashiell Hammett" is a man who looks like Dashiell Hammett not because an actor would perform the role if the play were staged, but because the "real" Dashiell Hammett is already an actor performing a role for public consumption. And the actors are literally consumed, or self-effaced, by the frivolity and meaninglessness of their interactions. With biting accuracy, Stein captures the triviality and tedium of party conversation: "This is what they all say, that anybody can get impatient with an aurora borealis" (422). "They hesitate about making witty remarks to each other but they do do it just the same" (423). "And the one who is like Dashiell Hammett what has he to say about money. / He says money I have money" (432).

Some disruption of the party's oppressive boredom seems to arrive when scene V ends, "Just then a noise was heard," but the next scene, all of nine words long, deflates our expectation of relief and merely sentences the actors to further confinement together: "There is no leaving when a noise is heard" (435). This statement is labeled "Scene VII," following which comes a "Scene VI" placed deliberately out of order. As a result of this disorientation, we expect the scene to deliver, as if in flashback, an account of what preoccupied the actors and prevented them from paying attention to the noise, but it turns out that, far from preoccupation, they cannot attend to anything at all:

> Scene VI.
>
> This is a short scene and the moonlight. None of them who look like any one of them are interested in the moon-light not even excepting the one who looked like Dr. Gidon or the one who looked like Mrs. Andrew Greene nor the one who looked like David Greene not even that one. (435)

Moonlight may seem like an incidental figure, but it is in fact a central motif in such other late dramas by Stein as *Listen to Me* and *Doctor Faustus Lights the Lights*. It also earns a significant mention in Stein's other account of the dinner party in *Everybody's Autobiography*:

> I said [to Charlie Chaplin] . . . I wanted to write a drama where no one did anything where there was no action and I had and it was the Four Saints and it was exciting, he said yes he could understand that, I said the films would become like the newspapers just a daily habit and not at all exciting or interesting after all the business of an artist is to be really

exciting and he is only exciting when nothing is happening, . . . I said that the moon excited dogs because it did nothing, lights coming and going do not excite them and now that they have seen so many of them the poor things can no longer see the moon and so no lights excite them, well we did not say all this but that is what we meant. (292)

Like the poor dogs, the partygoers in Stein's play "can no longer see the moon," and their inability to rouse an interest in it is an indictment not just of their attention spans but of the very condition of their subjectivity. Their overexposure—both *to* flashy stimuli and *as* flashy celebrities—has the ironic effect of rendering them dull. Implicit in the play and explicit in the anecdote to Chaplin is a crucial distinction for Stein between the seeming dullness of "nothing happening" and the actual dullness of a person who cannot be excited when nothing is happening. Thus a play about people habituated to boredom can nevertheless be exciting itself.

Or not. Richard Bridgman writes of the play, "The disparity between the public and private selves [of the characters] is expressed in a repeated locution—'The one that looked like . . .' . . . The technique is so strenuously used however, that the play as a whole is very dull."[24] Alternatively, I would argue that it is precisely in the strenuousness, if not outright aggression, of Stein's approach to her material that the interest of *A Play Called Not and Now* inheres. The violence of her relentless repetitions communicates sharply the masochistic self-injury of the partygoers, who have become like Gass's empty mirrors, "not even glass." In turn, the masochism of all the guests is matched by a kind of sadism among the men, whose insistent, hungry eyeing of the women conveys a sense of menace, a sexual threat, lurking beneath the boring surface of the party: "And then they all looked at the women. None of them who looked like Anita Loos or Gertrude Atherton or Lady Diana Grey or Katherine Cornell or Daisy Fellowes said yes" (423). One of the men manages, however, to escape the implicit indictment of the male gaze and even to earn Stein's sympathy: Lord Berners, a British aristocrat and composer who hosted and befriended Stein during a visit to England and who later wrote the music for the 1937 production of *A Wedding Banquet,* a balletic adaptation of Stein's play *They Must. Be Wedded. To Their Wife.*[25]

Lord Berners literally does not belong in this play. He, like Picasso and a few others, is a friend of Stein's who was not present at the original Hollywood party but who nevertheless makes the guest list for its imaginary re-creation. As an openly gay man, Berners also seems figuratively out of place among his lusty, heterosexual counterparts. Indeed, he is cajoled by a kind of peer pressure into joining the other men in their ogling of the women: "The one who looks like Dashiell Hammett looks at the one that looks like Picasso and both together look at the one that looks like Charlie Chaplin and the three of them look at the one that looks like Lord Berners, and then they all say, we do not look like any other one and they did not and do not. And then they say all together we will look at the women" (423). In this passage, the referent for "they" is deliberately unclear. "They" who say that they will look at the women could be "the three of them" ganging up on a silently acquiescent Lord Berners or could include Berners, forced uneasily into the group-speak. In either event, Berners is the only one who seems ashamed of his participation in the ensuing ocular frenzy and aware of the schism in self imposed by the party: "The one that looked like Lord Berners said. / I do not look at me" (423). No doubt Berners, described by his biographer Mark Amory as "the last eccentric," would be more comfortable back at his baronial seat in Faringdon, where he presided magisterially over parties whose guests (often young gay men) became part of Berners's queer menagerie of "flamingos, fed on shrimps to keep them pink; birds of paradise; storks; . . . a trumpeter bird," and multicolored pigeons that Berners claimed were "dyed each year on Easter Sunday and dried in the linen cupboard."[26] Indeed, Berners went so far in his pursuit of campy entertainment that in 1935 he erected a giant folly, replete with belvedere room and pinnacled parapet, whose opening was celebrated with fireworks and a bonfire. As Amory recounts, "Guests were allowed up to six effigies of enemies to be burned on the bonfire; this was deemed 'most inadequate'" (150).

Some of the enemies may well have been friends, or even guests on this occasion. In the same year that Berners built his tower, he also created another folly: *The Girls of Radcliff Hall,* a privately printed and circulated roman à clef penned under the pseudonym Adela Quebec. Set at a girls' school meant deliberately to invoke and deride *The Well of Loneliness,* the short novel describes a dizzying series of crushes, assignations, affairs, and treacheries among a group of gossiping adolescent lesbians, supervised by the voyeuristic headmistress Miss Carfax. This grand dame of Radcliff Hall represents none other than Berners himself, who, as John Byrne testifies in a republication of the book, re-creates faithfully the shifting attachments and allegiances among the gay set who partied at Faringdon: "So all the girls were boys, and far from being innocuous the little book must have caused acute embarrassment to those it did not actually hurt. All will have recognized themselves and each other: none can have wanted 'her' parents to read it. And the worst of it is that virtually nothing had been made up. . . . All the infidelities were real, and all the foibles observed with such malicious glee."[27] Among the artist friends subject to Berners's mockery are Cecil Beaton (Cecily Seymour), Oliver Messel (Olive Mason), Pavel Tchelitchew (Madame Yoshiwara), and Christian Bérard (Mademoiselle Gousse). In one particularly devastating and hilarious scene, Berners expends considerable venom on Peter Watson (Lizzie Johnson), David Herbert (Daisy Montgomery), and Robin Thomas (May Peabody):

> One day, toward the end of term, there occurred what Olive Mason described as an "ugly incident." It happened during the Old Girls' Lacrosse Match. The girls sometimes got very excited at Lacrosse, especially at the Old Girls' Match, where ancient passions and hatreds were often revived, and occasionally they would hit out rather wildly with their lacrosse sticks. In the course of the game Daisy Montgomery hit Lizzie a terrific blow on the head, and of course everyone said afterwards that Daisy had done it on purpose. Whether this was true or not, the fact remains that she felled poor Lizzie to the ground, where she lay prone, bleeding profusely from a cut on her forehead. At the sight of this, little May Peabody lost all control over herself, rushed forward and threw herself down in the mud, kissing Lizzie and crying out in a despairing voice, "Oh, she's dead, she's dead!"
>
> However, Lizzie was not so badly hurt as it had appeared at first sight, and when she got up from the ground she was very annoyed with little May and hissed at her in an angry whisper, "You have compromised me in front of the whole school, you slut."[28]

Apart from the great amusement offered by its wicked observations, *The Girls of Radcliff Hall* interests me as a kind of closet drama akin to Stein's own writing in this period. The book's quick pace and snappy dialogue lend it a dramatic quality, and the new edition's key of "Characters in order of appearance," aligning the fictional names and the real ones, cannot help but read like a cast list (95). At one point in the novel, Cecily stages a school play ("A Night with the Fairies") to reattract the attention of wayward Lizzie (25), whom one student's mother describes in a letter to another as "a *dreadful* girl, a very wicked girl indeed, and what they call a Thespian" (29). This comically malapropistic confusion of sexual deviance and theatrical performance reminds us that Berners has, in a sense, made the boys "play" the girls—and, like a good closet drama, their play is intended for a coterie audience of intimates to whom Berners sent the limited copies of the book.

One such recipient was Gertrude Stein, who enthused in a March 1935 letter to Carl Van Vechten, "I am awfully pleased that you like all of Berners' work because I do too, he wrote another book called Radcliffe [*sic*] Hall privately printed which is very funny and I am asking him if I may send it to you."[29] Stein did indeed receive Berners's permission and forwarded the book to Van Vechten, but she must have liked it so much that she requested another copy; among her papers in the Yale Collection of American Literature is an edition of the book inscribed by Berners and dated a year later:

> *Gertrude Stein*
> *from*
> *Gerald Berners*
> *with his*
> *Love*
> *March 1936.*

Around the same time that Stein received her second copy of *The Girls of Radcliff Hall,* she was also at work on *A Play Called Not and Now,* and I would argue that Stein's enjoyment of Berners's book, hovering in the background of the drama, comes to the fore to motivate an unusual pair of scenes, seemingly disconnected from the rest of the play:

Act III

A mysterious assemblage of women.

Three boys who look like men.

The mysterious assemblage of women did not look like Gertrude Atherton and Anita Loos Diana Grey Katharine Cornell and Daisy Fellowes, they did not look at all like them not at all, they did not look like a mysterious assemblage of women, they were a mysterious assemblage of women and they were all in their ordinary clothes and sitting down in chairs under a shelter in the Luxembourg Gardens, there were no men or children with them and what were they doing, they were talking not much but some.

Three boys who looked like men.

The three boys who looked like men did not look like Charlie Chaplin or like Picasso or like Lord Berners or like Dashiell Hammett they did not look like any one of them the three boys who looked like men nor like all of them.

Scene I

The three boys who looked like men were not very near the mysterious assemblage of women. (430)

Stein, a great fan of detective fiction, offers us here something like a modernist whodunit, which might be more accurately described as a "who-is-it." After several pages that enumerate obsessively the names of celebrities, we are confronted by the announcement of—ostensibly—two groups of anonymous characters: "A mysterious assemblage of women. / Three boys who look like men." But what if the phrase "three boys who look like men" is not meant by apposition to designate a second cluster of figures, but to describe the first further? What if, like the girls of Radcliff Hall, the mysterious assemblage of women is really an assemblage of queer men? Such a solution to the riddle would explain both why the women don't resemble the play's other women and why the slangily designated "boys" look like men but don't resemble the play's other men (including Berners, who was significantly older than the youthful company at Faringdon).

In this case, scene I could be a sort of red herring that provides truthful but misleading information in the manner of an oracle: "The three boys who looked like men were not very near the mysterious assemblage of women," because they *are* the women. Like the unstably gendered girls of Radcliff Hall, Stein's womanish boys could also be boyish women, unfettered from the bothers of heterosexual life ("there were no men or children with them"); indeed, the text could be prompting us to use a double vision to see not only Faringdon's partygoers but also Parisian lesbians (hence the mention of Luxembourg Gardens). Through whatever particular lens we view the gender trouble generated by these anonymous—and pleasurably underdetermined—characters, the passage invites the observation that quotidian forms of queer address, traded at parties or in letters, may provide a crucial, meaning-making referent not only for their campy refigurations in romans à clef like *The Girls of Radcliff Hall* but also (if less apparently) for high modernist aesthetic strategies like those deployed by Stein in *A Play Called Not and Now.* Moreover, the passage's juxtaposition of these anonymous characters with the maligned Hollywood celebrities offers an implicit valuation of a "mysterious" life over an empty one, of a queer sensibility over a lack of sensibility altogether. In a related move, the passage may also provide an important, albeit oblique, valuation of the violence of "hitting out rather wildly with one's lacrosse stick" over the violence done by identity and human nature. The "boys" may have catfights, but at least they know how to throw a party.

A ROSE (IS A ROSE IS A ROSE IS A ROSE) BY ANY OTHER NAME?

Lord Berners's professional association with Stein did not end with his musical composition for *A Wedding Banquet* in 1937. Stein, who attended and was delighted by a performance of the ballet at Sadler's Wells, approached Berners as a potential collaborator on a new project that she had in mind: an opera of the Faust story. Originally conceived with no reference to Faust and as a novel called *Ida* (a version of which was later completed and published), the project mutated into *Doctor Faustus Lights the Lights* in early 1938.[30] Sarah Bay-Cheng convincingly dates this turn to Stein's attendance of a performance of *Don Giovanni:*

> Apparently, Stein decided to shift from novel to drama during the performance of Mozart's *Don Giovanni* on February 23, 1938, at the Académie Nationale de Musique et de Danse. Among the notes she scribbled in her production program that evening were an opening stage direction for *Doctor Faustus*. . . . The program notes themselves for *Don Giovanni* may have also influenced Stein's decision to combine the woman from *Ida* with the Faust myth. An announcement of upcoming productions listed the performance of Charles-François Gounod's *Faust*. . . . Also included in the program was a photograph from the Académie's production of Hector Berlioz's *The Damnation of Faust* (1846) presented earlier in 1938. (76)

Stein began writing *Faustus* shortly after this performance, and two months later she had already seduced Berners into providing the music to accompany her words. On April 28, 1938, Berners wrote to Stein, "Please send me the first act of Doctor Faustus. I was very thrilled by what you showed me [on a visit to Stein's home in Paris] and read to me—and I want to have it by me and as soon as I've finished my present business I'll start on it."[31] Between May and October 1938, Stein sent Berners drafts of the opening acts of *Faustus* and modified them according to his suggestions: "I think that perhaps in the 1st act the sentences ought to be a little longer at the opening. Doctor Faustus ought to start off with an aria—this is from a musical point of view—but we can discuss all this when we meet."[32] "Perhaps I may ask you to alter one or two words here and there that are difficult vocally. Words like 'miserable' are sometimes awkward—but we can easily fix that together when I start the music."[33]

How much music Berners ever wrote for *Faustus*—or whether he really started at all—is unclear, but in December 1939, long after Stein had completed the libretto, Berners announced, in a moving letter, his inability to continue work on the project:

My dear Gertrude

I was delighted to get your letter and to hear that things are not too bad with you. What I want to say is, and it makes me very sad to say it —that all inspirational sources seem to have dried up: I can't write a note of music or do any kind of creative work whatever and it's not for want of trying and I don't believe I shall be able to as long as this war lasts. I feel confronted with the break-down of all the things that meant anything to me and the thought of it has got into my subconscious and filled it up to the exclusion of anything else. Not being able to find a note of music is driving me mad. I don't know when I shall be able to go on with Faust. That is why I very reluctantly suggest that you give it to someone else. Virgil Thompson [*sic*] perhaps. It makes me miserable to think of anyone else doing it. But it is unfair to you if I keep hold of it when I can't do it. And I really feel at present that I shall never be able to write music again. I had a letter from Francis he is in Cornwall. He stayed for a long time with Cecil and I gather they ended by getting on each others [*sic*] nerves. Give my love to Alice and bless you both.

Love from Gerald

Honoring her friendship to Berners, Stein never did send *Faustus* to Thomson or to anyone else—and so, with Berners's retreat from the music, *Faustus* retreated into the closet. Though Stein began and revised the play, unlike almost any of her other dramatic works, with an assumption of and an eye toward eventual performance, I would nevertheless argue that *Faustus* was always a sort of closet drama. Stein writes stage directions and assigns dialogue to specific characters in *Faustus* more obviously than she does, say, in *Byron*, but she is not consistent in her approach. At times, she lapses into explanatory prose that reads more like a novel than a play ("As she went she began to sing . . ."; "The dog sighs and says . . ."), and she renders so poetically lines that could be construed simply as stage directions that they, too, demand to be set to music: "Faustus gives him an awful kick, and Mephisto moves away and the electric lights just then begin to get very gay."[34] As with *Four Saints in Three Acts*, Stein must have assumed that others (Berners, for instance) would worry about the details of adapting her words and making them suitable for the stage.

One particularly difficult performative decision concerns the character Marguerite Ida and Helena Annabel. Though she has two names, she is one woman—but ought that necessarily mean that one actress should play the role? Two actresses speaking or singing her lines in unison might allow for interesting physical choreography and vocal harmonies. Moreover, Marguerite Ida and Helena Annabel speaks at times to "herself" in such a way that she seems to divide into Marguerite Ida on the one hand and Helena Annabel on the other. Consider the pivotal moment at which she is stung by a viper:

> There is a rustling under the leaves and Marguerite Ida and Helena Annabel makes a quick turn and she sees that a viper has stung her, she sees it and she says and what is it. There is no answer. Does it hurt she says and then she says no not really and she says was it a viper and she says how can I tell I never saw one before but is it she says and she stands up again and sits down and pulls down her stocking and says well it was not a bee not a busy bee no not, nor a mosquito nor a sting it was a bite and serpents bite yes they do perhaps it was one. (96–97)

Practically, Marguerite Ida and Helena Annabel's dialogue with herself, posed as a series of questions and answers, begs the possibility that one actress could ask about the viper and another respond to her. At the same time, the scene's comic potential might be best mined by one actress speaking all the lines. "Was it a viper," she would ask, no doubt earning a laugh when she replied to herself with exasperation, "How can I tell I never saw one before." Yet for all of its humor, the scene is also full of menace; and Marguerite Ida and Helena Annabel's division from herself, as a result of the viper sting, raises important thematic implications as well as theatrical conjectures.

When she first appears onstage, Marguerite Ida and Helena Annabel is stably two in one, and this paradoxical status represents her erotic communion with herself. Something like Luce Irigaray's famous "two lips" touching each other,[35] her simultaneous singularity and duality represent a woman's desire not simply or narcissistically for herself but for her self's other, in a complex constellation that escapes any sort of phallic economy —until the viper sting, that is. Suggesting at least in part some sort of sexual violation, if not an outright rape, the sting threatens Marguerite Ida and Helena Annabel's autoerotic completeness and plunges her into an existential confusion about her singly multiple (or multiply single) identity:

> *And I am I Marguerite Ida or am I Helena Annabel*
> *Oh well*
> *Am I Marguerite Ida or Helena Annabel*
> *Very well oh very well*
> *Am I Marguerite Ida very well am I Helena Annabel.*

This doubt about her own nature is mirrored by a doubt about the nature of her injury: "She stops she remembers the viper and in a whisper she says was it a sting was it a bite am I alright; was it a sting was it a bite, alright was it a sting, oh or was it a bite" (97). Ironically, her desire to continue to resist easy categorization or classification—to be both Marguerite Ida and Helena Annabel—gives way here to a desire to categorize or classify her hurt as either one (a sting) or the other (a bite). Indeed, the "poison" that runs now through her veins, and for which she eventually seeks a cure from Doctor Faustus, seems to be the poisonous impulse of which Wordsworth writes,

> *Our meddling intellect*
> *Mis-shapes the beauteous forms of things:—*
> *We murder to dissect.*[36]

The dominion that comes with (misrepresentative) linguistic mastery and fixity—and for which Marguerite Ida and Helena Annabel earns "an artificial viper there beside her and a halo . . . around her"—comes at the price of her own eventual domination (104). Prefigured by the viper sting, a "man from over the seas" called Mr. Viper comes to subjugate Marguerite Ida and Helena Annabel sexually and to make her his "pretty pretty pretty dear . . . all my love and . . . always here" (107). He is egged on by a little boy and girl who insist repetitively and creepily on the heteronormativity of their gender assignments (and who, through a slippage of language, admit inadvertently that they are "annoying"): "Mr. Viper dear Mr. Viper, he is a boy I am a girl she is a girl I am a boy we do not want to annoy but we do oh we do oh Mr. Viper yes we do we want you to know that she is a girl that I am a boy" (109). Through a sinister tautology that provides the scaffolding for an even more sinister logic, boys are boys, girls are girls, and women belong with and to men—certainly not with or by themselves. Following this verbal assault by Mr. Viper and the children and a further threat from Faustus, Marguerite Ida and Helena Annabel makes one last valiant effort to defend her sexual autonomy—"I am Marguerite Ida and Helena

Annabel and I know no man or devil no viper and no light and I can be any-thing and everything and it is always always alright"—but as she says these words "she falls back," like the swooning heroine of a nineteenth-century melodrama, "fainting into the arms of the man from over the seas" (118).

Before Marguerite Ida and Helena Annabel comes to this tragic end, it is none other than Faustus who recognizes the power of her name and who denies her a cure to the viper sting. As he insists to the little dog that is his companion, "She will not be . . . never never never, never will her name be Marguerite Ida and Helena Annabel" (95). No doubt the doctor would pre-fer to inhabit an earlier and simpler version of his legend, in which he could identify without complication Marguerite and Helena as a modern woman and an ancient Greek adulteress, respectively—and Ida and Annabel wouldn't even enter the picture. Nor is Faustus the only one to be troubled by or puzzled over Marguerite Ida and Helena Annabel's name(s). Critics have expended a great deal of energy tracing the various mythological, classical, literary, and historical allusions embedded in the quadruplicate;[37] and while I applaud this effort and assent largely to the findings, I want to suggest an alternative inspiration and genesis for the character. Consider the follow-ing list of names:

Bella, Anna
Black, Ida
Griffin, Marguerite
McCoy, Helen

These four full names are culled from the thousands of entries (among whom many other Marguerites, Idas, Helens, Annas, and Bellas might be cited) in a Storyville *Blue Book* preserved among Stein's papers in the Yale Collection of American Literature. Storyville was a red-light district of New Orleans where, between 1898 and 1917, prostitution was legal, and the blue books were directories of the women who worked there. Based on infor-mation provided by Al Rose in *Storyville, New Orleans: Being an Authentic, Illustrated Account of the Notorious Red-Light District,* Stein's edition of the *Blue Book* (the fifth and final) can be dated to a period from 1912 to 1915.[38] It remains unclear whether Stein received the *Blue Book* from a friend who had been to New Orleans during that period or acquired it as a curio dur-ing her own visit to the city in the 1930s.[39] Indeed, it is unclear whether Stein would have known anything, beyond the information that the *Blue Book* itself provides, about the women who lived in New Orleans's self-proclaimed "Queer Zone"—and just how queer some of them were.[40] Perhaps Stein could not have known, for instance, of Norma and Diana, the proprietresses of the French House, that "both women were reportedly lesbians" (77), but her imagination could certainly have been piqued by the innuendo of the following *Blue Book* advertisement: "Why visit the playhouses to see the famous Parisian models portrayed, when one can see the French damsels, Norma and Diana? Their names have become known on both continents, because everything goes as it will, and those that cannot be satisfied there must surely be of a queer nature" (unpaginated). As Stein wrote *Doctor Faustus* in her own French house, might not these "model-quality" prostitutes have provided the models for Marguerite Ida and Helena Annabel? It is certainly no stretch of the imagination to suppose that Stein could have had enough interest in the *Blue Book* for it to influence the composition of *Faustus*. Stein loved names and also loved to list them; her play *Short Sentences,* which she wrote just six years before *Faustus* and in which she names a long series of characters who each speak one line, reads less like a play than a directory—and at times like a directory of prostitutes (consider the sequence of "Frederika Holding," "Marguerite Line," and "Madge Cotton").[41]

In proposing the *Blue Book* as a background for and subtextual current in *Doctor Faustus,* I do not mean to underestimate the importance to Stein of such precursors as Marlowe and Shakespeare, nor even to diminish the fruitful connections to be drawn between *Faustus* and the novel *Ida.* Rather, I wish only to underscore further a point that I have also tried to develop through a strictly intratextual reading: Marguerite Ida and Helena Annabel's story, like many stories that emerge from Storyville, concerns a queer woman who is bought (metaphorically, at least) by a man. She finally has as much in common with Goethe's Gretchen as she does with Emma Johnson, a "wench . . . early drawn to lesbianism, [who] exercised a strange power over many of her sex and took great pride in the fact" (50).[42] This description could apply equally well to Marguerite Ida and Helena Annabel, whose viper sting grants her a similarly strange power over an ever-growing audience of female followers: "See how they come," Stein writes, punning, of her performance. "See how they come / To see her. / See how they come" (106). It is only a matter of time before the man from over the seas joins the country women to admire her, and then she, like Emma Johnson before her, must stage a show for his benefit. Just as the play's electric lights thematize technological anxiety and its eponymous protagonist points us toward religious and ethical conundrums, so too is *Doctor Faustus* a queer meditation on shifting sexual power relations. No readers of the play have understood this better than the Wooster Group, whose *House/Lights*—first produced in 1999, then restaged for a limited run in 2005—pays a special and kinky homage to Stein's preoccupation with sex and violence.

"GOING THE LIMIT"

In a foreword to David Savran's book *Breaking the Rules: The Wooster Group,* Peter Sellars (then director at the American National Theatre) offered the following prognostication: "Anyone with an interest in theatre in the United States of America in 1986 owes it to themselves to know what some of the latest developments are. If theatre in the United States is to become large again, the Wooster Group is out there, up ahead, scouting the way. They are inventing theatrical vocabulary that ten and twenty years from now will become the lingua franca of a revivified American Theatre. For my money, they are the most important theatre company in our country today."[43] Despite the controversy that some of the Wooster Group's productions have provoked and the distaste that certain critics have for their methods, at least some parties would still assent to Sellars's claim that "they are the most important theatre company in our country today." And now that the ten and twenty years that he projected have elapsed, even more would concur that Sellars's prediction has come true and that the Wooster Group's theatrical language has become American theater's lingua franca; as Nick Kaye attested in 1996, "Through its challenging and innovative nature, the Wooster Group's work has become the focal point around which much contemporary practice as well as performance theory and criticism positions itself."[44] In his description of the "challenging and innovative nature" of the Wooster Group's work, David Savran identifies five common, salient "objects" or elements in such diverse early productions as *Rumstick Road* (1976–80), *Nayatt School* (1978–82), and *L.S.D.* (1983–90)—elements that persist in such later pieces as *Brace Up!* (1989–94), *To You, the Birdie! (Phèdre)* (2001–3), and *Poor Theatre* (2004): "recordings of private interviews or public events"; "previously written dramatic material"; "prerecorded sound, music, film and video"; "the performance space that is left from the last piece, containing various architectonic elements that will be used in the development of a new piece"; and "improvised action-texts: gesture, dance and language to be used either as an independent strand in the work or as an elaboration of material from one of the other categories."[45] As the Wooster Group synthesizes these various elements of performance in the manner of a collage, no hierarchical relationship is established in advance among the different elements. Perhaps more important, no idea or theme is explicitly sought outside a persistent emphasis on the forms, patterns, rhythms, and movements that inhere necessarily in their structurally complex performances. As Liz LeCompte, the group's director, explains, "The most important thing in all of this is that . . . I don't have any thematic ideas—I don't even have a theme. I don't have anything except literal objects—some flowers, some images, some television sets, a chair, some costumes I like. . . . And then the ideas come after the fact. It's a total reversal of most of the processes."[46]

The "object" with which the group's 1999 piece *House/Lights* began was a 1964 film, *Olga's House of Shame,* directed by Joseph Mawra (*All Men Are Apes, The Peek Snatchers, Chained Girls*) and now considered to be a camp classic. *Olga's House of Shame* was a sequel to the popular *White Slaves of Chinatown,* a film with an auspicious pedigree as the cinema's first "nudie-kinkie," "a subgenre obsessed with sadistic bondage and fetish situations" and distinct from "the 'nudie-roughie,' which primarily dealt with rape themes, and the 'nudie-ghoulie,' which threw graphic violence and horror elements into the mix."[47] Both films concern the escapades of Olga Petroff (Audrey Campbell), a sadistic procuress with lesbian inclinations and a high-ranking member of a nebulously defined crime syndicate. Olga taunts, whips, burns, stockades, racks, and otherwise brutalizes young women until they acquiesce to her commands, which usually amount to prostituting themselves to her "business associates," peddling drugs, or smuggling jewels. *Olga's House of Shame,* like its predecessor, is a grainy, black-and-white film with low production values, sparse dialogue, and a heavy reliance on sleazily and melodramatically intoned narratorial voice-overs, such as the following gem: "Olga was still playing her cat-and-mouse game with Nadja. She would tie her to a tree and leave her there as long as a day at a time without doing anything else. This method eventually disturbed Nadja and slowly began working on her nervous system. Nadja never knew what to expect. Did Olga really know what to do with her? Was Olga stalling for time? What was Olga up to?"[48] After several years and incarnations of pieces that deconstructed the work of Eugene O'Neill, the Wooster Group decided in 1996 that *Olga's House of Shame* would be a crucial element in their next project, though they, perhaps like Olga, didn't "really know what to do with it" or "what they were up to" yet. As Clay Hapaz, the assistant director of *House/Lights,* explained to me, *Olga* first came to the attention of the group when it was privately screened for him, Liz LeCompte, and the actress Kate Valk (the "star" of *House/Lights*) by their friend the film critic Dennis Dermody.[49] Immediately upon seeing the film, LeCompte and Valk exclaimed that they had found "it"; shortly thereafter, the company began doing improvisational work with and around the film during rehearsals at the Performing Garage on Wooster Street, the Manhattan performance space that the group has inhabited since its formation in the 1970s. Along the way, the decision to juxtapose pieces of the film with excerpts of Stein's *Faustus* was something of a happy accident. In an interview that I conducted with LeCompte and Valk, LeCompte explained that she had been long encouraged by friends and colleagues to work with a Stein text, and specifically with *Faustus*. She had been reading Stein for some time, but she had shied away from undertaking *Faustus* because she feared the overdetermining influence of the play's many earlier incarnations in the hands of other avant-garde directors and luminaries: Judith Malina at the Living Theatre (1951); Lawrence Kornfeld at Judson Church (1979); Richard Foreman at the *Festival d'Automne* (1982); and, most recently, Robert Wilson at a variety of international theaters (1992).[50] Nevertheless, as LeCompte worked with *Olga* and continued to read Stein, she realized that she couldn't avoid the "perfect fit" that *Olga* and *Faustus* made with each other, and so the play joined the growing brew of rehearsal elements. Some members of the group would read Stein aloud as others acted out scenes from the film, and slowly the two began to converge.

When I first viewed *Olga's House of Shame,* my knee-jerk academic response was an objection to what I perceived as an improbable male fantasy of lesbian S/M. But it was precisely the fantastic elements of the film—the strange camera angles and stylized acting, which *Olga* shares with contemporaneous 1960s "art" films—that drew in the Wooster Group. I asked LeCompte and Valk whether their initial enthusiasm for *Olga* stemmed from attraction or revulsion, and they responded without hesitation that theirs was an unalloyed attraction to the film. In addition to the aesthetic appeal that *Olga* held for them, as a piece that could call into question the boundary between highbrow art and lowbrow entertainment, they must also have been intimately interested in the film's exploration of power dynamics between women. LeCompte and Valk described *House/Lights* as, in part, a reflection upon and assessment of their own working and personal relationship (interview). This observation invites a measured comparison between Olga and LeCompte, who has responded with ambivalence and even self-contradiction to the suggestion that she is an "autocratic director": "I think I have an autocratic style. I don't think that the way I work is autocratic. I like to run a tight ship. I like to have the final say, not so much because I want the power of it, but because otherwise, I lose my way. These workers bring this material to me, and I sift and siphon through it. . . . It's a slow process, and it's not democratic in any way. But *autocratic* is the wrong word for it."[51] In Olga's syndicate, there is no question that she is an autocrat, and a successful one—until, that is, her power is challenged by the upstart Elaine, whose relationship with Olga is at the center of the film and who double-crosses Olga in a jewel-smuggling operation. Elaine says, as she subsequently cuts a deal with her boss, "I think it would be nice to be the hunter this time instead of the hunted." Olga grants Elaine more and more power in the organization, and the film ends with the narrator's description of a newly forged unholy alliance between them:

> This day marked another triumph for Olga. The day that her protégée took over the reins as second in command. This was a day that Elaine had been waiting for, and she wasn't going to let anything or anyone stop her now.
>
> Yes, this was a proud day for Olga. She had created Elaine in her own image and likeness. Now there were two of them. Two vicious minds working as one. Set upon the destruction of all who stood in their way, by whatever means possible.

References to viciousness and destruction aside, this passage must have conjured for LeCompte and Valk a sense of the evolution of their own collaboration. Though earlier pieces by the Wooster Group focused chiefly on performances by male members of the company, including Spalding Gray, Willem Dafoe, and Ron Vawter, *House/Lights* places the reins firmly in Valk's hands.

With Valk at center stage, and given *Olga*'s emphasis on the "twinning" of Olga and Elaine, whom Olga creates "in her own image and likeness," we might expect the collision in *House/Lights* of *Olga's House of Shame* with *Doctor Faustus Lights the Lights* to focus on the patently queer and arguably lesbian figure of Marguerite Ida and Helena Annabel. Indeed, Kate Valk exclaimed to me with an almost childlike glee, "This is our lesbian piece!"— but the seeming innocence of this declaration belies the complex ways in which *House/Lights* construes and constructs lesbianism as such (interview). In the "final" version of the piece (if any performance of the Wooster Group's endlessly retooled works can be called final), Valk plays the role of "Elaine/Faustus," and Suzzy Roche joins her onstage as "Olga/Mephistopheles." Much of the piece's minutely detailed choreography focuses on longing glances and slow caresses between Valk and Roche—that is, when Roche is not cracking the whip at Valk or holding Valk aloft and upside down to mime a bite of her inner thigh. This last moment, placed at the end of the first act of *House/Lights,* comes as Valk delivers the line, "A viper has bitten her she knows it too a viper has bitten her believe it or not it is true, a viper has bitten her and if Doctor Faustus does not cure her it will be all through her a viper has bitten her a viper a viper." Like nearly all of the Stein text incorporated into *House/Lights,* this account of the viper sting figures as part of one long (though frequently interrupted) monologue, assigned to Elaine/Faustus and delivered by Valk in an electronically modified "dew-drop Betty Boop voice."[52] Marguerite Ida and Helena Annabel's sexual plight is subsumed under Faustus's presiding consciousness, as Faustus in turn morphs into Elaine and embodies aspects of her alternation between masochistic victimization and sadistic domination.

As Marguerite Ida and Helena Annabel says in Stein's play, "Doctor Faustus a queer name" (98), and LeCompte certainly mines the latent queer potential of the character in her cross-gender casting and her fusion of Faustus with Elaine. Just as Faustus resists and denies his pact with Mephistopheles, to whom he has sold his soul "to make white electric light and day-light and night light" but without whom, he claims, he can still "do everything" (89), so too does Elaine chafe against her servitude to Olga ("I think it would be nice to be the hunter this time instead of the hunted"). In the end, neither Faustus nor Elaine can escape the alliance with Mephistopheles and Olga, respectively. Elaine joins Olga in her torture of the other girls, and Faustus, who cannot resist Mephistopheles' "will of iron," "sinks into the darkness" with the devil (118). As *Olga's House of Shame* plays almost continuously on television monitors placed at the front and back of the stage, and as the actors shift between imitative re-creations of the film's action and impressionistic riffs on Stein's text, the parallels between *Faustus* and *Olga* become clear—just as they are distorted and reconfigured. Faustus's spiritual indenture to Mephistopheles becomes an erotic indenture to a sexually appetitive, lesbian devil; as Olga says when she stumbles upon one of her girls, Marianna, performing a belly dance for some of the others, "These kids were ready to go the limit. All that they needed was a little push in the right direction. And that's just what I was going to do."

For the Wooster Group, "going the limit" meant more than simply staging a confrontation between *Faustus* and *Olga.* As the piece developed gradually over a two-year-long period of rehearsals, other elements were also woven into the fabric of the production, either as video or sound: clips from various Hollywood musicals of the 1930s and from the Mel Brooks spoof

Young Frankenstein (1974); a musical number from an episode of the television series *I Love Lucy,* whose integration into the piece invites a comparison between Cuban band leader Ricky Ricardo (Desi Arnaz) and Stein's "man from over the seas"; and the Johnny Cash song "Ring of Fire" ("I fell into a burning ring of fire"), played in the first act after Valk describes the viper sting. In addition, the piece's second act, a loose rendering of the song and ballet from *Faustus*'s own second act, interpolates a comic routine between Valk and "Mr. Viper," represented here as a microphone "puppet" with a viper's head. The viper, who "speaks back to [Valk] in the hilarious, ventriloquist-dummy voice of John Collins,"[53] mouths lines that allude parodically to the act of Señor Wences, a Spanish ventriloquist and regular guest on American variety shows of the 1950s and 1960s. A detailed analysis of these various aspects of production is too complicated for the present discussion, but I do want, in closing, to focus on one element in particular: the Powerbook sound improvisations provided by Tanya Selvaratnam (Christine and Nadja), who used a Mac laptop computer to generate a series of disruptive "bings," "bongs," "quacks," "bip-bips," "blips," "crows," "waa-woos," "beeps," "klinks," and musical notes (piano, organ, and flute) throughout the course of the piece. As LeCompte recalls, Selvaratnam, who was an intern with the group, clashed heatedly during the development of *House/Lights* with the male sound designers and operators, who felt that her "intrusions" marred the effect of their carefully calculated score (interview). LeCompte defended the young woman, however, in what she perceived as a sort of battle of the sexes, and the Powerbook improvisations stayed, ultimately becoming a fixed and precisely timed group of sounds in the piece. In this victory for Selvaratnam, something of Marguerite Ida and Helena Annabel's spirit persists in the work, despite her otherwise complete integration, if not evaporation, into the role of Elaine/Faustus. Valk may say, at the end of the third and final act of *House/Lights,* that "you Marguerite Ida and Helena Annabel . . . you know I can go to hell and I can take some one too and that some one will be you," but the "klink" orchestrated to come fast on the heels of this line, as though "spoken" by the absent woman, derides and deflates it. Stein's text may air a grave suspicion of technology in the form of electric lights that "get brighter and nothing comes" (92), but I think that she would have been pleased to see that something *could* come from technological innovation. In this case, it preserved her heroine's voice and transmuted it into the idiom of another power(ful) book.

Ultimately, Selvaratnam's discordant noisemaking serves as a figure in miniature for the discordant pulses of *House/Lights* as a whole. By describing *House/Lights* as "discordant," I do not mean simply to suggest (though it is certainly true) that the piece's kaleidoscopic fusion of *Faustus, Olga, Frankenstein, Lucy,* et al. creates a sense of discomfort and dis-ease, as the constituent parts of the work crash into and bounce off each other like bumper cars. Rather, what *House/Lights* "illuminates" for us, ironically, is just how discordant and dark Stein's play about blinding electric lights has been all along. Reading retrospectively through the prism of the Wooster Group's interpretation, we want to say with LeCompte of Stein's play, "Of *course* Faustus is a sadomasochist." Indeed, how better to describe a man whose self-punishing desire to suffer hell's torments fuels his violent designs on Marguerite Ida and Helena Annabel, the boy, and the dog? As Faustus says in the play's third act, "How can I be I again alright and go to hell. . . . I will kill I will I will" (116). Significantly, Faustus's murderous impulse is linked here not only to his wish to go to hell but also to a hope that "I [can] be I again." In a highly disturbing translation, Stein reimagines her famous line, "I am I because my little dog knows me," as, "I am I because I kill my little dog." Human nature may depend in part on the little dog's recognition, but Stein must recognize in turn that the human nature thus constituted is nasty, brutish, and not as short in the duration of its bloodthirstiness as she or we might like.

This dark reading of Stein inspired by the Wooster Group redounds not just to *Faustus* but to Stein's other plays of the same period. If Faustus must kill his little dog to go to hell, then the Hollywood party of *A Play Called Not and Now* is, in a sense, a version of the hell to which he seeks access—with the crucial distinction that the partygoers have committed not canicide but a form of suicide to get there. Like a member of the tribe of the undead, the woman who looks like Gertrude Atherton has murdered a part of herself for the dubious privilege of wandering listlessly from living room to dining room and back again. And what of the woman who looks like Gertrude Stein? One way out of hell is to refuse the invitation to the party and to stay at home with Alice, but as *Byron* demonstrates, the domestic cocoon provides no certain protection against the human inclination toward violence. The play may provide Stein with a space within which to revivify her dead dog, but there's no guarantee that she won't, like Faustus, send him back to the grave: "Byron, when Byron droops he droops because he has been not only not invited but compelled to face the cold. He droops" (373). Even if drooping doesn't necessarily equate with or lead to dying, the owner who compels her dog to face the cold also compels her lover, the "hot little sacrifice," to face a heat that is similarly ravishing. I began this discussion of

Stein with reference to her off-the-cuff ruminations on sex, but it is important to remember that Stein spoke to John Preston in the same breath of sex *and* death—and, by implication, the death that inheres in sex, playwriting, or any other passion. As *Olga*'s narrator says of Elaine at the beginning of *House of Shame,* "She dared not get caught again. Capture could mean death. It was a very rare case when Olga was known to spare the life of one who tried to escape. Their lives were spared only when Olga could find some very special use for their services." Elaine may escape literal death, but the brutal service for which Olga enlists her invariably reeks of it—deferred, displaced, and sexualized, but death all the same.

Gertrude Stein is not a preeminently moral or ethical writer. She does not ask with, through, or of the figures in her fictions and dramas, "Who is right and who is wrong?" but rather, "Who is weak and who is strong? Who has the power?" And almost invariably, Stein's own identification is with the strong. If Stein is, as she reports in lectures and essays, a great fan of detective fiction, she comes to the genre from the perspective of the hard-boiled, hard-nosed, flat-footed cop, not the victim. In "What Are Masterpieces and Why Are There So Few of Them," Stein says of detective stories, which she considers the "only really modern novel form": "In real life people are interested in the crime more than they are in detection . . . but in the story it is the detection that holds the interest and that is natural enough because the necessity as far as action is concerned is the dead man, it is another function that has very little to do with human nature that makes the detection interesting. And so always it is true that the master-piece has nothing to do with human nature or with identity, it has to do with the human mind and the entity that is with a thing in itself and not in relation."[54] Stein makes a crucial distinction here, as we have seen elsewhere, between human nature and the human mind. If she presents human nature at all, as she does in *Doctor Faustus,* she will present it in all of its ugliness. But how preferable, in her view, to do away with human nature altogether and focus scrutiny on the cold, calculating human mind. As for the human body, so much the better if it should appear, as it does in detective fiction, as an outright *dead* body. "The hero is dead to begin with," she writes approvingly, "and so you have so to speak got rid of the event before the book begins."

Conversely, in the theater, the human body is arguably the one indispensable element, the sine qua non, of live performance. Indeed, it is perhaps just this intractable human body that Stein resists when she writes plays that resist performance. The Wooster Group understands this impulse, and they account for it in their production of *House/Lights.* If the human body must appear, then it will appear disfigured. Costumes contain weird bulges that prohibit graceful movement, and LeCompte describes the corseted actors on stage as "lumpy women" (interview). And if the lumpy body must appear, and speak, then it will appear only to be flagellated, and speak only through electronic mediation—or, even more ideally, it will speak as a corpse. In *Doctor Faustus,* the final line of the play may be given to the little boy who may have also died, suddenly and unceremoniously, a page earlier.[55] From beyond the grave, and presumably disembodied in Stein's imagination, he says, "Please Mr. Viper listen to me . . . please Mr. Viper listen to me" (118). This is also the final line of *House/Lights,* which Kate Valk delivers as the eponymous houselights go down and, in the darkened theater, her voice temporarily achieves the disembodiment that Stein imagines.

If we, along with Mr. Viper, are asked plaintively and insistently to listen to these words, then what is the message we receive when we hear? Most simply, both the play and its adaptation seem to suggest that death is certain, and the life that leads there is likely to be full of suffering, struggle, violence, and torture. It is not an uplifting message, but neither Stein nor the Wooster Group flinches in its delivery. Like Olga and Elaine, whom *House of Shame*'s narrator describes as "two vicious minds working as one," Stein and her transmitters work as one to convey an unnerving vision of hell on earth. If we like, we can choose to dismiss or ignore the vision, which is, after all, packaged as a fable. But *Faustus,* written in Europe in 1938, is also a wartime play, and I suspect that the Wooster Group chose to revive it in 2005 precisely because it is a fable for us. Turning from Stein to Barnes, who is likewise obsessed with representations of death and (at times) its relationship to war, it would be tempting to describe, too, a turn from Stein's identification with the aggressor to Barnes's empathy for the victim; but as we shall see, Barnes's relationship to victimization is a complex one that demands a nuanced analysis sometimes absent from criticism of her work.

4

backing barnes

CLOSET TRAUMA?

In an interview given to James Scott late in her life, Djuna Barnes, never one to pull any punches, offered a biting portrait of fellow American expatriate Gertrude Stein: "[Stein] couldn't write for beans! But she did write 'A rose is a rose is a rose'—that was good. The only thing she ever wrote that was. D'you know what she said of me? Said I had beautiful legs! Now, what does that have to do with anything? She said I had beautiful legs! Now, I mean, what—what did she say *that* for? I mean if you[']re going to say something about a person . . . I couldn't *stand* her. She had to be the center of every-thing—a monstrous ego. Her brother, what was his name? Leo Stein. Poor thing. He was a nice boy. She simply *ate him up!*"[1] This account corrobo-rates impulses that we have already seen at play in Stein's work: the asser-tion of force and the desire for dominance, manifested at times in a de-vouring cruelty ("She simply *ate him up!*"), at times in an implicit dismissal or denigration of a fellow artist ("Said I had beautiful legs!"). But just as il-luminating in this account of Stein's condescension toward Barnes is Barnes's refusal to submit to Stein's animus: "I couldn't *stand* her"—and she didn't. Though they traveled in overlapping artistic circles in the 1920s and 1930s, Barnes kept a calculated distance from Stein and "found infuri-ating," as her biographer Phillip Herring attests, "the general assumption that she had been a friend of Gertrude Stein's in their Paris days" (176).

No mere victim, Barnes. And yet a strong strain of scholarly work seeks to emphasize precisely the element of victimization in her writing. Some-times hovering in the background of this criticism, and sometimes boldly asserted, are two unsubstantiable claims about Barnes: that she may have been molested as a young child by her paternal grandmother, Zadel Barnes Gustafson; and that she may have been raped as a teenager either by her father, Wald Barnes, or by a family friend goaded or at least permitted by Wald to violate her. Great weight has been placed particularly on the latter charge, because Barnes renders just such a violation in her most autobiographically inflected works, the novel *Ryder* and the play *The Antiphon*. Barnes herself was the explicit model for these two works' respective female protagonists, just as the members of her immediate family provided the basis for the texts' other characters; and to ignore entirely the biographical dimensions of these intimately personal documents would constitute a serious critical omission.

At the same time, any scholar who equates Barnes's work with her life commits an equally serious—and double-hinged—interpretive error. On the one hand, he treats unskeptically as truth what Barnes has presented as fiction, despite the fact that the biographical record (family correspondence, written and oral testimonies provided by Barnes and her friends) offers no conclusive proof that Barnes was the victim of abuses exactly like those suffered by her characters. On the other hand, and perhaps more troubling from the perspective of literary criticism, he reduces the self-conscious complexities of Barnes's writing, with its many elisions and opacities, knots and brocades, to the product of a damaged consciousness incapable of processing clearly and directly its own damage. If the author is traumatized, such a reading goes, then the textures of the writing will record that trauma; or, as Anne B. Dalton, in an account of Barnes's play *The Dove*, puts it, "One critic stated that [Barnes's] writing 'suffers from that most irritating offense of difficult writing—the mysterioso effect that hides no mystery, the locked box with nothing in it.' I would argue that Barnes's work is more like Pandora's box: once one manages to open it, the contents stream out irrepressibly."[2]

In turn, I contend that neither Dalton nor the critic whom she cites[3] represents Barnes's work accurately. Her challenging, often extravagant style does not amount to nothing, but at the same time, it does not conceal any easy truth that we must simply know enough about Barnes's life to understand. Dalton, for instance, reads *The Dove* as a coded protest against the putative sexual abuse of Djuna that she attributes unflinchingly to Zadel Barnes. But Barnes's attitude toward incest and toward sexuality in general —as expressed in *The Dove*, her most famous novel *Nightwood*, and elsewhere—is much more complex than such an account would allow.[4] It is not incest per se but nonconsensual sex and the objectification that it entails (objectification against which Barnes chafed, on a less extreme scale, in her interaction with Stein) that Barnes protests in her writing; as Louise DeSalvo rightly observes of father's violation of daughter in *The Antiphon*, "In refusing to use the word 'incest' to refer to what Titus has done to her, Miranda calls incest by its proper name: rape."[5] Though DeSalvo would surely disagree with any distinction between rape and incest that leaves room for a positive valuation of the latter transgression, I would argue that precisely such a distinction animates Barnes's work. Though Barnes condemns rape categorically, she points to various configurations of lesbian incest—between mother and daughter, grandmother and granddaughter, sister and sister—that would not only provide a consolation for male violation but also constitute ideal ends in themselves. If this trope of lesbian incest remains a fantasy in Barnes's writing, posited but unrealized, it is because cultural taboo prohibits such an expression of sexuality and because such sexuality, were it ever to be expressed, could only be a compromised version of the utopic consummation for which Barnes longs. Especially in her dramatic writing, Barnes's method can be described as tragic and violent, yet the tragedy results not from incestuous desire as such but from the impossibility for incestuous desire to be fulfilled nonviolently, given the conditions, in Barnes's view, of the cruel world in which such fulfillment would have to take place.

This account of Barnes's work is admittedly troubling. While there is certainly no easy distinction between "bad rape" and "good incest" in Barnes's work, Barnes nevertheless upsets our unilaterally negative view of the meanings of incest, and this radicality of vision outstrips the unorthodoxies of most of her modernist contemporaries.[6] In the face of such a radical, and perhaps radically distasteful, conception of desire, it would be easy to fall back on a psychologization of Barnes that contains and constrains her imagination of lesbian incest. Indeed, my reading could easily fuel the contentions of those who wish to avow categorically Zadel's supposed abuse of Djuna. If Barnes's characters long for sexual attachments to the fellow women in their families, the counterargument to my own would maintain, then they do so because Barnes, like many survivors of abuse, has internalized the permissibility of incest and cannot distinguish between (so-called) healthy and unhealthy desires. Quite apart from my refusal to weigh in on the unknowable details of Barnes's private life, I reject this argument because it fails to reflect accurately the subtlety of Barnes's writing, in favor of a sanitized, reductive, and ultimately impoverishing reading of her work. While the readings that I propose here are indebted to—indeed, would be impossible without—the precedents established by feminist scholars, some of those scholars miss a crucial aspect of Barnes's writing: it disorients us not just because of the contortions and convolutions of her style but because of the discomforting ideas, especially about incest, that her stylistic intricacies force us to confront. In my view, to honor the complexity of Barnes's literary output means not to speculate without great care about what personal experiences might be at the back of her writing, but to back that writing in all of its disturbing dimensions.

Another way to frame this argument rhetorically is to propose a move away from Barnes's closet trauma—the purported abuse that leaves her capable of only quasi-coherent expression—and toward her closet drama, a deliberately nonnormative and possibly unperformable theatrical idiom that reflects the nonnormative nature of her subject matter, taboo sexuality. Indeed, it is in Barnes's dramatic writing—her short play *The Dove,* her long verse play *The Antiphon,* and her unpublished play *Biography of Julie von Bartmann*—that she explores most acutely and provocatively her failed utopic visions of lesbian incest. Moreover, these works are best understood alongside some of her other dramas (the short play *An Irish Triangle,* the unpublished play *Ann Portuguise*); the more broadly performative dimensions of her early journalistic "stunt pieces," which articulate her notions about transgressive and alternative, if not specifically incestuous, desires and behaviors; and Jackson Mac Low's performative revisions of her work in *Barnesbook,* which emphasize, too, her preoccupation with and celebration of sexual transgression. Ultimately, the most important contexts for Barnes's ruminations on lesbian incest are not her real relationships with the women in her own family (whether sexual or not) but her and others' championships, as expressed in performative writing not chiefly concerned with either lesbianism or incest, of the plurality of sexuality and the freedom to express one's sexuality as plurally as possible. As her friend Emily Coleman once reminded Barnes in a letter, "When I asked you if you considered yourself really Lesbian: 'I might be anything. If a horse loved me, I might be that.'"[7] Barnes's joke to Coleman says nothing serious about her own proclivities, but it does point tellingly to her belief in and advocacy of sexual heterogeneity. And in her earliest writings that bear on these issues, it's not a horse but a gorilla that provides the focal point for discussion.

GORILLA IN THE MIDST

From 1913 until 1920, when she moved to Europe, Djuna Barnes rose quickly to prominence as a New York journalist. As a regular correspondent for the Brooklyn *Daily Eagle;* a freelance writer for the *Press,* the *World,* and the *Morning Telegraph;* and an eventual contributor to most of the other New York papers, Barnes enjoyed a fair amount of her own celebrity (initially by proximity but ultimately for a unique style of writing) through interviews of such other celebrities as Lillian Russell, Diamond Jim Brady, Alfred Stieglitz, and Jack Dempsey. In addition to the celebrity interviews, Barnes garnered most attention for another genre of journalism, "stunt pieces" for which she performed such quirky acts as riding the "slides, chutes and whirling disks of Luna Park Steeple Chase" and "allowing herself to be lowered at the end of a rope from the top of a building for an article on firemen's rescues."[8] Among these performative pieces, often frivolous in design and outlandish in execution, one more sober foray stands out and has generated more recent critical commentary than all the others: "How It Feels to Be Forcibly Fed," written in September 1914 for *New York World Magazine* and inspired by the experience of British suffragettes. As Alyce Barry explains: "In their effort to get the vote, British women committed acts of civil disobedience by the hundreds. Finding, however, that their imprisonment had little effect upon government policy, they adopted the tactic of hunger striking while in prison. Many became ill, and the Home Office, unwilling to allow prisoners the popularity of martyrdom, ordered that hunger strikers be forcibly fed by prison officials."[9] At a hospital in New York, Barnes submitted to a tube-feeding much like that of the suffragettes and chronicled the details of her experience in an article whose immediacy is still palpable nearly a hundred years later.

Critics have sought in a number of ways to understand the significance of this strange piece and its relationship to Barnes's more mature work. Not surprisingly, Anne Dalton reads "Forcibly Fed" as a rehearsal for such plays as *The Dove*—that is, in her view, yet another recapitulation of Barnes's childhood trauma. She writes: "By participating in the force-feeding, Barnes was engaged in a destructive, yet revealing, form of acting out. Barnes's position in the 'voluntary simulation' was a symbol of her former position in her family—in which her father and grandmother conflated nurture and violence in their violation of her bodily integrity" (123). To my mind, Dalton is too eager here to dismiss Barnes's agency in the stunt of force-feeding and too capricious in her scare-quoting of "voluntary simulation." In so doing, she glosses over the most challenging and provocative ambiguity at the heart of Barnes's experiment, which is perhaps best described not as a voluntary simulation (the circumstances of the feeding may simulate the reality of the suffragettes' imprisonment, but there is nothing unreal about the feeding itself) but paradoxically as a voluntary coercion, a "constrained act" in which "some level of consent" has, nevertheless, occurred.[10] To submit willingly to a compulsory act is a seeming contradiction in terms, and one toward which Barnes gestures in the account of her equally contradictory response to the feeding, which she describes alternately as "passive revolt" and "futile defiance."[11] At one point, she tries to separate neatly these two dimensions of the experience from each other: futility and passivity belong to the capitulating body, while revolt and defiance belong to the mind angrily comprehending the body's capitulation; or, as she puts it, "The spirit was betrayed by the body's weakness. There it is—the outraged will" (178).

This distinction belies, however, the complexity of Barnes's project and the extent to which, even at the bodily level, she maintains some level of volition. Barbara Green suggests that "How It Feels to Be Forcibly Fed" might be more aptly titled "How It *Looks* to Be Forcibly Fed" because of the ways in which Barnes makes her body a spectacular object for the consumption of both the doctors who force-feed her and her eventual readers;[12] yet Barnes is concerned in her article not only with the way her body looks *to* others, but also with the ways in which it looks *at* the world as she undergoes the feeding. For every description of the gaze upon her—"The doctor's eyes were always just before me"—there is a description of what her own gaze registers—"The electric light to my left took a hazy step or two toward the clock, which lurched forward to meet it" (178). Though Barnes's throat may open, despite her desire to choke, and swallow "the hated flow" of milk through the rubber tubing, she can still actively watch "the pitcher as it [rises] in the hand of the doctor" (179, 177). Finally, it is this meticulously observant eye, the journalist's eye, that preserves the quality of performance—what Barnes herself calls her "playacting" (178)—in the piece and dissociates this performance from Barnes's putatively traumatic childhood.[13]

Dalton's emphasis on the force-feeding as "a symbol of [Barnes's] former position in her family" ignores the crucial historical dimension of the stunt as, rather, a symbol of, or at least a commentary upon, the force-feeding of the suffragettes. Barbara Green, who takes up this task admirably and offers a useful overview of these force-feedings and their place in the suffrage movement, reminds us of an important aspect to this feminist trial that Barnes knew all too well but that we could easily forget: the force-feedings were just as much a performance—just as much a weirdly "voluntary coercion"—for the suffragettes as they were for Barnes. Far from a simple tactic that physicians used "to break [the suffragettes'] spirit[s]," as Dalton maintains (123), the force-feedings were events that the suffragettes turned to their own strategic advantage as a recruiting method. As Green explains, "the militant Women's Social and Political Union produced a constant stream of images of feminine protest as part of the struggle to win the vote," including images of forcible feeding intended to garner sympathy for the suffragettes and outrage on their behalf (71).

It is just this ambivalent element of calculated martyrdom that Barnes reproduces in her own performance—but in so doing, she repeats it with a critical difference. Green posits that Barnes was uneasy about the ways in which "activists position[ed] themselves as exhibitions" (82), and I would add that a subtle but pervasive—even campy—irony permeates her supposed commendations of the suffragettes in "Forcibly Fed." When she writes, "If I, playacting, felt my being burning with revolt at this brutal usurpation of my own functions, how they who have actually suffered the ordeal in its acutest horror must have flamed at the violation of the sanctuaries of their spirits," she writes, tongue firmly in cheek, as someone who knows both that her physical pain is just as "actual" as the suffragettes'—and that their violation is just as performative. Her tone seems sober and even somber when she declares that "science had at last, then, deprived us of the right to die" (178), but she undercuts this rumination when she remarks, with a kind of cruel wit, just a few paragraphs later, "At least I have never heard of a militant choking herself into eternity" (179). Through such moments of gallows (or perhaps it would be better to call it "swallows") humor, Barnes's article becomes a strange satire on the practice of forcible feeding—and, to boot, a multipronged and omnidirectional satire in which no one, including herself, emerges unscathed. If the suffragettes are to be slyly chided for manipulating their own objectification, then so must the journalist who recapitulates their objectification in order to critique it: "I had shared the greatest experience of the bravest of my sex," she concludes, her sardonic deflation showing through her overwrought superlatives. Then, too, the doctor and his attendants are not let off the hook just because, as Barnes declares at the beginning of the article, the "experiment . . . was only tragic in [her] imagination" (174–75). To perform such an invasive procedure and then blithely return to the business of everyday life is a chillingly dissociative capability that Barnes makes sure to register at the article's close: "The little, red mustache upon [the doctor's] upper lip was drawn out in a line of pleasant understanding. He had forgotten all but the play. The four men, having finished their minor roles in one minor tragedy, were already filing out at the door" (179). Ultimately, the men's casual indifference to the woman's ordeal, more than the particulars of the force-feeding itself, is the most horrifying aspect of the spectacle.

This element of detached male superiority, along with other uncanny similarities, links "How It Feels to Be Forcibly Fed" to another article that Barnes wrote for *New York World Magazine* about a month later, "The Girl and the Gorilla," and broadens the context in which we might understand the resonances of the former piece. In a headnote to "The Girl and the Gorilla," reproduced in the volume of Barnes's articles *New York*, Alyce Barry explains the occasion of the piece's composition and the fate of its eponymous gorilla, Dinah: "When Dinah the gorilla's captors, from the New York Zoological Society, found her in the spring of 1913, they kept her in Africa for eighteen months to accustom her to captivity before bringing her to the U.S. in the fall of 1914, when Barnes wrote this 'interview.' By Christmas, Dinah had outlived any other gorilla in captivity but was suffering from paralysis. She eventually stopped eating and died of malnutrition the following August."[14] From this account of the story's background, clear correspondences between Dinah and the suffragettes immediately emerge: both the gorilla and the political activists are prisoners subject to male will—in Dinah's case, her keeper Engelholm and the zoology professor Robert L. Garner[15]—and both have only their bodies, specifically their refusal to eat, with which to protest their confinement. To draw parallels between adult, human women and a female gorilla might seem absurd, but this is precisely the conceit of Barnes's article, which might have been more aptly called "The Girl *Is* the Gorilla." At the outset of the piece, Barnes approaches her subject almost immediately—and quite wryly—as "neither very feminine nor very fragile," but nonetheless a woman: "We thought we had a line on all the different kinds of femininity in the world, their fads, fancies, and fashions, their virtues and their indiscretions—when suddenly enters Dinah, the bushgirl" (180). What follows is a mock-interview in which Dinah tells Barnes "what conclusions [she has] come to regarding our United States" —or rather performs such gestures as "[cupping] her hand about her ear and [dusting] a piece of lint from her shoulders," behaviors that Barnes "freely interpret[s]" and translates into English "according to Professor Garner's rules" (181–82). Not surprisingly, Dinah, whose name uncannily echoes *Djuna*, "speaks" to Barnes in an idiom that sounds much like the journalist's own polished and witty discourse, as when she ruminates on the fad of chewing gum: "I would like to find out what it is in that little delicacy that keeps so many people rotatory beneath their hats. But I have been getting the most weird and winsome feed here at the zoo that ever passed my understanding" (183). As a surrogate mouthpiece for Barnes, Dinah expresses observations, bordering at times on the poetic and poignant, that are patently her interlocutor's own: "The sun has no chance in New York and . . . the moon is only a past memory. I couldn't make out whether it was daylight or electricity" (182–83).

But Dinah is not simply an object for the journalist's projection, alternately joking and serious; indeed, Barnes emerges in the article as the only human capable of an empathic identification with the gorilla. Over the course of the interview, Barnes makes a clear and stark distinction between the rough male keeper, Engelholm, who "caught [Dinah] by the scruff of neck and paused in full view of the crowd, wiping his forehead, hauling her off like luggage from back home" (184), and herself, a gentle female presence who is "willing to hug [Dinah] and have her embrace [Barnes] in return" (183). More subtly, Barnes intimates that there is something faintly and curiously erotic about the gorilla's embrace: "Three feet of the newest womankind in the world was making me feel—well, awkward, to say the least" (182). The awkwardness gives way to a feeling that is "rather agreeable," as Dinah "[lays] her head upon [Barnes's] knees" and "[finds] something in [her], as representative of the women she had come among, to make her trustful" (183). In this lightly drawn moment, Barnes prefigures the much darker moment of embrace between human and gorilla with which O'Neill, her colleague in the Provincetown Players, concludes *The Hairy Ape*. She also prefigures the darker moments of female sexual intimacy— or rather failed attempts at intimacy—in her own more mature, literary work. The crucial element of trust, which she finds so easily with the gorilla, is more complicated to achieve and often unavailable entirely to the women in her fictions, hemmed in as they are by cultural prohibitions and domestic oppressions that foreclose the possibility of tenderness so comparatively effortless to the gorilla "looking out of faraway eyes upon a life called civilized" (180).

In addition to dovetailing with the preoccupations of Barnes's later novels and plays, the issues raised in this seemingly trifling article also redound to its chronological companion piece, "How It Feels to Be Forcibly Fed," in intriguing ways. Dinah is in part a figure of fun who can "spoil" Barnes's meditations on womanhood "by gravely putting an orange peel upon her head" (183), but she is, unlike the suffragettes, also the subject of serious and untainted pity. Whereas the suffragettes' imprisonment is transitory and their force-feedings part of a collectively endured and enjoined struggle, Dinah's sentence is permanent and her trials solitary, as "the only living captive of her race" (180). When Engelholm chases her around her cage, he is "Germany gaining upon Africa with difficulty," a metaphor by which Barnes highlights the implicitly political dimension of Dinah's experience, even as she evacuates the force-feeding of its political purpose and reduces it to a stunt. To render the plight of force-feeding as a sideshow and Dinah's sideshow as a plight is an inversion typical of Barnes's writing in all the phases of her career. We see this strategy at work in such early plays as *An Irish Triangle* and *Ann Portuguise,* where inversion is not only a structural method but also the subject—specifically in the form of so-called sexual inversion—of a drama that will become increasingly focused on the problems of sexual repression and taboo.

"THERE'S WAYS AND WAYS OF TYING A RIBBON"

Among her plays, Barnes's short 1920 piece *An Irish Triangle* may seem like a strange work with which to begin a discussion of her closet drama, because it is not one. First performed by the Provincetown Players in 1920 and published in *Playboy* the following year, the play was never closeted;[16] nor does it resemble superficially those plays that could more arguably be called closet dramas, given its straightforward linguistic idiom and uncomplicated dramaturgical representation. The play does, nevertheless, point in crucial ways toward the retreat that Barnes's dramatic writing would soon take into the closet. As Douglas Messerli says of this work and some of Barnes's other early efforts for the stage, "Barnes wipes away all the action, and explores instead the dialogue of wit. . . . [She] returns to the Socratic dialogues, one of the roots of theatre, in order to push away from a naturalist drama toward a theatre in which language, as opposed to setting, character, or thematic structure, dominates."[17] Taken to a further extreme, at which the language would become more opaque and the length of this logocentric drama would increase substantially from, say, ten pages (roughly the length of *An Irish Triangle*), this antinaturalistic tendency could—and did—push Barnes's drama off the stage and into the closet. Consider the full-length, three-act play *Ann Portuguise,* written shortly after *An Irish Triangle* and weighing in at more than a hundred pages.[18] Also indebted to the Socratic model, the play is composed almost entirely of slow, talky scenes between two characters at a time; because Barnes persists in this method of dramatic composition for so long, and because the characters' language is so evasive and their meanings so shrouded in ambiguity, it would not be unfair to deem the play unperformable. As one commentator declared while processing the manuscript for the archive, "I am quite clear that the play could not be done in such a way as to be understood, not to speak of being profitable, but it is the product of a mind of genius."[19] The arguable genius of the work notwithstanding, *Ann Portuguise* has indeed never been performed; and at the time of this writing, it also remains unpublished.[20]

In terms of the two plays' respective representations of sexuality, and specifically of male homosexuality, we can chart a similar trajectory away from comprehensibility and toward a more "closeted" mode of expression. While *An Irish Triangle* is not exactly frank in its discussion of homosexuality, its revelation of a homosexual encounter is decidedly unambiguous —though the revelation may come as something of a surprise. The play is set in the "neat little sitting room" of the O'Rune cottage, where Kathleen O'Rune, "a rather tall handsome woman" with a "general appearance . . . much above that of the usual poor," entertains her friend Shiela O'Hare, by contrast "a middle aged woman, thin small and sad."[21] Almost immediately we get the sense that Shiela's friendly visit is an errand to gossip. The door is barely closed behind her when she begins, through unsubtle innuendo, to indict Kathleen with the rumor of her husband John's infidelity, which has become common knowledge in their village:

> KATHLEEN: And how are you this fine day, Shiela, and the winter scarcely over and the spring coming?
>
> SHIELA: It's grand, fine I am, and glad to see yourself my eyes have not been clapped on since last October, and me watching your man going down into the woods quiet like, and it the poaching season. (97)

Kathleen knows full well that Shiela is less interested in John's poaching of hares than the game to which he has access "since he saw the inside of the Manor door" (99), and it isn't long before she brushes breezily past Shiela's barely veiled insinuations and admits what her friend longs to hear: "But I'll be telling you, John is the envy of my heart and it's a great thankfulness I have that I ever met him at all, and no keening and swinging of the body this side and that, because he has gone up on the hill and found her ladyship beautiful" (102). Shiela is appalled that Kathleen can treat her husband's adultery so lightly, with no concern for either her "own honor" or "the honor of other women with husbands who do be going to the fishing or the hunting" (103); but Kathleen, who has already shown off her stylish blue gown and her memorization of a poem from a Parisian journal, is quick

to point out the benefits of education and refinement that come from contact with "her ladyship": "For there's nothing she says or does or thinks, but
he does be telling me also, and she hasn't put a thing on her back this six
months he hasn't described fine and it's the world will be seeing something
this spring, I'm thinking, when I take my butter to market, for there's ways
and ways of tying a ribbon, and there's ways and ways of greeting and
farewelling, that the likes of us poor know nothing about at all, until we
marry a lad with the sun in his hair, who is fit to nose it out at the end of a
good love-making" (103–4). It's clear from the enthusiasm with which
Kathleen speaks earlier of "the glory and beauty of [her] limbs, and the independent ways of [her] breasts" that John's tutelage isn't confined to what
he can nose out at the end of a good lovemaking, but includes what he can
nose out *during* one, too; and as he describes all the things that her ladyship has put on her back, he no doubt shares with Kathleen all the things
that she's done on her back as well (101).

Just when we think that this erotic mastery has proven enough to shock
and dismay Shiela, Kathleen makes a final admission that leaves her friend
"blind mystified. . . . and all turned about and mazed":

SHIELA: And it's I don't know what to make of you, and the ter-
            rible triangle that's come into your life! [*raising her head*]
KATHLEEN: It's the triangles that do be raising Ireland. [*She removes
            her cap.*] And it's the master of the Manor himself who is
            soft of tongue and charming, and John says there's a way
            he's dying to know, the master has of wrapping his put-
            tees, that can be learned by close contact only. (106)

Right down to the removal of her cap to show, almost literally, what she's
been keeping underneath it, Kathleen clearly savors the delay of her disclosure that it's not a triangle at all but a quadrangle that has the ability to
raise John up, so to speak. Once we learn that John has engaged in a liaison
with the Master, too (or soon will), an entirely new level of meaning is lent
retrospectively to many earlier lines that were already pregnant with sexual
connotation. "And there's a rare mighty change come over things John does
be putting his eyes on," Kathleen says at the beginning of the play; and we
understand, looking back, that the "stupendous change [that] has come over
nature," to which Shiela unwittingly assents, encompasses, among other
things, homosexuality (98). Nor is the homosexuality, or at least the homoeroticism, limited to John's exploits with the Master; for how else but
as a kind of paean to lesbianism are we to interpret Kathleen's final line: "It's

a grand night coming on, and it's the moon and I will be climbing the hill, for I've nothing more to learn, but John is rare ignorant" (106). John must still learn "by close contact" all the things that the Master can teach him, but Kathleen is satisfied that she has experienced just such a closeness to the lady through John's mediation: "And where my man can go in body there I go in spirit. . . . What he knows, I know, and what he sees, I see" (103). In a sense, Kathleen has "known" the lady, and this knowledge adds a further twist to Shiela's exasperated question, "Where would the likes of the glory of Ireland and its women be if they were all as strange as yourself, Kathleen O'Rune, I'd like to know?" (105).

Of course, it is the "strangeness" of Kathleen O'Rune that Barnes so obviously prizes and champions—and that she uses to make *An Irish Triangle,* among other things, a parody of Yeats's dramatic writing for the Abbey Players, in which he "[insists] on the superiority of dream to daily life" and "celebrates the deathlike superiority of dream as more 'real' than the world of banal convention that the world calls reality."[22] Far from needing to depart the world to escape its banality, Barnes suggests, one might stay in it and reshape its conventions. Unlike, for instance, Yeats's eponymous protagonist Cathleen ni Houlihan, who "pressures [her spouse] Michael to choose between the careful husbandry of marriage and the glorious immortality promised to those who die in the service of Ireland"—and who thus makes it clear "that death and immortality constitute the only heroic course of action"[23]—Kathleen O'Rune expands queerly the notions of marriage, love, and life so that they, too, can constitute the "glory of Ireland," even if (that is, precisely because) Shiela doesn't think so. As Douglas Messerli observes, Shiela's "bourgeois shock is simply a tool to keep the language and [Kathleen's] story moving" (10). Counterpoising Shiela as a fairly one-dimensional straw man, Barnes makes Kathleen her mouthpiece for a platform of unencumbered sexuality. The play is light in tone and simple in its doctrine, but it ought not to be underestimated as a trifle. Here we see Barnes accomplish a feat that she will never again attempt in her dramatic writing—the positive statement of her ideals about love and sex, which she must assign to the entirely unfamiliar (and admittedly stereotyped and fantastic) setting of "Ireland" to make plausible, especially perhaps to herself. Once she begins in any way to draw on real, lived experience, even as she fashions that experience into an antinaturalistic idiom that borders at times on the surreal, she can communicate her sexual vision only negatively and obliquely. Beginning with plays like *Ann Portuguise,* Barnes writes a series of cautionary tales and laments in which we see the nightmarish obverse of Kathleen's bright bubble—dimly lit corners of human experience where no one is "sitting among the hedges like the elves or the Queen, . . . smiling with the straight smile that knows no sorrow, . . . lying down in the dark and rising up in the dawn with a sense . . . that [one] had not stopped the great progress of the world" (105).

ANTHONY, GET YOUR GUN

Ann Portuguise begins with a detailed character list that paints the central figure of act one, Cassius Povlin, as an unmistakable gay dandy in the mold of Oscar Wilde:

> *Cassius Povlin*
>   A man of fifty years. Clean shaven, with long dark hair. His face is pale, heavy, quiet, such a face as was common during the Restoration. He wears an indescribable wardrobe, consisting of an officers [*sic*] coat, a pair of evening trousers and a visored cap. He is never seen without a cane of strong rough wood, studded with silver nails, neither is he ever without a pair of large yellow gloves. He is evidently a man of wide culture and roaming disposition. No one knows just where he hails from. He always seems very fond of women, but where other men continue he concludes with a pat ~~on the bottom~~.[24]

How fitting that Barnes should have struck through the last phrase "on the bottom," as if it signaled too clearly the homosexual desire that Cassius seeks desperately to banish. When the play opens, he and his companion, Ann Portuguise, are visiting the country estate of fey Anthony Scarlett, "a young man, thin[,] nervous, pale, slightly under height and decidedly underweight" (2). Anthony has invited them to his home with the ostensible intention of wooing Ann away from Cassius, but as he says when Ann asks him whether he loves her, "Yes, but we're all confused" (18). In his sexual confusion, he is also drawn to his supposed rival for Ann—"I think I love Cassius" (17)—and Barnes uses the ensuing complications among the three to distinguish Ann, brazenly and perhaps even polymorphously perverse, from secretive and repressed Cassius.

Ann announces her perversity exactly as such during her first appearance, which conveys immediately her disregard for propriety. Fluttering excitedly around the dining room, she has dodged the company of the other houseguests to gossip with the two maids: Lena, who is hardened and suspicious of Ann's flirtatious chatter; and Olga, a younger woman captivated by what Barnes calls Ann's "biting, brilliant" "manner" (1). Her captivation gives Ann an opportunity for seduction that she seizes readily: "I'm perverse —as they say. Come here (*Olga reluctantly comes forward*) put your hand on my shoulders[.] (*Olga obeys timidly*) See, they are as limber as a bird's[.] (*Moving them*) That's the secret of perversity—(*Laughing*) now you know everything" (14). If the secret of Ann's perversity resides in her limberness, then the open secret of her perversity lies in her infinite capacity to desire whoever is at hand. It's incredible that Olga should be swayed by an attention that is a transparent variation on a similar seduction practiced on Lena —in Olga's presence—just moments earlier:

ANN: . . . I'll tell you something about myself. I positively graze life, you see. Don't hold that against me, either. See—I'll stroke your hair (*She reaches forward*)

LENA: (*Drawing back*) Don't put your hands on me!

ANN: (*Shaking some money in her hand*) Would you deny me? See, for a silver piece let me stroke your hair—Christ only brought thirty, you know—

LENA: (*Crossing herself in fright*) Merciful heaven! (*She inclines her head ever so slightly toward Ann*)

ANN: (*Stroking it*) It's because of that, perhaps, that so many of us have gone for less—

LENA: (*Defiantly*) Now get out!

ANN: There, I feel better, elevated as it were (*She begins to move about with a quick lively step*) (10)

After just a few minutes of conversation, Ann knows exactly what strings to pull to effect a capitulation from Lena, a woman who likes to be "outraged"—and in this regard a more complex version of Shiela O'Hare— but for whom a direct insult dispels the erotic moment. Once Lena has consented to the "stroke," Ann has no further stake in her, pushes her away, and directs her "quick lively step" and her restless desire toward Olga; but Olga is such easy prey that the moment of her arousal has barely begun when Ann loses interest and focuses her attention on bigger game—Anthony, who has entered the room and who, unlike Lena, thrills precisely and masochistically to Ann's repeated insults. What's more, he gets a further satisfaction from the self-conscious analysis, the open admission, of his thrall to torture. "You are always saying things to make me feel dull—childish—to hurt my throat," he charges Ann (24), but he says as much only with the hope that Ann will continue to berate him. For her part, Ann wants to "hurt his throat" so fully that she will push him to the brink of savagery—to flip the switch that will make of his masochism a sadism to rival and ravish her own: "You are young, gentle, romantic, yet you think you are strong, passionate and perverse perhaps," she tells him. "In other words you are adolescent, you must be very young indeed or you would not leave the party to follow me in here and say 'Ah no' like that. Still I repeat, I could be torn apart like a rotten rag under the right question" (19).

Given Cassius's succession from Shakespeare's great manipulator, it is fitting that he, not Ann, should be the one to ask "the right question" and to spur Anthony to violent action. Shortly after his entrance, Cassius makes chillingly clear what's on his mind:

ANN: . . . What are you thinking about, Cassius?
CASSIUS: What I always think about at a party.
ANN: What?
CASSIUS: Death. (26)

That Cassius's more specific agenda should be to effect his own death emerges only slowly and cryptically; we might think rather that his goal, like Ann's, is to seduce Anthony, whose stimulation he monitors and encourages. "I'm beginning to get that giddy sensation in the pit of my stomach," Anthony says, to which Cassius responds, "*looking directly at him*," "Here's to the pit then" (30). Indeed, we wouldn't be wrong to read this exchange as an erotically charged one: Cassius's desire for Anthony and his desire for death are inextricably bound, as his pun on the word *pit* (of the stomach, in the ground) begins to intimate. Full of self-loathing, he wishes to annihilate his body and its homosexual urges—to be, as he says to Anthony, "nothing, nothing in front or behind" (45).

Yet Cassius cannot fully part with his desire, so he must transmute it into an act of violence. Rather than merely commit suicide, he waits until he and Anthony are alone and goads Anthony to kill him—the only sublimated consummation of his passion that he can tolerably imagine. In the initial throes of their contretemps, Cassius's words read equally as sexual innuendo and death wish:

CASSIUS: . . . [Ann's] a dove, Anthony, a pure-hearted dove. I've drunk out of her shoe often, Anthony, my boy, but it elevates me too much. To drink out of a woman's shoe is to ascend, and I must descend. Have you felt that too? Do you know what I'm driving at?
ANTHONY: I do not drink and tell.

CASSIUS:	A fool's answer, but let it pass. Can you hold your hand steady?
ANTHONY:	What are you trying to say?
CASSIUS:	(*Looking ~~keenly~~ into his eyes*) Can you hold your hand steady?
ANTHONY:	(*Annoyed, puzzled*) I've never tried (*Holding it out*) As you see, well enough. Why?
CASSIUS:	Could you still do that if there were let us say, a weight at the end?
ANTHONY:	(*Dropping his hand*) What are you driving at?
CASSIUS:	Never mind. Now tell me what you think about death. (33)

Of course, the "weight" that Cassius wants Anthony to hold in his hand is finally not a body part but a gun, the phallic connotations of the weapon notwithstanding. Cassius's clarification of his wish horrifies Anthony, who refuses to abet him and shouts for help; conveniently, no one heeds the call until Cassius has tormented and enraged Anthony with a series of nihilistic blasphemies—and tempted him with the prospect of Ann, on whom he can bestow "real kisses, kisses that mean nothing and so last long," once Cassius is out of the way (42). Before Anthony pulls the trigger—and as the rest of the characters return to the stage just in time to witness the bloodshed —Cassius makes one last speech in which he comes as close as he ever will to confessing his homosexuality outright. Even in this moment of revelation, however, his language is evasively metaphorical: "Let us say for the moment that you and you alone in all the world know a bullet for a bullet and all the rest of the world thinks it a boiled pea. You'd go mad, because you, out of all the world had to stand the terrific impact of that [undivided] truth. Well, that's me" (42). Cassius camouflages an ontological crisis (his feeling of isolation as a homosexual) as an epistemological dilemma (the possession of knowledge that no one else can understand), but we can nevertheless infer that he longs for death because he desires something that he sees as self-annihilating (a bullet) rather than sustaining (a boiled pea).

Thus ends the first act of the play. The second opens on the same setting, four years later, at which point Ann and Anthony are married. We might wonder how Anthony has managed to avoid prosecution (indeed, whether anyone ever called the authorities), by what means this callow murderer convinced Ann to wed him, and how exactly they disposed of Cassius's body. But these are questions for the literal-minded. Suffice it to say that the real consequence of Anthony's act is the long shadow that Cassius

casts over his union with Ann. As if in surrogation of Cassius's own lacer-
ating and self-abnegating tendencies, the haunted couple leads a sexless life
in which they find their only libidinal outlets in punitive recriminations of
themselves and each other. With the exception of one preposterously devised scene in which Ann taunts Anthony's bastard son, Savalee, so acutely
that the boy hurls himself down a flight of stairs, the rest of the play is pure
static and reads like a tepid rehearsal of the marital hell so expertly explored
by playwrights like Strindberg and Albee. If my tone here borders on glib-
ness, I can only plead the appropriateness of my response to Barnes's structural miscalculation: what could have been a much tauter and more startling one-act play, ending with Cassius's shooting and Anthony's addled
rationalization—"He said horrible things—horrible, horrible—terrible,
terrible" (46)—devolves into an aimless and tedious series of dialogues. But
the point toward which Barnes attempts to drive her language and characterizations—the dire effects and tragic legacy of sexual denial—is, nevertheless, a compelling one. With more practice and assurance as a dramatist, and the wisdom of economy to guide her, she succeeds in matching
the appeal of her writing to the appeal of her ideas in the short play *The Dove*,
where she also begins to explore sexual transgression in its more specific
form as lesbian incest.

WHEN DOVES CRY

Like her earlier short play *An Irish Triangle*, Barnes's *The Dove* is not exactly
a closet drama. Though it was first published for a readership in *A Book*
(1923) and only later produced for the stage, both at Smith College and at
Bayes Theatre in New York City,[25] the play is eminently performable; but
it nevertheless shares features with Barnes's other closet plays that place it
on the same dramatic spectrum. From the very start, the play's setting—
"the Burgson apartment, a long, low rambling affair at the top of a house
in the heart of the city," whose single door and overfurnishing evoke the
claustrophobia of its inhabitants—could be described as a kind of closet.[26]
At the same time, with its "garish" decoration, "dealing heavily in reds and
pinks," "reclining" furniture, and array of pistols and swords, the space also
gestures beyond the cramped, modern closet and back toward the type of
boudoir in which Sade would have set one of his kinky closet dramas (149).
Indeed, Barnes poises the tensions of the household precisely on this frac-
ture line between closet as cloister and closet as bedchamber. On the one
hand, Sade may himself be part of the Burgson syllabus; as middle-aged Vera
Burgson explains of her and her sister Amelia's (self-?) tutelage, "our en-

tire education has been about knees and garters and pinches on hindquar-
ters— . . . and our beds are full of yellow pages and French jokes as a bird's
nest is full of feathers" (150–51). On the other hand, and for all that racy
reading, the self-described virgin sisters will, by Vera's account, "never, never
be perverse," and it is in the repression of their own desires, which find fulfillment only in acts of displacement (when they are not deferred entirely),
that the "closet drama" of *The Dove* is most keenly felt.

In one such displacement, of the voyeuristic variety, Amelia suggests
that she, Vera, and the apartment's other inhabitant—the young maid
whom they call "the Dove"—"come and see Carpaccio's Deux Courtisanes
Vénetiennes now, the sun is shining right in on the head of the one in the
foreground" (158). Fittingly, both the reproduction of the sexually charged
painting and the sunlight are in another room, and the sisters never do leave
the stage to see it: so mired are they in the dark stasis of their self-denial
that they can't even complete a symbolic act of erotic sublimation. Ironically, their immobility casts them somewhat in the likeness of Carpaccio's
courtesans, who, in "apparent boredom," "gaze fixedly past [a] spectacle"
beyond the edge of the canvas. As Anne Dalton explains, because "the original painting was cut on both the right and left sides some time before the
nineteenth century," "the nature of this central, yet unfigured, drama is impossible to decipher" (131). The sexual drama in which the Burgson sisters
long to participate remains likewise unfigured—closeted, as it were—just
past the edge of the stage; but where the courtesans, saturated with experience, ignore a likely "violent or visually arresting event" out of apathy and
cynicism, Barnes's untouched sisters resist sexual exploration out of hesi-
tancy and fear.

But what exactly do they fear—and, for that matter, what do they want?
Dalton rightly identifies the Burgsons' desire as lesbian, but I think she
misses some of the subtlety of Barnes's drama when she assumes that this
lesbian desire is focused by both sisters on the Dove and that the incestuous element of their desire is maternal and symbolic: "The opening dialogue
indicates that the two Burgson sisters are significantly older than The Dove.
Although the sisters are not related to the younger woman, the age difference, coupled with the fact that they take her in, casts them as her adopted
maternal figures. Throughout Barnes's writing, as in folktales about child
theft, adoption by pseudomaternal figures often proves ominous. Certainly,
in this case, the way in which the older women 'mother' the girl seems sinister at best" (127). In emphasizing the attitude of the Burgson sisters toward the Dove as motherly and ominous, Dalton overlooks the root of their

relationship not in family dynamics but in class: the Dove is their servant, and the play opens with her words, "Yes, I'm hurrying," as she polishes *"the blade of an immense sword"* (150). This blade belongs to just one of the apartments' many swords and guns that we must imagine she has been made obsessively to shine. Yet for all of this imposed drudgery, the Dove, whom Vera calls "the only dangerous thing [they] ever knew," seems, much more than either of the sisters, to be the most "sinister" presence in the household (157). *Sinister* is Dalton's word, at any rate, for the power that she thinks the sisters wield over the Dove; but if it is rather the Dove who, to use Vera's word of choice, is truly "dangerous," then the danger that she poses comes not from any active or aggressive menace that she threatens (a menace that could legitimately be described as sinister) but from her passive and tacit encouragement of illicit behavior:

VERA: You know, I'm afraid of you!

THE DOVE: Me?

VERA: Yes, you seem so gentle—do we not call you the Dove? And you are so little—so little it's almost immoral, you make me feel as if—

THE DOVE: As if?

VERA: Well, as if your terrible quality were not one of action, but just the opposite, as if you wanted to prevent nothing.

THE DOVE: There are enough people preventing things, aren't there?

VERA: Yes—that's why you frighten me.

THE DOVE: Because I let everything go on, as far as it can go?

VERA: Yes, because you disturb nothing. (154)

When the Dove says that "there are enough people preventing things" and that she would "let everything go on, as far as it can go," she recalls the equally insouciant attitude and liberationist philosophy of Kathleen O'Rune. In this case, the farthest reach to which things can go, however, exceeds the taboos of *An Irish Triangle*'s quadrangle. Finally tired of merely "disturb[ing] nothing," the Dove asks the question that threatens to disturb everything: "What do you want, Vera?" (155).

Like Cassius, Vera will not state outright what she wants and will only define it by its obverse: "Some people would say a lover, but I don't say a lover; some people would say a home, but I don't say a home. You see I have imagined myself beyond the need of the usual home and beyond the reach of the usual lover—" (155). Vera's imbrication of the sexual and the familial, along with her further claim that the imbrication she imagines is an "unusual" one, suggests that she desires none other than Amelia. Far from the complex and metaphorically incestuous feelings that Dalton imagines Vera directing toward the Dove, Vera longs, simply and literally, for her actual sister. When the Dove pushes her to name this longing more explicitly— "Then?"—Vera, again like Cassius, can imagine only obliteration in place of confession, violence in place of tenderness: "Perhaps what I really want is a reason for using one of these pistols!" (155). The Dove, prescient beyond her twenty or so years and perhaps as a result of "wild, insane" experiences (153) that stand in pointed contrast to the sisters' "advanced [virginity]" (152), sees through the innuendo that Vera's sexual disposition is intolerable to her because of the incest taboo. In sympathy, and echoing Vera's statement that her desire is "beyond the reach of the usual lover," she says, "I wish every man were beyond the reach of his own biography" (157). For all of her self-denial, Vera's response is tellingly acute:

VERA: You are either quite an idiot, or a saint.

THE DOVE: I thought we had discussed that.

VERA: [*dashed but not showing it*] Yes, a saint. (157)

Only someone with a utopic vision—only a saint—could imagine the paradisiacal conditions under which "biography" would not impose a limit on Vera's love for Amelia. But as the Burgson sisters live in New York, not heaven, Vera feels "that her bones [are] utterly sophisticated but that [her] flesh [is] keeping them from expressing themselves": whether or not her spirit is willing, her flesh is, quite literally, weak.

For her part, Amelia has urges that simmer much closer to the surface. She wears red heels and dances around the room in them (160); she "slurs" notes passionately on the violin (158); and—one step closer to violence than Vera, who only dreams of shooting a pistol—she sticks pin holes in a "Parisienne bathing girl's picture," as her sister relates with disapproval (152). When Amelia returns from an errand to the market, she is immediately associated with another picture—the Carpaccio reproduction, upon which she longs to gaze and whose place in the entryway has begotten the errand in the first place: "It's because of that picture of the Venetian courtesans that I send Amelia out for the butter," Vera explains to the Dove; "I don't dare let the grocer call" (158). Though the Dove can only pick Vera's brain and try to spur her desire through conversation, Amelia is ripe for another kind of picking; perhaps it is because she hovers nearer to the brink of genuine sexual expression that the Dove says, early in the play, that she loves her (152). Vera is patently jealous of the rapport between sister and servant and leaves the room with a cry of "Rubbish!" when their conversation turns euphemistically to "get[ting] the corks out of bottles" (159). Alone with Amelia, and exasperated by her circuitous and ineffectual disquisition with Vera, the Dove tries just such an uncorking and makes a move toward which, we must infer, she has been slowly building:

AMELIA: ... [*She has danced until she comes directly in front of* THE DOVE. *She drops on her knees and lays her arms on either side of* THE DOVE.] I hate the chimneys on the houses, I hate the doorways, I hate you, I hate Vera, but most of all I hate my red heels!

THE DOVE: [*almost inaudibly*] Now, now!

AMELIA: [*in high excitement*] Give me the sword! It has been sharpened long enough, give it to me, give it to me! [*She makes a blind effort to find the sword; finding* THE DOVE's *hand instead, she clutches it convulsively. Slowly* THE DOVE *bares Amelia's left shoulder and breast, and leaning down, sets her teeth in. Amelia gives a slight, short, stifled cry. At the same moment* VERA *appears in the doorway with the uncorked bottle.* THE DOVE *stands up swiftly, holding a pistol. She turns in the doorway hastily vacated by* VERA.] (160–61).

Vera's cry of "Rubbish!"—all too easily interpreted as anger at the flirtation between Amelia and the Dove—turns out to have been a too literal-minded challenge to the Dove's assertion that only she can uncork a bottle. In her attempt to outstrip the Dove and please her sister with wine, Vera falls ironically short of the Dove's own explicitly erotic gesture. Yet Amelia, who has finally been given a chance to rise to the occasion of sexual contact, also falls short of the Dove's expectations. Instead of responding to the bite with pleasure or with a reciprocal physical overture, she gives "*a slight, short, stifled cry.*" Too slight her response; too stifled, still, her sexuality—and so the Dove, in frustration, retaliates with an appropriately symbolic act. Crying, "For the house of Burgson!" she leaves the stage and shoots a hole through the picture of the Venetian courtesans (161). Recapitulating Amelia's own act of sticking pins through the picture of the bathing girl, but with considerable amplification, the Dove's puncture of the painting punctuates her disgust with Amelia's sexual inhibition, as if to say, "The house of Burgson will never consummate a greater act than this one."

Tragically, albeit modestly so, Amelia misinterprets the meaning of the Dove's rebuke. Rushing offstage and then "*reappearing in the doorway*" with

the damaged picture, she says "*slowly, but with emphasis*," "*This* is obscene!"
(161). For the Dove, the patron saint of sin, the obscene act is the unven-
tured one; as she says to Vera, "I want the beautiful thing to *be*" (157, emphasis added). But Vera—and finally Amelia, too—can imagine only shame
and disgrace, certainly not beauty, in the fulfillment of their desires. Amelia
must draw attention, deictically, to the picture's bullet hole in order to draw
it away from her own bared shoulder and breast; if she insists on the obscenity of the painting's damage, then she can repudiate the much more
lurid moment that preceded it. Despite the Dove's effort to effect a change
in the family dynamics, the curtain closes on the Burgsons as it opened:
Amelia is "*vitally hysterical*" instead of happily vital (149), and Vera's "*eyes
are closed*" (150).

"CLAIMS ON ECSTASY"

The three-act *Biography of Julie von Bartmann* (1924) presents us with further domestic dysfunction and might more aptly be called the biography
of the Borns, a widower and his three children who live claustrophobically
and in near-isolation on their family farm. In returning from the conci-
sion of *The Dove* to the challenges of a full-length drama—and in writing
a play that remains both unperformed and unpublished—Barnes also re-
turned more fully to the closet; one of her archivists writes in a headnote
to the play, "This play contains some of the most vigorous and pungent writings that ha[ve] come to my attention in some time. The style indeed belongs to some other form in literature aside from drama. . . . The play would
be perplexing to an audience, but for the reader it has many stimulating
qualities in the midst of a little that is confusing."[27] Though this anonymous
commentator adds that he or she cannot "state clearly the theme and the
plot of this play," I think that the headnote's emphasis on style is more
telling. Characters often speak elliptically, figuratively, almost surreally, and
the dialogue might indeed be "a little confusing" for an audience compared
with an industriously close reader; but the play's plot is, by comparison, very
simple. The famous and beautiful singer Julie von Bartmann arrives in the
Borns' part of the world and stays with them on their farm; father Basil
seems to have been a man of some connections before his retreat to an idyll
of his own making, where the children have been homeschooled in defiance
of the state. After Julie's arrival, each member of the family attempts to seduce her: Basil, elder son Gart, younger son Costa—and, perhaps most surprising, daughter Gustava. Just as Gustava's erotic overture toward Julie
might hold the most interest for us, so too does it capture Julie's attention

most strikingly—not simply for its lesbianism, but for its weirdly incestuous character, as Gustava tries to make of Julie both lover and mother.

The centrality of the absent mother to Gustava's sexuality emerges slowly and cryptically, but her primacy more generally in the family dynamic is foregrounded in the play's first scene. Basil, who boasts of having "known many women," describes his late wife to Julie:

JULIE: Was she beautiful?

BASIL: No madame, beautiful women do not make good martyrs. I got her from a burlesque house in the Haymarket, she played the part of a drummer, she was young then, and had a long melancholy face, like the faces of kings who have not ruled. I could see in the way she lifted her legs that she wanted to settle down, to become gross, to be a mother, to drink strong coffee, to sleep in the daytime, and at night to pour [*sic*] over the destiny of the Corsican. She was very simple, very lewd, she laughed at one time and not at another, she was strong but not healthy, she was pure but much handled; she had dignity but she was powerless. That[,] madam, was the mother of my children.

JULIE: (Simply) And what will become of your daughter?

BASIL: She will follow her mother. She is both buxom and coarse, I mean that in the best sense. She will become stout, it will save her from the pale existence of those women who from the cradle to the grave, have but two odors; celibacy and monogamy. My daughter will be frank, neither promiscuous nor childless, these things are for flat chested women whose hearts beat sideways for lack of room. She will eat, function, die, looking neither backward nor forward.

JULIE: Yet—What will she do with that ecstatic moment when she lies, for the first time, with her lover?

BASIL: The simple, madame, put no claims on ecstasy.[28]

Here Barnes offers us no innocent account of the late Mrs. Born, but a litany of the qualities that Basil projected onto her and an exposition of the role into which he cast her: like a director, he "could see" in her an aptness for motherhood and martyrdom that suited his own typological and misogynistic view of women. If she was "powerless," we must intuit, such powerlessness could be calibrated only in proportion to the power that domineering Basil arrogated to himself. This powerless and subservient role is one into which Basil would also like to fit Gustava, but it is a part for which she is remarkably ill-suited. Contrary to his interpretation of her character, she "look[s]" both "backward" and "forward"—but especially backward, with a longing for her mother; and far from "simple," she makes "claims on ecstasy" that are quite complicated and unusual.

After having shown Julie to her bedroom at the end of the play's first scene, Gustava returns at the beginning of the next to watch Julie as she sleeps. When Julie wakes, Gustava confesses her sexual intentions with deliberation and after some subterfuge; first she says that her appearance in the bedroom "is nothing" (21), then that she would like the worldly Julie to explain her father to her (22), and finally that she wants to "put [her] head on [Julie's] arm, [her] perfume is so strong and so sweet" (24). "I love you," Gustava declares as she lies beside Julie in the bed, "it is like that" (25) —but what exactly "it" is like exceeds this simple declaration and hinges on Gustava's identification of Julie with her dead mother. Indeed, Gustava tells Julie indirectly what her love is like by telling Julie what (or whom) she supposes *Julie* is like:

GUSTAVA: . . . It is like this. You were born. You were laid in a bassinet, you did not cry. You learned to walk before other children, you watched everything, and then one day, when you were three or four, you realized that you were terrible, a child of destiny. . . . And then one day a man took your fancy, you walked together under the trees, you went to a small town together, you took a boat, you were in foreign parts, you became sleepy, you went to a hotel, and he did not dare to defile you until you had shut the door, there was a great clock under a glass, and it did not go, there were a lot of vulgar red cushions and gilt chairs, and you said, "Aren't the French funny people, they have so many dead clocks."

JULIE: Where did you get all this?

GUSTAVA: I have travelled, mother travelled, she travelled to keep herself from thinking, father was everything, but that's different. (23–24)

In recounting her mother's early life story as though it were Julie's, Gustava asks Julie implicitly to *be* her mother—and, more specifically, to be the carefree and autonomous woman prior to her marriage to Basil, when "everything" became "different." Ironically, this desire to eradicate her father and to possess an imagined version of her mother makes Gustava precisely her father's daughter. Just as Basil sought to mold first wife and then daughter to his liking, so too does Gustava seek to mold Julie—and so does she accordingly fail. As Gustava proceeds to describe "Julie," the confused guest corrects her and denies any likeness to her mother: "No, no, that's not it [at] all" (24). Gustava persists, and Julie continues to challenge the imposition of Mrs. Born's narrative onto her life. Given Julie's intransigence, Gustava's fantasy of a life with her is finally and utterly dispelled, at which point she can only lament the misfit of her desire and its potential object: "I could have loved you without regret or shame, . . . and I would have died then and been buried happily, and people could have come and looked at me, quite as they pleased, just in their usual way, looked at me and have found no sin. Not to have one remorse, nor one regret, because you would have been mine" (31). Implicit in Gustava's use of the conditional tense is the one condition that Julie resists: performing the girl's maternity.

What's so extraordinary about Gustava's imagined life as Julie's lover is her conviction that it would be shameless and sinless precisely in proportion to its resemblance to—and not its deviation from—incest. Ironically, the bubble bursts, in Gustava's view, not because incest is culturally impermissible but because it is literally impossible (with Julie, at any rate). If Gustava functions as Barnes's radical mouthpiece for the championship of incest without "remorse, nor one regret," then her brother Gart is the foil who realizes more explicitly the failure of such a vision in practice. In a scene parallel to the one in which Gustava climbs into bed with Julie, Gart—somewhat like Ham at Noah's tent—asks to join his father in bed, where Basil consents to "[put] *his arms over him*" but then commands him to "go to sleep" (51). Just as Gustava began her failed seduction of Julie with the pretense that she wanted to know more about her father, so too does Gart purport to wake his father with questions about what sort of woman Julie is and what she does (52–54). Soon, however, the conversation turns to the nature of father and son's relationship. Gart confesses that he wants "to lay open the heart, yours or mine" (60), but, much like Cassius in *Ann Portuguise* or Vera in *The Dove,* he can imagine this vulnerability of feeling only as violent rather than affectionate in expression. When Basil demands what his son "want[s] to know," Gart cannot admit that he wants to know his father sexually, but only "whether I must kill myself, or you" (59). Basil is terrified and leaps from the bed at Gart's further declaration, "I am not afraid, I will take what comes. If one thing fails, there is still another. I will go all the way." This deeply ambiguous line suggests that Gart's two perceived options, in "[going] all the way," are to fornicate with Basil or, more likely in the face of his father's refusal and his ensuing abjection, to murder him; the extremity of his feeling permits no lesser choice. Confronted with the intensity of his son's incestuous attachment, Basil cries, in direct opposition to Gustava's dream of a shameless mother-love, "Wait, this is your father's body, your father's body! [*He falls against the door, Gart turning over on his face, weeping.*] Shameful, shameful! It is all shameful!" (61).

We can perhaps easily imagine a much more conventional—and Freudian—version of this startling scene, in which Gart, vying with his father simply for the affections of Julie (the most proximal mother figure), must kill Basil in order to displace him. Barnes challenges, however, the orthodoxy of the heteronormative Oedipal complex with an opposing vision of same-sex incest. If psychoanalysis posits son's identification with father as the necessary condition for the maintenance of the incest and murder taboos, then son's alternative desire for father (or daughter's for mother) exposes the tenuous balance of those taboos much more devastatingly: "If one thing fails, there is still another." In Barnes's negative vision, it is the fantasy of incest that invariably fails and the reality of murder that is more likely to erupt. Yet *The Biography of Julie von Bartmann* avoids at last this eruption of violence: the second bedroom scene ends rather with an interruption, as "*someone is heard running up the steps toward the door*" (61); and the play's third act, similar to the final two acts of *Ann Portuguise* (where death comes too soon), devolves into lengthy and opaque speeches that fail to deliver the tragic crisis and resolution Barnes has led us to expect. It may be the case here, as in the earlier *Ann Portuguise*, that Barnes is attempting to create a deliberately anti-Aristotelian anticlimax that would challenge dramatic conventions in proportion to her challenge of sexual conventions. But if this is the case, her execution of such a technique is so hesitant and the thematic purchase so unclear that the result seems more muddled than meddling.

Only in her final and most fully realized drama, *The Antiphon*, does Barnes master the structure of a three-act play—although it is a strange form of mastery, with its own closet complications. Like *The Biography of Julie von Bartmann*, *The Antiphon* is the drama of a tortured and torturing family, but it is written, in the 1950s, from a completely different vantage point. In the gulf of years between Barnes's composition of these two plays, O'Neill and Williams—and, in a more startling way, the Beckett of *Endgame*—boldly reinvent the domestic tragedy, and Barnes's intervention in the genre must be understood as a pointed response to these renovations. *The Antiphon* shares the penchants for excess that characterize both O'Neill and Williams, but with hardly any of the concessions to realism with which they accommodate their audiences. Rather, she, not unlike Beckett, aims for intense and symbolically charged obliquities, but with none of the streamlining that makes Beckettian minimalism, finally, so playable. Style, as we shall see, is what makes *The Antiphon* simultaneously intoxicating and forbidding.

"LET IT BE THE HEAVY MOTHER LODE"

Without even reading a word of *The Antiphon* (1958), we can begin to get a sense of the text's linguistic difficulties from a small sample of manuscript notations made by T. S. Eliot, who helped Barnes edit the play for publication as she revised multiple drafts of it in the 1950s:

> Why does a widow's breath smell of hunting?
> How can a lip be "empty"?
> How can anything scamper slowly?
> Abdiction. Abdication? Why should his ears abdicate?
> "Fat girl with an orbit in her lap." EXPLAIN.
> Why do the patients practise *clockwise*?
> What on earth is a Moslem holy man doing sitting in chocolate and brandy?
> This whole speech defeats me.[29]

Fittingly, Barnes, in a marginal annotation of her own, called these questions "Eliot's queeries," for there is certainly something queer about both the semantic fabric of *The Antiphon* and the baffled responses, Eliot's among them, that it has generated. This queer language is, in fact, the most signal factor in the play's designation as a closet drama. If even such a dense writer and close reader as T. S. Eliot should feel "defeated" by the often opaque idiom of *The Antiphon*—at times faux-Baroque, at others quasi-Jacobean—then surely, it has been supposed, no audience hearing the dialogue aloud could make sense of its intricacies and nuances? What's more, this closeted quality of the drama is one of which Barnes herself was eminently aware and that she deliberately thematized. The very setting of the play ("England, Burley Hall, in the township of Beewick, formerly a college of chantry priests, in the Burley family since the late seventeenth century") is an abandoned house that once served as a cloister (6); and the characters are pointedly self-conscious not only of their own theatricality but also of this theatricality's sequestration from the stage. Consider the coachman Jack Blow's speech to his employer, Miranda Hobbs, when they first arrive at Burley Hall in search of her uncle, Jonathan Burley:

. . . But where's your uncle Jonathan?
You said you came to kiss him fond farewell.
The scene is set but seems the actor gone.
No tither, weeper, wait or cicerone;
No beadle, bailiff, barrister, no clerk
In short no audience at all:
My hands will have to be your clamor, lady. (9)

The time of Burley Hall's eerie emptiness is "during the war of 1939" (6). According to Barnes's "Notes toward a Definition of *The Antiphon*," Miranda's "first intention, when she met Jack Blow, was to get to Beewick and her uncle because there was war," and we must assume that Paris, her most recent place of residence, has become unsafe.[30] Little does Miranda know that she has walked into an even more unsafe environment, where Jack Blow has arranged for her to confront unwittingly her estranged mother, Augusta, and two brothers, Dudley and Elisha. Or, rather, I should say her *other* two brothers, because Jack Blow is himself Miranda's youngest brother, Jeremy. As Jack explains to Jonathan of his "first" meeting with Miranda, "Say I fell in a time ago in Paris. / I, with the single, she, the compound eye / Met back to back—a kind of paradox" (38). When he describes the meeting "back to back" (rather than face to face), Jack assumes that Miranda does not recognize him, but her "compound eye" apprehends more than he supposes. She knows that he is Jeremy, but she lets him assume in turn that he is indeed a stranger to her. For Miranda, there is a certain comfort in feigning anonymity with her youngest and only loved brother: the pretense allows her to enjoy his company and express affection for him without being crushed by the weight of their painful family history. Alternatively, Jack wants precisely to confront the demons of their shared childhood—to provide, as it were, an antiphonal corrective to the family's dominant narrative of the past. In his real person as Jeremy, he has summoned Augusta; she longs to see the son who abandoned her twenty years earlier but doesn't recognize "Jack" when she sees him. Once this party, with its complicated and varied levels of recognition, has assembled, Jack plans to "[spring] a trap" (10) in which to catch the "villains" (202) of the family. As he says in a soliloquy in act one,

I've seen a judge
Sitting in the credit of his chair,
So abandon justice that his ears
Stood, in abdication, on his head.
Yet did the astounded air gag up the verdict? It did not. (23)

Justice, it would seem, is no longer only blind but deaf, and has refused to hear any appeals; nor will crime's victims speak out without prompting. With a mysterious prop that he has brought from Paris—"a beast-box, say, a doll's house, or an Ark," as he ambiguously nominates it to Jonathan— Jack will set the stage for a forced, overdue trial among his mother and three siblings (28).

But which member of the family is being indicted, who wronged, and what is the nature of the offense? At first it would seem that Jack's trial is intended for dead father Titus, a proponent of "free-love," "free lunch," "free everything" (71), who used his doctrine of liberation as a pretense for "the monstrous practice of polygamy" (110) and who filled his house with mistresses and their illegitimate offspring even as he "whipped" Augusta's sons in their infancy (93). But when Jack reveals his "beast-box," a dollhouse representing in miniature Titus's home and its inhabitants, we see that he means to unleash a "contagion" to "unhem[]" Augusta as well (144). Forcing her to look through a windowpane into the "cock-loft" made of Miranda's bedroom (148), he charges his mother with complicity in Miranda's rape by a brother of one of Titus's lovers:

> The eye-baby now you're pregnant with
> You'll carry in your iris to the grave.
> You made yourself a madam by submission;
> With, no doubt, your apron over-head,
> And strewing salt all up and down the stairs
> To catch whose feet? Hers alone, or his,
> Walked that last mile? Miranda not yet seventeen.
> Thrown to a traveling Cockney thrice her age,
> Indeed Brigid-Matilda's brother. Why?
> Titus had him handy for experiment;
> Though Miranda cried first, like the ewe,
> "Do not let him—but if my father wills it—!"
> Offering up her silly throat for slashing,
> Already bubbling in the lamentation,
> So I say between you both you made
> Of that doll's abbatoir a babe's bordel. (151)

According to Miranda, Augusta's chilling disregard for her extends beyond her role as "*madam* by submission" to a monstrous lack of love— all lavished instead on her sons—conceived at the very moment of her birth:

Of that luckless sprawl, three sons she leaned to fairly:
On me she cast the privy look of dogs
Who turn to quiz the thing they've dropped.
Yet in her hour, become by me, twice headed,
The one head on the other stared, and wept. (15)

For her part, Augusta, who denies this accusation and swears, "The virgin did not love / Her chirrup more than I my children," nevertheless cannot declare her love for Miranda singularly. Her alienation of her daughter, specific to Miranda's womanhood, must be understood as a crucible of jealousy and resentment—both displaced from Titus's other lovers onto her daughter and directed at Miranda's potential to escape the family and lead a different, happier life. As Augusta herself concedes to Miranda,

Think of it!
All through my beauty he enjoyed an ugly woman!
That man your father. I said his acts to me
Were never gentle, fond, nor kind;
Nor he never held nor stroked me anywhere;
And you stood up, as in a lost equation,
As you had mended such economy. (186)

Miranda responds to this maternal neglect by growing insatiable—at times masochistically so—for Augusta's love and attention. As Dudley attests to his mother,

You had her so convinced she was the devil,
At seven she was cutting down the hedges
To furnish brier to beat her to your favor,
Then went out hunting for the crime. (121)

This tendency to make herself abject for some contact with or from her mother persists even into Miranda's fifty-eighth year, at the time of their contrived reunion in Beewick. Though Miranda herself is "lame" as a result of "turn[ing] her ankle, coming down from church" (74), she stoops to massage her mother's foot the moment Augusta complains, "I think I've hurt my foot. / . . . / My foot, Miranda, I have hurt my foot!" (84). In turn, Augusta takes advantage of Miranda's prostration as an occasion for further complaint. "*Noticing Miranda's rings*," she charges, "You never gave me any rings," to which Miranda responds, "You never remember any rings I gave you," as she nonetheless "[*gives*] AUGUSTA *her rings*" (89). It is sig-

nificant that Miranda's desperate attempts at touch should alight on hands
and feet—the very instruments of various kicks, slaps, and strangles both
immediate and remembered throughout the course of the play—even as
she longs, more primally, not for a love (fetishistically?) displaced onto the
extremities but for its opposite: a return to mother's center, or womb, ecstatically described as "a palm-full of the belly's Thames" (161).

Radically outstripping this nostalgic wish—and so much the better,
from Miranda's perspective—is a desired communion with her mother's
sex that could be uncontaminated and unmediated by male penetration, the
repugnant precondition of pregnancy. In one of the play's strangest and
most powerful speeches, Miranda describes the love that she bore her
mother and the implied place that she had in (or at least toward) her
mother's body before she was even conceived:

> Hold, woman!
> There was a time when we were not related.
> When I first loved thee—I say "thee" as if
> It were to use a lost endearment
> That in the loss has lost the losing world—
> When I first loved thee, thou wert grazing:
> Carrion Eve, in the green stool, wading:
> In the coarse lilies and the sombre wood;
> Before the tree was in the cross, the cradle, and the coffin,
> The tragic head-board, and the victim door,
> The weeper's banister, the cunning panel.
> When yet the salt unspilt, the bread unbroken,
> The milk unquested, uncried and unsprung,
> You came braying for a victim lover.
> The cock crew, the spur struck, and Titus Adam
> Had at you with his raping-hook
> And you reared back, a belly full of thumbs. (160–61)

This passage echoes, much more lyrically, Gustava's similar wish in *The
Biography of Julie von Bartmann* to supersede her father and ravish her
mother before her mother's (male) ravishment. As she likens her mother
metaphorically to Eve in the Garden of Eden, Miranda imagines Augusta
not as an innocent—she is "braying" for a "lover"—but as an erotic being,
naked and "grazing" among the vaginally "coarse lilies," who would, as yet
undefiled by Titus, make an ideal partner for Miranda herself. Indeed, Augusta is not, in this incarnation, braying just for a lover but oddly for a "vic-

tim" lover—and who better such a victim than the daughter who has survived a rape? In this tenuously constructed fantasy, Miranda cannot, like
her brother Dudley, "watchmaker to the world" (32), keep good time. She
posits herself at once in an imagined past before her birth and in the real
past after her sexual abuse, as her repeated emphases on her "loss" and her
description of Titus's "raping-hook" intimate. But this temporal disorientation follows its own internal logic: Augusta, uninitiated to sex with a man,
must become Miranda's lover to compensate precisely—and justly—for
her daughter's rape, with its dimension of paternal complicity. Incestuous
lesbian desire becomes here the idyllic and idealized obverse of incestuous
heterosexual violation.

Miranda reformulates this dream at the very end of the play, when her
mother accuses her of not an incestuous but a murderous desire:

> AUGUSTA: I know you. You are the one would lay
> Me ticking down, ten cities deep!
> MIRANDA: Nay, sparrow.
> I'd lay you in the journey of your bed,
> And un-bed you, and I could, in paradise. (200–201)

Miranda's mention here of "paradise" calls to mind Vera Burgson's similar claim in *The Dove* that no one but a saint could sanction her erotic love
for her sister. It also links these lines to Miranda's own former speech about
Eden: only before this world, or in the next, could Miranda "un-bed" her
mother from Titus; only under utopic conditions could she herself "lay [Au-
gusta] in the journey of [her] bed." But in *this* world, as Julie L. Abraham
shrewdly observes, Augusta "cannot hear . . . a statement of love for herself."[31] In response to Miranda's desire *for* her mother, Augusta wishes instead to *be* Miranda and thereby undo her own pain, suffering, and culpa-
bility. She places herself literally in her daughter's shoes when, "*without
asking permission, [she] takes off* MIRANDA's *shoes, puts them on her own
feet, and in exchange puts her slippers on* MIRANDA" (166); and she tries to
imagine Miranda's exotic expatriate life as her own when she dreams of all
the different "ways to catch a world" (183). Finally, the women's conflicting desires come to a head when Miranda, who wishes to care for and live
with her mother, prevents Augusta from chasing after Dudley and Elisha,
who have cruelly left their aging, burdensome mother behind them as they
speed away from Burley Hall with a "*sudden derisive blast of the car-horn*"
(200). As we have come to expect of Barnes's drama, the hope of erotic communion dissolves into the reality of violent extinction. Augusta charges Mi-

randa with the "blame" for all that she has "lost"—including Jeremy—as she "*brings* [*a*] *ringing bell down on* MIRANDA. *Both fall across* [*a*] *gryphon* [*once a car in a roundabout*], *pulling down the curtains, gilt crown and all*" (201). Prior to this attack and struggle, the gryphon, one among many eccentric curios in Burley Hall that call attention to the setting's theatricality, was split in two but put together to make the "divided beast / An undivided bed" for Miranda (155). As such, it is a potent site and symbol for the fight, which results in both women's deaths. Murderous division triumphs over sexual union, the beast over the bed; and in the wake, no consolation but the further sting of Jack's seeming "*indifference*" as he surveys the wreckage and "*leaves the stage*" (203).

"PERSONAL IMPERSONAL ATTENTION"

The Antiphon has never been professionally produced for the American stage —or, for that matter, in English. In its only noteworthy performance, the play met with mostly favorable reviews when it was translated into Swedish by no less a luminary than Dag Hammarskjöld, a former chairman of the Nobel Prize Foundation, and premiered at the Royal Swedish Theatre in 1961—the same year that Hammarskjöld, then completing his tenure as the second secretary general of the United Nations, won the Nobel Prize for Peace. In a note among her personal papers from the previous year, Barnes recalls a conversation in which Hammarskjöld told her, "'The Antiphon is as the *Himalaya*[,] . . . Nightwood the lower range, just under, but under.' I found this surp[r]ising, he had shown such a very great liking for *Nightwood*. . . . It was so high an appreciation that as usual I felt the unhappiness always brought about in me when overpraise is being much too lavishly given. . . . In Hindu mythology the mountains are invested with great sanctity."[32] Despite such reverent praise—which has been shared by a number of other enthusiasts in the past half-century—no intrepid American director has yet dared to scale *The Antiphon*'s Himalayan peaks, though at least one critic has called "for a company of modern-day idealists—perhaps a feminist theatre company—with sufficient grasp of the play's depth and its politics to surmount apparent technical obstacles to production."[33]

Ironically, the play's words have been most often heard by audiences as they figure in a performance piece even *more* linguistically formidable —if not inscrutable—than *The Antiphon* itself: "Barnes 1," one of four poems in Jackson Mac Low's *Barnesbook,* in which the poet uses various sentences from Barnes's writings as the source texts for poems specifically designed for public declamation.[34] In *Barnesbook,* Mac Low continues the development of what he calls the "diastic strategy" that he had been using as the basis for poetic composition since the 1960s; he explains this strategy—and its evolution in the computer age—in an afterword to the four poems:

> I have been an admirer of the work of Djuna Barnes since the early 1940s when, not long after I had discovered and read her best-known work, the novel *Nightwood,* (and subsequently met in New York Dante Pavone, a nightclub singer who was said to be one of the "layers" of Dr. Matthew Mighty O'Connor), I was introduced to her wonderful archaizing novel *Ryder* by the late Robert Duncan. More recently I discovered her short story collection *Spillway,* her verse play *The Antiphon,* and her early uncollected stories brought together by Douglas Messerli as *Smoke and Other Early Stories.*
>
> Then in June 1989 the poet, scholar, critic, and teacher Charles O. Hartman sent me a computer program called DIASTEXT, which is an automation of one of the "diastic reading-through text-selection methods" that I first developed in January 1963 and have used in various ways since then to compose many poems and performance pieces. These methods are "nonintentional" in that the author cannot predict what will be drawn from a source text, but "deterministic." . . . Most of these methods use a "seed" or "index" word or phrase that is spelled out by reading through a source text to find words that have, successively, the seed's letters in corresponding places, e.g., if I use "Barnes" as the seed and these first two paragraphs as source text, I produce the line:
>
> *B*arnes *ea*rly wo*r*k O'Co*n*nor wond*e*rful compo*s*e
>
> The seed is used to select words (or other linguistic units) that *spell it through* repeatedly throughout a poem, hence, "diastic" < Gk. *Dia* through + *stichos* row, line, verse, on somewhat imperfect analogy with "acrostic": the seed is spelled *through* in the poem's *lines.*[35]

DIASTEXT allowed Mac Low, in *Barnesbook* and other works, to develop an even more complex version of the diastic strategy than the one explained above, and he likewise made the compositional method even more "nonintentional" by using "chance operations" to select the sentences from Barnes's work that would serve as his source texts (49). Mac Low doesn't identify, in his afterword or elsewhere, exactly which sentences he used, or how he arranged them during the process of "seeding," but a couple of striking words help us to locate at least some of the lines in Barnes's *The Antiphon* dismantled and reconfigured diastically in "Barnes 1." Consider the two sentences "I heard you call her vixen at fifteen" (87) and "Once on the stairs, she mounted like a lizard, / Crying, 'Are you intense?'" (111), alongside their dramatic reformulations (juxtaposed with other pieces of Barnes's language) on the opening pages of "Barnes 1":

> *Once on.*
>
> *Once like.*
>
> *Once on the she them sea attention.*
>
> *That stairs,*
> *"lizard intense?"*
>
> *Mounted brings mounted fifteen.*
>
> . . . .
>
> *Crying brings.*
>
> *Crying asking attention.*
>
> *Crying:*
> *"Are her vixens you mounted intense?*
> *Know you*
> *with water,*
> *asking stairs:*
> *'Intense?'"* (7–8)

Much of the appeal of Mac Low's diastic writing stems from such formal features as the accidental, almost Steinian repetitions ("Mounted brings mounted fifteen") and the surprising puns ("sea attention" implies the word *see*) that his procedure generates. Readers also delight in the sheer sonic exuberance and surreally vivid imagery of lines like, "That stairs, / 'lizard intense?'" Indeed, some would claim that the admiration of these qualities provides the only legitimate access to a writing that does not, in the absence of "intention," make "sense" in conventional ways; in other words, Mac Low's work would demand a strictly semiotic interpretation and would forbid our usual, semantic mode of reading.

Alternatively, I would argue that some measured amount of close reading is warranted and even productive in understanding what and how Mac

Low's work means. Whatever the problematic status of intentionality, some element of choice persists in Mac Low's compositional method: after all, he selected Barnes's work, and not some other texts, as the basis for *Barnesbook*; he edited the output, if sparingly; and if he didn't like the poems produced by DIASTEXT, he could have used different input or left the results unpublished. As Mac Low himself concedes, "The very devising methods must involve the author's taste at certain points" (51), and, more important, "Nonintentional operations and intuition seem made for each other! The former free the latter from the pressure of self-expression" (52). As though "intuiting" such a rejection of an ego-based form of expression, "Barnes 1" makes this very metatextual point when it reads,

> Impersonal impersonal impersonal impersonal
> "fortitude,"
> nor for that
> "fortitude"
> attention. (12)

Despite the almost farcical, tongue-in-cheek (but whose tongue? and whose cheek?) insistence on impersonality, and the "fortitude" that it may or may not take to evacuate the lyric "I" from the poem (the scare quotes leave us in doubt), the work still requires as much of the reader's "attention" as—if not more than—a more conventionally produced piece of writing.

Similarly, "Barnes 1" intuits not only Mac Low's ideas about composition and selfhood but also some of Barnes's ideas from *The Antiphon*. By choosing to seed through a sentence that names the character "Miranda," Mac Low foregrounds her as a figure in the poem—and gives voice anew to some of her hopes and laments, frustrated love and righteous anger. As though "Mac Low" or his proximate persona has not been entirely obliterated, he seems to address Barnes when he writes, "I heard her death, / inordinately heard you" (8). Moreover, the poem registers that Miranda's "death" is not just the one that she suffers at Augusta's hands but her prior one—the loss constituted by her rape and her parents' complicity in it: "Death, / fifteen." Likewise, the poem comprehends Miranda's conflicting feelings toward her family in the wake of her violation, her simultaneous desire to confront her mother with her crime—"Asking should, / Miranda" (10)—and to receive her love—"needing / needing attention" (12). Finally, Mac Low grants Miranda the healing purification that the play denies her—"Will wash was was wash us. / . . . / Will with wash"—

and makes real the fantasy of her mother's love that she can only posit "in paradise":

Inordinately inordinately inordinately inordinately inordinately
pleased
pleased she lizard pleased neither mounted
what? (11)

With almost infinite abundance, the poem gives Miranda pleasure and, as she dreams in *The Antiphon,* undoes through this implicitly erotic pleasure both her rape and her father's role in Augusta's conception: "neither mounted." As if in quiet awe of language's capacity to grant Miranda's illogical wish, the poem asks quite simply of itself, "what?" "Barnes 1" makes possible the reconciliation formerly unavailable to the Hobbses, who are, as Jeremy describes them in the play's final speech, "utterly bereft of home" (203). Conversely, words here have the magical, almost incantatory power to transform the dollhouse from a "beast-box" into a benign toy. As Mac Low says,

They pleased them home.

Love home. (9)

The poem, when read aloud, also enabled Mac Low to (im)personate Miranda. "Barnes 1" calls its own reading of *The Antiphon* "impersonal impersonal attention" (11), but, as embodied by Mac Low in performance, I would instead call the procedure, paradoxically, "personal impersonal attention." As Mac Low attests, "The fact that Charles O. Hartman has automated some of my diastic text-selection methods seems to free me to interact with his programs' outputs in other ways than those required by my 'nucleic' methods. . . . But then, this has also always happened in performances of my simultaneities and other indeterminate performance works" (51–52). Giving voice to the piece, Mac Low could make the indeterminate more determinate and *become* Miranda; or, as the poem itself says (twice), "He her" (8, 11). And indeed, when I saw Mac Low perform "Barnes 1" at one of his last public appearances in June 2004, he somehow, strangely —queerly?—made himself Barnes's heroine despite his obvious physical misfit for the part. Though he was very frail and needed assistance to the podium, he filled an auditorium at the University of Maine with a sonorous and chameleonic voice that seemed untouched by age and that Charles Bernstein has described as an "immaculate enunciation of constructed word patterns."[36] Ranging from a girlish twitter to a thunderous roar, he communicated the various, fragmented parts of Miranda, at once the injured teenager called a vixen by her mother and the aging actress who, according to Barnes, "can rise to impassioned fury."[37] As a kind of patriarch to the community of poets and scholars assembled to hear him, Mac Low might more obviously be aligned with Titus than Miranda—or, perhaps even more aptly, with the professor who purports to have a special (and specialized) interpretive understanding of the gorilla-girl's language. But I think that such an analysis of the performance would be a mistake. Listening to Miranda's voice come out of the mouth of an old man gave me a poignant, almost perverse thrill. It seemed as though the failure of justice in Barnes's revenge drama received an antiphonal corrective in Mac Low's revision— as though father were resurrected and made to speak daughter's truth. Mac Low himself wondered of Barnes, had she been alive to read or hear his poems, "Would she have been indignant, considered my borrowings and rearrangements of her words desecrations of her texts? Or would she have accepted these poems as acts of homage?" (52). Would Mac Low figure as another doctor with rubber tubing, or as a coachman who could, at last, take Miranda farther than Beewick Hall? At the risk of my own personal impersonal transgression, I imagine Barnes's response and describe it with the last words of "Barnes 1" itself:

Looks?

Pleased. (14)

conclusion: other closets, other rooms

When I saw Jackson Mac Low perform the opening piece from *Barnesbook* at a National Poetry Foundation conference in the summer of 2004, I had the uncanny and exhilarating feeling that all of the strands of this project were coming together and being enacted—emerging from the closet, as it were—before my very eyes. Other audience members at Mac Low's reading included Lyn Hejinian and Bob Perelman, both of whom had participated in the performance of the *L.Z. Masque* in San Francisco, 1978. At the same conference, a colleague delivered a paper on Stein's *Ida*, a text whose composition grew out of her work on *Doctor Faustus Lights the Lights;* and Marjorie Perloff gave an address in which she celebrated the life and career of Hugh Kenner—and during which she spoke at length of her daughter Carey's production of *Elektra*, indebted in its conception (at the elder Perloff's suggestion) to Kenner's *The Pound Era*. I was on the right track, I told myself. All of the pieces fit together, and the proof was in this constellation of events that touched, in one way or another, on the texts and performances that I had already chosen to constellate critically.

But perhaps the pieces fit together too neatly. After my initial feeling of enthusiasm came the more sobering recognition of the potential limitations of my work. This recognition was, in some ways, analogous to Judith Butler's grim description of coming out of the closet: "Conventionally, one comes out of the closet; . . . so we are out of the closet, but into what? what new unbounded spatiality? the room, the den, the attic, the basement, the house, the bar, the university, some new enclosure whose door, like Kafka's door, produces the expectation of a fresh air and a light of illumination that never arrives?"[1] Was my work addressed only to the small, self-selective, and mutually reinforcing group of scholars and artists who trekked to places like Orono, Maine, to speak with, to, and about one another's work? For that matter, who constituted the audience not strictly or simply for my own work but for the work about which I had chosen to write? Could directors like Perloff and LeCompte really be said to "uncloset" modernist drama when the New York audiences for their productions were circumscribed and elite? Was *House/Lights*, for instance, just another "coterie" performance that took place in a space more similar to the closet than to other, larger stages? What were the stakes, purchase, and relevance of the writing and performance of closet drama—and my meditations thereupon?

By way of beginning to answer these questions, I want to explore the possibility that not just the Wooster Group's Performing Garage but most, if not all, theaters—even the much larger, much more expensive Jerome Robbins Theater that is slated, at the time of this writing, to serve as the group's new home base—are closets.[2] In an essay on the theater of (and critical responses to) Tennessee Williams, Anne Fleche makes the claim, which I would like to pursue and extend here, that theater as such configures a kind of closet because of the ways in which theatrical space "has to be bounded, modified, organized, relativized, [and] quoted" in order to appear legibly as theater; like the space of a closet, theatrical "space requires a frame, a garment, a proscenium, a limit."[3] One of the things that closet drama resists is this "limit" of the theater, which is variously defined in different contexts; but at the same time, closet drama follows a structural logic that likens it to this limited theatrical space. If, as Fleche observes, "theatrical space already *includes* the offstage, the outside, the invisible[,] and in this it resembles the [gay] closet," then theatrical space also resembles, paradoxically, the closet drama; for such drama, far from diametrically opposed to the theater, includes the onstage, the inside and the visible of the playhouse, in its complex resistance to theatricality (256). Just as a queer subject is never wholly in or out of the closet but "carries" the closet, "is on the *side* of the closet" (265), so, too, is closet drama never wholly separate from theater but exists alongside theater, both the real one that it rejects and the potential one that it imagines; and so, too, does theater itself exist alongside "the space [we] don't see, can't measure, haven't imagined yet," that is, the space beyond its boundaries toward which it gestures implicitly in its very boundedness (256). Closet drama, no mere aberration from theatricality, shows us in a queer way something that embodied, theatrical performance more directly —and fundamentally—shows us all the time: the edge of the theater and what may beckon from the other side.

This line of thinking suggests a reengagement with and departure from an aspect of the work of Martin Puchner, who writes, as he takes up the question of embodiment in live performance, that "limitations . . . make themselves everywhere felt in the theater. It is the closet drama alone that can actually change a man into a woman, place thousands of people on an impossible stage, and even turn objects and fragmented body parts into agents."[4] Bracketing the fact that it is not closet drama but surgery that can "actually" change a biological male into a female, and that what can change a man into a woman, including self-assertive speech acts, is a much more complex and culturally negotiated matter, I question Puchner's assertion that closet drama "alone" can effect transformations that test the permeable limits of human embodiment, including sexual embodiment. Whether we think of closet drama as a prosthesis of the theater, or theater as a prosthesis of the closet drama (or, ideally, keep both ideas aloft and in productive tension with one another), the theater that uncloselets drama is just as likely as closet drama itself to imagine the sorts of fantastic breaks with the everyday that Puchner enumerates; for it is in the realm of imagination and illusion, not of actuality (what would it mean, in Puchner's slightly uncareful formulation, to "actually" do anything "on an impossible stage"?), that both drama and theater traffic.

In such imaginative traffic, modernist closet drama looks, as I have suggested throughout this project, both backward and forward, and so, too, does this study of closet drama invite us to look backward and forward as a way of further assessing its implications. Where that which precedes modernism is concerned, I am particularly interested in how this work may make an intervention alongside prominent accounts of theatricality and privacy. In *Private Theatricals*, Nina Auerbach traces a direct line of descent from Victorian antitheatricalists like Thomas Carlyle and Matthew Arnold to twentieth-century critics like Lionel Trilling and even Erving Goffman, all of whom participate in an idealization of the sincere, stable, and single self whose "dearest privacy of mind" is threatened by the theater's multiplication of selves and their impersonations, or rather by the potential (sullying) extension of this theatrical impulse into the mental sphere and the practices of everyday life.[5] Modernism, as this book has demonstrated, interrupts and complicates such a narrative about antitheatricality. While in both the nineteenth and the twentieth centuries some prominent thinkers and artists rejected the theater because it threatened the fixity of the self, some modernists resisted the theater because it did not appear to do *enough* to threaten this self's fixity. A complex and theatricalized privacy, epitomized by the spaces of the closet dramatic text, became for modernists not a refuge from performance but a place to perform "denials of the ontological fixities that codify culture," which Auerbach calls "female by definition" (12) and I read as queer. Of course, modernists were by no means unique or unprecedented in experiencing their privacy as theatrical.[6] As Karen Halttunen observes in *Confidence Men and Painted Women,* middle-class Americans were, by the mid-nineteenth century, "actually beginning to take pride in the theatricality of their social conduct," and this "growing middle-class fascination with the theatrical arts of everyday life" was epitomized by the "explosive popularity" of parlor theatricals, tableaux vivants, and related games, such as charades.[7] But if, as Halttunen argues convincingly, the most interesting and revealing of these parlor theatricals were the "significantly self-conscious . . . [ones] that parodied the histrionic efforts of the performers themselves," then there persists, even in this private embrace of theatricality, a strong element of what I would identify as embarrassment, prohibiting the full and unqualified celebration of "posturings" (181). No such embarrassment (de)animates the modernists; as they look backward, often scornfully, to their immediate Victorian predecessors, their breaks with middle-class modesty point not only to their (on the whole) privileged defiance, but also to a more broadly identifiable historical shift marked by the interrogation of previous generations' pieties.

To consider backward-looking tendencies—both the modernists' and my own—from a different but equally important angle, I must also comment on the pervasive, if often tacit, role that camp plays in my interpretations of modernist closet dramas and, indeed, in those dramas themselves. As I have argued elsewhere—in an attempt to navigate among conceptions that are too narrow or too broad, too specific or too vague—camp is best defined as affectively ambivalent queer parody, a term that condenses three related postulates: to be plausibly identified as such, "camp must be understood as a practice that calls attention to the constructedness and performativity of gender and sexuality"; "camp must echo some preexisting text, tropes, or set of codes in this negotiation of gender and sexuality"; and "camp requires of its deployer a simultaneous *identification* with and *disavowal* of the object of its contemplation."[8] Given the detailed analyses offered in this book, my definition here of camp is both capacious and delimited enough to provide us a perspective from which to recognize how many modernist closet dramas, including Pound's *Elektra,* Zukofsky's *Rudens,* and Stein's *Doctor Faustus,* can be read as significant camp artifacts. Even Djuna Barnes's *The Antiphon,* in its queer renegotiation of the revenge tropes from Jacobean and Romantic drama to which it is ambivalently attached, discloses a dimension—perhaps the most melancholic—of the camp sensibility.

While camp is routinely associated with plays or novels by dandies at the various edges of modernism, such as Oscar Wilde and Ronald Firbank, readers may be dislocated by my suggestion that some of the most difficult or experimental high modernist texts are equally susceptible to camp nominations. No doubt the defamiliarizing effect of the suggestion owes a great deal of its force to its situation alongside truisms about modernism, cemented during the first waves of modernist criticism and common to both the left (the Frankfurt School, paradigmatically) and the right (the New Critics, most iconically). These critical truisms, which grew up alongside modernist literature, performances, and related artistic activity, are still deeply felt despite the ways in which scholars have more recently attempted to debunk them.[9] In a timely meditation on persistent and pervasive critical prejudices about modernism, Robert Scholes argues, in *Paradoxy of Modernism*, that the idea of a "High/Low distinction"—between the most celebrated modernist art and its mass or popular complements—is chief among such prejudices and continues to obscure from our view the ways in which high modernist texts "often have crucial elements that our critical discourse associates with [their] opposite[s]."[10] Though Scholes never engages directly the concept of camp (curiously, given his chapter-long meditation on what he calls Oscar Wilde's paradoxically "durable fluff" [143]), camp is certainly one of these "crucial elements" of so-called high modernism ignored or even made invisible by many of its critics. By going against that critical grain, I am asking us to see old modernists through new eyes: to begin, if only tentatively, to think about the ways in which, say, Barnes revising the manuscript of *The Antiphon* in the 1950s or Zukofsky correcting proofs of *Bottom* in the 1960s might have something in common—something oblique, qualified, but nonetheless powerful—with the gay Bette Davis fans described by James McCourt in *Queer Street* or the female impersonators interviewed by Esther Newton in *Mother Camp*, respectively.[11] (Doesn't Barnes obsessively generate citational representations of dangerous women, and isn't Zukofsky performing a writerly drag?)

Of course, camp gestures and postures are inhabited not only by modernists and their contemporaries but also by the performers who have uncloseted modernist drama (recall the Wooster Group's campy decision to collide *Doctor Faustus* with *Olga's House of Shame*)—and, likewise worthy of acknowledgment, by me, as a contemporary of these performers and as a critic of them and their modernist predecessors. In chapter titles, in section headings, and in scores of related stylistic choices and tonal inflections, I have allowed camp to percolate through the pages of this book, and so it is only right that I offer some metacritical appraisal of my approach. To embark on that appraisal, I find it helpful to invoke Heather Love's observation, in *Feeling Backward: Loss and the Politics of Queer History,* that "not only do many queers . . . feel backward, but backwardness has been taken up as a key feature of queer culture. Camp, for instance, with its tender concern for outmoded elements of popular culture and its refusal to get over childhood pleasures and traumas, is a backward art."[12] Though my prior remarks should make clear my divergence from the notion that camp must take up "outmoded elements of popular culture," I want to linger over Love's recognition of the "refusal to get over childhood pleasures and traumas"—and the possible identity of those pleasures and traumas, unexplored in this local claim of hers—as a key element of camp. Unlike some of the other objects of my camp attentions (the most publicly avowed, in my scholarship, are 1980s soap operas),[13] modernist closet dramas do not belong to my literal childhood; but they may belong to my "second childhood," if that term can be disarticulated from its associations with senility and old age (perhaps, more accurately, the third childhood) and yoked instead to a time when other "children" and I played dress-up in funny costumes, held marathon sleepovers, and ate junk food with abandon: our (avowedly privileged) undergraduate years. Not surprisingly, those years were the same ones during which I had my first intense, continuous, and loving exposure to difficult modernist texts—and during which the seeds of this book were first planted (though I couldn't know as much) in conversations, serious and casual, curricular and extra, about "*A,*" and *Last Operas and Plays,* and so forth. So how, at (what I flatter myself is) a substantial remove from that time, its affects, and the attachments that those affects encouraged, can I sustain a long-term relationship with modernism, a demand imposed by the exigencies of likewise long-term academic projects that, perhaps inevitably, begin in one time of life and end in another, often quite different one? To be frank, I find that the onetime pleasures of modernism would, from the vantage point of my adulthood, feel like traumas were it not for the (re)mediating access that I have to modernism through a camp perspective—one that finds its intellectual justification in the ways in which it allows me to meet modernist texts on their own, refreshingly campy terms.

I offer this personal account as a kind of gentle request for similar accounts from others engaged in scholarship about modernism. As currently

configured, it is a field of study where the frequent (though happily interrupted)[14] affectation of thoroughgoing seriousness not only reproduces,
with insufficiently critical self-awareness, what Scholes calls "the false [mod-
ernist] opposition between light and serious [that] really inhibits our vision" (16) but also provokes a cognitive dissonance in me (and, I suspect,
in many others) that prompts me to wonder: Is this Arnoldian high seriousness how we actually *live with* Pound, or Stein—or how their texts are
actually asking us to live with them? At the same time, I permit myself this
extended meditation on camp because of my sense that this project has
poised me to speculate about why camp has been, and continues to be, such
an enduring strain of queer lives, performances, and cultural formations,
despite the ways in which it has been critically repudiated as retrograde,
minor, and/or apolitical. To be sure, there are consequentially material and
historical differences, ones that I would not wish to overlook or deny, between, for instance, me and closeted gay subjects in the 1950s, for whom
camp was a much more immediate mode of survival; or between Jackson
Mac Low, writing and performing in the 1990s and 2000s, and those gay
subjects; or between Jackson Mac Low and me. But those consequential differences are so striking that they have the potential to occlude from view the
much more fragile stakes that may unite such diverse and otherwise disparate subjects—and camp may be one of those stakes. As long as prevailing categories of sex, gender, and sexuality fail to accommodate subjects'
bodies, affects, and desires; as long as those subjects' bodies, affects, and
desires refuse, likewise, to be seamlessly coordinated with dominant modes
of production, consumption, and value; as long as these failures and refusals
beckon for the creation of alternative spaces, psychic and material, that are
also alternative temporalities; in short, as long as ways of feeling "other"
are determined by the defining features of modernity and their postmodern legacies, camp will be one crucial response to those ways of feeling.

To direct attention away from camp, from myself, and from those who
have uncloseted modernist dramas, I'd like, finally, to consider the ways in
which our understandings of others who (in both senses of the word) *follow* modernists may be newly invigorated by this book's meditations on
closet drama. Specifically, I hope that my insistence on and development
of a supple and flexible use of the term *closet drama* may begin to suggest
to others ways to build on my approach and to embark upon even more
capacious explorations of how a new conception of closet drama, as a mode
rather than as a genre, can illuminate various cultural phenomena. David
Savran gestures toward such a possibility when he titles the second half of

A Queer Sort of Materialism, his recent collection of essays on American theater, "Part II: Closet Dramas." Not a single one of the plays that Savran an-
alyzes in these essays is a closet drama in the strict generic sense in which
the term is usually deployed. Instead, Savran uses *closet drama* to denomi-
nate commercially staged, post–World War II American plays that "facili-
tate an almost wild proliferation of queer desires only by keeping the homosexual perpetually out of sight, invisible, elsewhere" (157), as well as
recent films that "resuscitat[e] the closet drama" by "mobilizing [such] conventions" as "evasions, furtive cravings, innuendoes, withheld secrets, and
homicidal passions" (182). When Savran calls an essay "A Different Sort of
Closet Drama," he takes for granted the ability to depart entirely from the
conventional definition of the term; the difference he means is that of Jane
Bowles's *In the Summer House* from such coded queer plays as those of Tennessee Williams (158), not the difference of all of these "closet dramas" from
their unperformed and supposedly unperformable sister texts.

Following Savran's cues alongside my own over the course of these
pages, we might ask: What other texts can be fruitfully interpreted through
the rubric of closet drama, and how and why? For instance, could R. Kelly's
outrageous Gesamtkunstwerk *Trapped in the Closet* be plausibly called a
closet drama, and if so, how would such an interpretation complicate the
prevailing notion that the closet drama is incompatible with—indeed, opposed to—the value and valences of theatricality produced by the total work
of art?[15] In what sense might anonymous pornographic videos (in which
the participants' faces are frequently concealed) posted to Web sites like
Xtube be construed as closet dramas that simultaneously circulate performance and withhold its acknowledgment—and to what extent are the viewers who watch such videos, typically alone in spaces understood as private
ones, closet audiences? And what of all the juicy (queer) backstage dramas
about which most theater audiences never know;[16] is the green room a kind
of closet? While it is beyond my scope in this book to probe these particular questions, I raise them suggestively as a gesture toward the ways in which
closet drama indexes not just a rich form of creative expression but a potentially rich mode of critical investigation for those scholars who would
seek new perspectives on the objects of contemplation that sustain us—that
is, new ways to unsettle our closures.

As for the closure of this book, I focus its last words on another, unsettling set of last words, those of a perhaps unexpected addition to the
project's foregoing cast of characters: Dutch Schultz, a major player in New
York organized crime in the 1920s and 1930s. After being shot in the men's

room of the Palace Chop House in Newark, New Jersey, in 1935, Schultz, delirious from peritonitis and morphine injections, uttered a largely bewildering and superficially nonsensical stream of words in response to questions from police officers hoping to learn the identity of his shooter. This hospital deathbed speech, recorded by a police stenographer and later published in the *New York Times,* has captured the imagination of a number of writers, including William S. Burroughs, who used the speech in his "closet film" *The Last Words of Dutch Schultz,* a novel in the form of a screenplay that, as John F. Keener argues, "Burroughs intends . . . to be read explicitly as a form of proto-filmscript."[17] More seamlessly than such phenomena as the Web 2.0 or MTV videos mentioned above, *The Last Words of Dutch Schultz* can be read contiguously with—and, as a closet film, extend the arguments about—the modernist closet drama discussed in this book, both because "Burroughs is . . . taken with [Schultz's] last words as a form of accidental, Steinian writing" and because Burroughs's own refashioning of those words, in a "media-specific extenuation of the 'cut-up' technique" that he used in such previous novels as *Naked Lunch,* is arguably also a radical extenuation of modernist techniques of fragmentation and collage (154, 153). As one inheritor and transmuter of the modernist closet drama's energies and attitudes vis-à-vis the theater, the postmodern closet film simultaneously courts and resists contemporaneous filmmaking conventions and parameters. Burroughs's screenplay, first published in England in 1969 and then reissued in an altered American edition in 1975, is no more daring or extreme in its visual and aural conceits than other experimental films of its period and is, indeed, in conversation with such films; but because it imagines such conceits on the lavish scale of commercial Hollywood cinema for which financing would be extremely unlikely, it remains in the closet.

The Last Words of Dutch Schultz also resembles modernist closet drama in its queer articulations and preoccupations. Where modernist closet drama sometimes anticipates and sometimes outstrips the logic of the postwar gay closet, Burroughs's screenplay is incubated directly in that logic, even as it defies it. Because Dutch Schultz was shot in a men's room, and because Burroughs, as an aficionado of all Schultz arcana, would surely have been aware of the legend that Schultz staggered out of that men's room to avoid a (to him) unbearably emasculating death on its floor, I cannot resist the temptation to read *The Last Words* alongside another queer text that was likewise written right before Stonewall and revised for republication in the mid-1970s: Laud Humphreys's *Tea Room Trade: Impersonal Sex in Public Places.*[18] Some of Schultz's feverish last words seem to express, accidentally or otherwise, an understanding of the ways in which the men's room, a site that troubles the distinction between public and private, might also trouble the distinctions among usually vivid (and vividly different) identities; and the last words thus seem to anticipate Humphreys's account of men's room sex that attracts straight, bisexual, openly gay, and closeted gay men alike and that erases many of the differences among them: "No business, no hangout; no friends, nothing," Schultz says. "Just what you pick up and what you need."[19] In turn, Burroughs elaborates much more aggressively the queering effect that the men's room gunshot, curiously analogous to men's room sex, has on Schultz. Discussing E. L. Doctorow's treatment of the Schultz lore in *Billy Bathgate,* Keener argues that "coming out," in his words, into gangster life means repudiating the body's inadequacies and nonnormativities—and thereby no longer being a "punk" (142); by this logic, being shot and departing gangster life might beget a descent to punk-hood (with all the implications that such a loaded word as *punk* entails), and it is exactly this possibility that Burroughs explores in *The Last Words.*

Throughout the screenplay, Burroughs characterizes Schultz as a hypermasculine man disgusted by the related weaknesses of junkies and queers—the very typologies most intensely associated with Burroughs himself. During a youthful stint in prison, Burroughs's Schultz rejects heroin, as well as sex with drag queen inmates who impersonate movie starlets. Yet after his gunshot, he has no choice but to submit to a shot of morphine administered by a nurse, and he is subject to a terrifying hallucination of penetrative sex that aligns his body with the disordered close-up of "dresses, thighs, buttocks" that images the sodomized drag queens.[20] "Why can't he just pull out and give me control?" Dutch, now similarly disordered, asks of the police detectives (19), one of whom responds with the same dictum of self-regulation by which Schultz has heretofore avoided such queer abjection: "Control yourself" (22). Rendered out of control by the injury received in the men's room, Schultz becomes like the other uncontrollable, even frenzied queer figures in the screenplay: Owney Maddon, a gangster "sweet on" one of his associates of whom Schultz says disparagingly, "When a queer gets the hots he don't think what he's getting into" (54); and the "pack of screaming faggots" who "fill [a nightclub] screeching and camping, . . . snatch tablecloths, curtains and drapes and do impersonation acts" (74). The faggots appear thus to Schultz in a nightmare vision as he says cryptically to the police, "The 400," real words of Schultz's deployed here by Burroughs to describe the gaggle of unruly men and their disturbance of both the imaginary nightclub and Schultz's peace of mind. Moreover, this pack of disturbers stands for Burroughs himself, who has disarranged the story of Schultz's life and death by grafting onto it his own obsessions with queer life and junk. A self-conscious announcement of this strategy comes in the form of a joke: in the Arcade edition of the book, period photographs of Schultz and his world accompany the text, and one of these photographs, given the caption, "Police stenographer, looking remarkably like Big Bill Burroughs" (115), is in fact a picture of Burroughs. Usurping the place of the passively objective recorder of the last words, Burroughs shapes language actively—virally—to make Schultz's water closet drama a queer one.

Burroughs's palimpsestic mapping of his authorial agenda onto the figure of the stenographer encourages similar critical moves, such as the overlaying of chop house bathroom and tearoom that I sketched in my invocation of Humphreys. In tandem, we might look to Lee Edelman's critical overlaying of the men's room and another charged, circumscribed space: that of the theater. Writing of the relationship of the men's room to the gay closet, "to which it is nearly allied (both as 'water closet' and as site of bodily relations discursively tabooed)," Edelman suggests further that the space of the men's room is constructed to incite theatrical performance: "The men's room gives the male subject his body in its relation to symbolic space . . . by allowing him . . . to enact, as if in a theater, the law of its mandatory closeting."[21] In this formulation, closeting is not the denial of performance, not a silence or gap that stands in the place where performance might otherwise happen,[22] but the very condition that prompts performance— or, from another perspective, the condition engendered by performance. In the study of modernist closet drama, I have elaborated these very insights and their conjunction: that closet provisions are not necessarily hostile to but queerly constitutive of possible performance provisions, and that performance provisions, especially theatrical ones, can themselves be understood as closet provisions. To point, with these ideas in mind, to the dramas that take place in other closets, other rooms—from men's rooms, real and imagined, of the 1930s and the 1960s, to so many other modern interiors whose enclosures produce effects that are at once disarming and comforting, dispiriting and exhilarating—is to go as far as this book's own enclosures will allow.

NOTES

INTRODUCTION "Half In and Half Out"

1   Waters, Introduction to *Trash Trio*, vii.

2   One of the screenplays included in the volume, *Flamingos Forever* (a sequel to *Pink Flamingos*), conforms most neatly to this definition of closet drama. Stymied first by lack of funding and then by Divine's death, Waters never realized the script for the screen—and how we might realize it in our own living rooms also remains questionable, given that the text ends with "*Divine and family flying on turd over Baltimore, wind in their hair, happy . . . as turd flies away like magic carpet over skyline*" (258).

3   Raber, *Dramatic Difference*, 13.

4   Straznicky, *Privacy, Playreading, and Women's Closet Drama*, 1, 16.

5   Gould, *Virtual Theater*, 1, 7, 37.

6   Archer, *Play-making*, 21.

7   Hardy, preface to *The Dynasts*, x.

8   Williams, *Playing the Race Card*, 17, second emphasis added. See also Brooks, *The Melodramatic Imagination*, and Gledhill, "The Melodramatic Field."

9   Stein, *Four Saints in Three Acts*, 445.

10 Zukofsky, *Rudens*, in *"A,"* 487.

11 Cox, *In the Shadows of Romance*, 43.

12 Szondi, *Theory of the Modern Drama*.

13 Ackerman and Puchner, "Introduction," 8, 12.

14 Worthen, *Print and the Poetics of Modern Drama*, 9, 73.

15 Quigley, *The Modern Stage and Other Worlds*, 29, 36, 40.

16 Puchner, *Stage Fright*, 2.

17 Davenport, "Zukofsky's 'A'-24," 23.

18 Sedgwick, "Queer and Now," 8.

19 Boone, *Libidinal Currents*, 3.

20 Herrmann, *Queering the Moderns*, 6–7.

21 Herring, *Queering the Underworld*, 22.

22 Bersani, *Homos*, 27.

23 A notable exception to this generalization is David Savran, who "believe[s] that 'queer' remains a provocative way for thinking about the intersection between certain theatrical forms and certain sexual subjects" and who uses the term to analyze the ways "in which ostensibly stable meanings and identities (sexual and otherwise) are routinely displaced by notions of mutability, instability, and polyvalence." See Savran, *A Queer Sort of Materialism*, 58.

24 Solomon, "Great Sparkles of Lust," 9, emphasis added.

25 Senelick, "The Queer Root of Theatre," 26.

26 Peters, "Performing Obscene Modernism," 210.

27 Goldberg, "Performance Anxiety."

28 For an account of the emergence of "queer" theatrical practices in the 1960s—and, indeed, for the first (if contested) use of the term *queer theater*—see Brecht, *Queer Theatre.*

29 Roach, "Imagined Communities," 45.

30 Grosz, "The Time of Architecture," 268.

31 Auslander, *Liveness*, 40–41.

32 Dolan, *Utopia in Performance,* 13.

33 Villarejo, *Lesbian Rule,* 203.

34 Burroughs, *Closet Stages,* 8.

35 For an account of the ways in which "the link between scholars and artists has been alternately disavowed and celebrated, touted and feared, re-termed and re-organized," both inside and outside the academy, see Jackson, *Professing Performance,* 2–3.

36 Athanases, "When Print Alone Fails Poetry," 120.

37 Conquergood, "Rethinking Elocution," 335.

38 Worthen, "Disciplines of the Text," 12, emphasis added.

39 Ackerman, "The Prompter's Box," 6.

40 *Oxford English Dictionary Online,* entry for *closet.*

41 Sedgwick, *Epistemology of the Closet,* 72.

42 Chauncey, *Gay New York,* 6.

43 Howie, *Claustrophilia,* 4, emphasis added.

44 Miller, *Place for Us,* 132–33.

45 O'Hara and Rivers, *Kenneth Koch,* 129.

46 Stein, *Doctor Faustus Lights the Lights,* 98.

47 Ezra Pound, "Drafts of Canto XX," Yale Collection of American Literature, quoted in Marsh, "Letting the Black Cat Out of the Bag," 125.

48 Auerbach, *Private Theatricals,* 13.

49 James, Note to *Theatricals,* 255.

50 Edel, Foreword to *The Complete Plays of Henry James,* 9.

51 James, "After the Play," 237.

52 James, "Tennyson's Drama," 181.

53 Kurnick, "'Horrible Impossible,'" 111, 123, 126.

54 James, "Owen Wingrave."

55 James, *The Saloon.*

56 Moon, *A Small Boy and Others,* 4.

57 Edel, Editor's foreword to *The Saloon,* 648–49. Alan Ackerman reads *The Saloon* as crucially invested in "a dangerous act of spectatorship" (Wingrave's of the ghost); thus he interprets James's reaction to the materialization of the ghost as disgust at the circumscription of the act's danger, since "the ghost's materiality immediately reduces . . . the dramatic to the comic." See Ackerman, *The Portable Theater,* 219.

CHAPTER 1 **Fronting Pound**

1 Rabaté, *Language, Sexuality, and Ideology,* 73–74.

2 Pound, *The Cantos,* 65–66.

3 Savran, *Communists, Cowboys, and Queers,* 17.

4 E. Patrick Johnson, "Manifest Faggotry," 74.

5 The body of critical literature on Pound's life and work is vast, but for some of the most useful readings of *The Cantos,* in particular, see Bush, *The Genesis of Ezra Pound's "Cantos"*; Davie, *Ezra Pound;* Hesse, *New Approaches to Ezra Pound;* Kenner, *The Poetry of Ezra Pound* and *The Pound Era;* and Perloff, *The Poetics of Indeterminacy.*

6 Pound, *"Noh" Plays,* 213.

7 For a detailed account of the working and personal relationship between Pound and Yeats, see Carpenter, *A Serious Character.*

8 Reid, Introduction to *Elektra,* xiii.

9 Classic Stage Company, "History."

10 Perloff, Introduction to *Elektra,* xi.

11 Fenollosa letter to Pound.

12 Pound letter to Williams, 22.

13 Litz, "Pound and Yeats," 141.

14 Pratt, *Ezra Pound and the Making of Modernism,* 163.

15 MacDuff, "Beautiful Boys in Nō Drama," 248.

16 Hare, *Zeami's Style,* 16. For a further account of the role of same-sex desire in Nō theater, see Leupp, *Male Colors.*

17 Zeami, *On the Art of the Nō Drama,* 5.

18 Masakazu, "The Aesthetics of Ambiguity," xxxix–xl.

19 This anecdote is also told approvingly by Yeats as he contemplates the transformation of acting in the modern theater. For an account thereof, see Puchner, *Stage Fright,* 125.

20 Grosz, "Bergson, Deleuze, and Becoming." See also Bergson, *The Creative Mind.* That Pound, in one of his more querulous moods, said of the philosopher, "DAMN Bergson and frog diarhoea [*sic*]" (quoted in Carpenter, *A Serious Character,* 114) makes it all the more delightful to find a Bergsonian tendency at play in Pound's queerest work.

21 Deleuze and Guattari, *A Thousand Plateaus,* 276.

22 Letter from John Keats to George and Thomas Keats, December 21, 27(?), 1817, 60.

23 Savran, *Communists, Cowboys, and Queers,* 42.

24 Tsukui, *Ezra Pound and Japanese Noh Plays,* 46–47.

25 Fenollosa, "Outline of *Aoi No Uye.*"

26 Shikibu, *The Tale of Genji,* 168.

27 Albright, "Pound, Yeats, and the Noh Theatre," 47–48.

28 Pound Letter to Kitasono.

29 Pound and Fleming, *Elektra,* 38.

30 Syros, "Beyond Language," 107.

31 Laks, *Electra,* 1–2.

32 Lucian, "The History of Orestes and Pylades."

33 Eliot, *The Waste Land,* 61.

34 Packard, *Queer Cowboys,* 3.

35 For accounts of Electra's marriage to Pylades, see such commentators as Apollodorus and Pausanias.

36 See Sedgwick, *Between Men.*

37 Barthes, *A Lover's Discourse,* 73.

38 Schechner, *Between Theatre and Anthropology,* 36.

39 Churchill, *Cloud Nine,* 248.

40 Gainor, "*Elektra* by Ezra Pound," 130.

41 For excellent accounts of Pound's complicated attitudes about race, see the essays in Coyle, *Ezra Pound and African American Modernism*.

42 Wilmer, "Maker of Songs," 10.

43 Feingold, "Ludlam Wise, Pound Foolish," 109–10.

44 Gussow, "Stage: Pound's *Elektra*."

45 Carey Perloff, quoted by Gainor, "*Elektra* by Ezra Pound," 127.

46 Sontag, "Notes on Camp," 275, 279.

47 See, for instance, Moe Meyer, ed., *The Politics and Poetics of Camp* (New York: Routledge, 1994); and Cleto, *Camp*.

48 Feuer, "Reading *Dynasty*."

CHAPTER 2 **Bottoming Zukofsky**

1 Zukofsky letter to Pound, Yale Collection of American Literature.

2 Letter from Louis Zukofsky to Ezra Pound, September 6, 1927, in *Pound/Zukofsky*, 5.

3 Zukofsky, "Poem Beginning 'The,'" 11.

4 For a less explicitly sexual but nonetheless queer reading of this passage and Zukofsky's mention of it to Pound, see Rifkin, "The Legacy of Louis Zukofsky," in *Career Moves*, 82–84. I might also mention that such readings need not emerge from studied consideration; indeed, the queer interpretation may even be the most innocent one of the passage in question. As a colleague and fellow Zukofsky scholar recently related to me with some surprise, "When we read 'Poem Beginning "The"' in my undergraduate class, all my students just assumed that Zukofsky was gay—it wasn't even a point of argument or speculation, just an obvious given to them" (Dworkin email).

5 Letter from Zukofsky to Pound, December 12, 1930, *Pound/Zukofsky*, 77.

6 On the paternal nature of Pound's relationship to Zukofsky, see Barry Ahearn's introduction to *Pound/Zukofsky*.

7 Letter from Pound to Zukofsky, *Pound/Zukofsky*, 144–45.

8 Letter from Zukofsky to Pound, April 15, 1933, *Pound/Zukofsky*, 147.

9 Killian and Stefans, "The American Objectivists."

10 The American Poetry Archive and The Poetry Center at San Francisco State University, outtakes from the NET Film Series *USA: Poetry*.

11 Edelman, "Homographesis," 12, 10. In debt to the Derridean concept of *différance*, Edelman uses the word *homographesis* to express both the idea of resistance to codified sexual identity categories *and* the opposite of that idea. As he explains, "Like writing, then, homographesis would name a double operation: one serving the ideological purposes of a conservative social order intent on codifying identities in its labor of disciplinary inscription, and the other resistant to that categorization, intent on *de*scribing the identities that order has so oppressively *in*scribed" (10).

12 Perelman, Foreword to *Bottom*, ix–x.

13 Worthen, *Print and the Poetics of Modern Drama*, 22–24.

14 Zukofsky, *Bottom*, 13, 39.

15 Spears, *Slang and Euphemism*, 44.

16 Zukofsky, *Autobiography*.

17 Emphases added.

18 Most critics agree that Spinoza's thoughts about the mastery of the passions play a central role in *Bottom*, but the specific implications of Zukofsky's reliance upon Spi-

noza have been a matter of some debate. For alternative interpretations, see Melnick, "The 'Ought' of Seeing"; and Scroggins, *Louis Zukofsky and the Poetry of Knowledge*, 72–74.

19 Zukofsky's "position" vis-à-vis Celia in *Bottom* may also shed light on his oft-quoted statement of poetics in *"A"*-12: "An integral / Lower limit speech / Upper limit music" (138). Though most critics emphasize the upper limit of Zukofsky's integral and discuss the ways in which his poetry imitates musical composition and privileges sound over sense, I would suggest that Zukofsky remains squarely at the bottom of the integral and consistently places others—namely, Bach, Celia, and his son Paul, a violinist —at the top. One of the only critics to gesture toward such an understanding of Zukofsky's relationship to music is Bob Perelman, who claims, in a reading of *"A"*-24, that "to hear the piece [*L.Z. Masque*] performed is to be struck by the fact that words, no matter how 'musical' their sound or their syntax, are *not* music. . . . The simultaneity of sound and significance that constitutes music and allows for single lines to build up into immediately perceptible chords does not occur with words." See Perelman, *The Trouble with Genius*, 185.

20 Román and Miller, "Preaching to the Converted," 221.

21 See Zukofsky, "Year by Year Bibliography."

22 For a few of the many excellent critical discussions of *"A"*-9, see Ahearn, *Zukofsky's "A,"* 100–115; Peter Quartermain, "'Not at All Surprised by Science': Louis Zukofsky's *First Half of 'A'-9*," in *Disjunctive Poetics*, 70–89; and Twitchell-Waas, "Tuning the Senses."

23 Ovid, *The Metamorphoses*, 333.

24 Zukofsky's play on letters—turning a T into an H—can also be read in the context of his fluency in two alphabets, English and Hebrew. The T resembles a cross, while the aspirated H resembles the central Hebrew letter (ה) for God's unpronounceable name. Turning a Christian symbol (back) into a Jewish one may be Zukofsky's tacit, secular homage to the traditional Judaism of his parents and to the tricks of Talmudic sages, who regularly "misread" words by changing a letter in order to make passages of Torah better fit their interpretations. I thank Alan Ackerman for making clear to me these important aspects of Zukofsky's writerly performance in *Bottom*.

25 Wray, *Catullus and the Poetics of Roman Manhood*.

26 David Wray has recently observed that Zukofsky's *Catullus* is also no *merely* homophonic translation. See Wray, "'Cool Rare Air.'"

27 Plautus, *Rudens*, trans. Nixon, 297–99.

28 Whitney et al., *Century Dictionary*, 1: 631. Here and elsewhere I refer to this dictionary in particular because it was Zukofsky's own favorite and most often-used lexicon during the composition of *Rudens* and other projects.

29 Ibid., 8: 6522.

30 Wray, "'cool rare air,'" 22.

31 Whitney et al., *Century Dictionary*, 5: 3863, emphasis added.

32 The performance took place in the context of the Louis Zukofsky Centennial Conference, held at Columbia University in September 2004, and was directed by Giles Scott.

33 Similarly, Ahearn observes, "Within the poet there lurked a frustrated dramatist, anxious to hear his words uttered and in motion. '*A*'-12's listing of aborted projects includes 'notes for different plays / I'd have done in my twenties /At the slightest en-

couragement' (p. 252). Celia's masque at least satisfied the poem's tacit striving toward public performance" (176).

34 See Gilman, *Jewish Self-Hatred* and *The Jew's Body*.

35 For an excellent account of the ways in which Jewish composers and librettists shaped American musical theater in the twentieth century, see Most, *Making Americans*.

36 Zukofsky and Zukofsky, "*A*"-24.

37 Perelman, "'*A*'-24," 293. When Perelman assigns to "Zukofsky" the goal of "trying to hook up the . . . act of hearing with the fullest possible range of thought," he encounters the difficulty faced by any critic who attempts to ascribe intention to the authors of "*A*"-24. While we can say with certainty that the work is a collaborative effort, exactly how much of the piece's aims and design are attributable to Louis Zukofsky remains unclear. As Perelman observes earlier in the same piece, "'*A*'-24 really is 'Celia's L.Z. Masque,' a most accurate portrait of him. The scoring and text selection were hers. (I assume the 'idea' of the piece was both of theirs.)"

38 Parsons, "A More Capacious Shoulder," 247.

39 For more details, see Guy Davenport, "Zukofsky," in *The Geography of the Imagination,* 105.

40 Perelman, "'*A*'-24," 292.

41 Bob Perelman, "Language Writing and Literary History," in *The Marginalization of Poetry,* 16. This essay also examines with insight and objectivity the knotty question of what language writing is and to what ends (and with what effects) that descriptive term has been deployed by various individuals and groups.

42 Harryman interview.

43 Sloan, "'Crude Mechanical Access,'" 242.

44 Perelman interview.

45 "Louis Zukofsky: A Performance of '*A*'-24."

46 Roach, *Cities of the Dead,* 2.

47 Perelman, *Ten to One,* xv–xvi.

48 I owe this attribution to a collaborative project edited by Jeffrey Twitchell-Waas, "Z-site: A Companion to the Works of Louis Zukofsky," where a fuller version of Stein's text is quoted as follows: "'Well we took off and went up the Rhine to Cologne, we flew low over and over Cologne and then we found that the airports there were not functioning so we went on to Coblenz where they were not functioning either and so back to Frankfort. Cologne was the most destroyed city we had seen yet, it is natural, of course it is natural to speak of one's roof, roofs are in a way the most important thing in a house, between four walls, under a roof, and here was a whole spread out city without a roof. . . . That evening I went over to talk to the soldiers, and to hear what they had to say, we all got very excited, Sergeant Santiani who had asked me to come complained that I confused the minds of his men, but why shouldn't their minds be confused, gracious goodness, are we going to be like the Germans, only believe in the Aryans that is our own race, a mixed race if you like but all having the same point of view. I got very angry with them, they admitted they liked the Germans better than the other Europeans. Of course you do, I said, they flatter you and they obey you, when the other countries don't like you and say so, and personally you have not been awfully ready to meet them halfway, well naturally if they don't like you they show it, the Germans don't like you but they flatter you, dog gone it, I said I bet you Fourth of July they will all be putting up our flag,

and all you big babies will just be flattered to death, literally to death, I said bitterly because you will have to fight again. Well said one of them after all we are on top. Yes I said and is there any spot on earth more dangerous than on top. You don't like the Latins, or the Arabs or the Wops, or the British, well don't you forget a country can't live without friends, I want you all to get to know other countries so that you can be friends, make a little effort, try to find out what it is all about. We all got very excited, they passed me cognac, but I don't drink so they found me some grapefruit juice, and they patted me and sat me down, and there it all was' [137]. From *How Writing Is Written*, ed. Robert Barlett Haas (Black Sparrow Press, 1977)."

CHAPTER 3 Topping Stein

1   Preston, "A Conversation," 191.

2   For useful accounts of aspects of Stein's life and work (dramatic and otherwise) that I do not consider here, see Benstock, *Women of the Left Bank;* Bowers, *Gertrude Stein and "They Watch Me as They Watch This"*; DeKoven, *A Different Language;* Ruddick, *Reading Gertrude Stein;* Ryan, *Gertrude Stein's Theatre of the Absolute;* and Sutherland, *Gertrude Stein.*

3   Bay-Cheng, *Mama Dada*, 35.

4   Stein, "Plays," xxxv. Bay-Cheng locates Stein's handful of references to the cinema in an effort to controvert this claim, but she fails to realize the extent to which, occasionally, cinema provided Stein with a handy *metaphor* for certain ideas about time, space, and movement, rather than a practical model for dramatic writing. As Stein says earlier in the same essay of the "thing[s] heard" and the "thing[s] seen" in the theater, "I suppose one *might* have gotten to know a good deal about these things from the cinema . . ." (xxxv, emphasis added). The fact remains that Stein was not indebted to the cinema for her ideas about theatricality; she simply recognized the usefulness of the cinematic metaphor as a way to make her ideas more readily understandable and accessible to her readers.

5   See, for instance, Stein's correspondence with Virgil Thomson in the Yale Collection of American Literature, to get a sense of the enthusiasm with which she greeted his 1934 production of her opera *Four Saints in Three Acts.*

6   Though Sarah Bay-Cheng promises a reckoning with the queer dimensions of Stein's drama in *Mama Dada*, the book almost invariably gestures toward queer readings without actually positing them. The aspects of Stein's writing that Bay-Cheng designates "queer" also are largely limited in her account to Stein's attitude toward gender roles.

7   Marranca, Introduction to *Last Operas and Plays*, xi.

8   Stein, *Byron A Play*, 349.

9   To "begin again and again" is in fact a phrase that Stein uses in the essay "Composition as Explanation" to describe her more or less phenomenological attempt to write "a continuous present." Stein recognizes the inherent difficulty, even impossibility, of expressing the immediacy of a moment, let alone of sustaining such a sense of immediacy throughout a piece of writing. In her "groping toward a continuous present," which ipso facto she cannot reach, she must settle for the compromise formation of beginning again and again to capture the present, which will always have passed by the time of writing. See *Composition as Explanation*, 1–7.

10 W. B. Worthen is also interested in the ways in which "Stein's plays addressed, engaged,

and troubled the design of printed drama as cognate with dramatic form, as a register of 'the play,' and so also troubled the ways the space of the page at once implicates and resists the rhetoric of modern performance." Bringing this shared preoccupation to bear on *Byron,* he comes to a slightly different conclusion about the play's "Acts," about which he claims that "the 'Act' divisions mark less the narrative progression of a conventional drama than point to a series of 'acts,' moments in Stein's effort to mark the continuous present of her writing as a visible (theatrical?) event." See Worthen, *Print and the Poetics of Modern Drama,* 62–63, 66.

11   Robinson, *The Other American Drama,* 13.

12   In her most recent book-length study of Stein, Ulla Dydo is so preoccupied with the idea that *Byron* constitutes an elegy for Stein's dog that she insists categorically that the play "is not about the poet, though he is the stuff for drama and the name seems to put him in the play"; *Gertrude Stein,* 554. Nevertheless, textual evidence repeatedly suggests otherwise, from Stein's naming of "George Byron" (362) to her mention of "Byron and clothing" (386), a subject that preoccupied the poet both in life and in such works as *Beppo* and *Don Juan.*

13   Stein, *Everybody's Autobiography,* 50.

14   Trask, *Cruising Modernism,* 89.

15   See *Byron* (manuscript notebook).

16   Worthen, *Print and the Poetics of Modern Drama,* 67.

17   I choose this formulation, rather than one that would attribute "coming again and again" to both Stein and Toklas, because of Janet Malcolm's recent observation, echoing a similar one made by Ulla Dydo, that "Stein regularly gave Toklas orgasms—called 'cows' in the notebooks—but [probably] received none herself." See Malcolm, *Two Lives,* 227.

18   Stein notes to Toklas.

19   Sometimes, as at one point in the first note quoted above, Stein identifies herself as "baby," but this moniker is also used for Toklas.

20   Toklas note to Stein.

21   Stein, "Identity," *A Stein Reader,* ed. Ulla Dydo (Evanston: Northwestern University Press, 1993), 588. The quotation in the subheading is from Stein, *A Play Called Not and Now,* 435.

22   Gass, Introduction to *The Geographical History of America* (Baltimore: Johns Hopkins University Press, 1973), 17.

23   Toklas, *What Is Remembered,* 152.

24   Bridgman, *Gertrude Stein in Pieces,* 285.

25   See "Appendix C: A Chronological List of Dramatic Adaptations" in *Mama Dada,* 166. Berners also describes his compositional practice and the production of the musical in his correspondence with Stein, preserved in the Yale Collection of American Literature.

26   Amory, *Lord Berners,* 138.

27   Byrne, Postscript to *The Girls of Radcliff Hall,* 97.

28   Berners, *The Girls of Radcliff Hall,* 16–17.

29   Stein letter to Van Vechten.

30   As Stein wrote in a letter to Thornton Wilder on May 11, 1938, "Ida has become an opera, and it is a beauty, really is, an opera about Faust, . . . some day she will be a novel

too, she is getting ready for that, but as an opera she is a wonder." See *The Letters of Gertrude Stein and Thornton Wilder,* 217–18.

31 Berners letter to Stein, April 28, 1938.

32 Berners letter to Stein, May/June, 1938.

33 Berners letter to Stein, October 15, 1938.

34 Stein, *Doctor Faustus Lights the Lights,* 97, 99, 91.

35 See Irigaray, *This Sex Which Is Not One,* 24.

36 Wordsworth, "The Tables Turned," 377.

37 See, for instance, Neuman, "'Would a Viper Have Stung Her?'"

38 See Rose, *Storyville, New Orleans,* 146. The different editions of the *Blue Book* can be easily distinguished from one another based on variations in their prefatory material.

39 For Stein's account of her and Toklas's trip to New Orleans, see *Everybody's Autobiography,* 263–66.

40 See the preface to the *Blue Book,* Yale Collection of American Literature: "This Directory and Guide of the Sporting District has . . . proven its authority as to what is doing in the 'Queer Zone'" (unpaginated).

41 Stein, *Short Sentences,* 329.

42 Emma Johnson is just one prostitute and proprietress among many described in Rose's *Storyville* who invite a greater or lesser degree of comparison with Marguerite Ida and Helena Annabel. Take, for instance, Fanny Sweet, a "thief, lesbian, Confederate spy, poisoner, procuress, and brawler" (14), or Marie Rodrigues, "whom the police had arrested in a vile den of infamy . . . where she was consorting with the worst characters —male and female—in the city" (18).

43 Sellars, Foreword to Savran, *Breaking the Rules,* xvi.

44 Kaye, *Art into Theatre,* 253.

45 Savran, *Breaking the Rules,* 51.

46 Interview in Kaye, *Art into Theatre,* 260.

47 "*Olga's White Slaves of Chinatown.*"

48 *Olga's House of Shame.*

49 Hapaz conversation.

50 LeCompte and Valk interview. For a detailed account of these earlier productions of *Faustus,* see Bevya Rosten's unpublished dissertation, "The Fractured Stage."

51 LeCompte interview in *Breaking the Rules,* 115–16.

52 Sebastian, "Stein Soup."

53 Ibid.

54 Stein, "What Are Master-pieces," 149.

55 The text invites the interpretation that the little boy who appears with Faustus is the same figure as the little boy who is traveling with the man from over the seas.

CHAPTER 4 **Backing Barnes**

1 Barnes unpublished interview.

2 Dalton, "'This Is Obscene,'" 117.

3 See the review of Barnes's *Selected Works, Time,* April 20, 1962, 108.

4 For accounts of incest and lesbian desire in *Nightwood,* see Backus, "'Looking for That Dead Girl'"; and Martins, "Gender Trouble and Lesbian Desire."

5 DeSalvo, "'To Make Her Mutton at Sixteen,'" 308.

6 Katherine Bradley and Edith Cooper, writing collaboratively and pseudonymously as Michael Field, are notable and equally exceptional figures for their literary treatment (and personal practice) of lesbian incest. Tellingly, and as Kate Thomas notes in one of the most recent evaluations of Bradley and Cooper, critics "[hide incest] in plain view" as they "pass over or smooth out the extraordinary oddness of their lives, poetry, and drama." See Thomas, "'What Time We Kiss,'" 328, 330.

7 Coleman letter to Barnes.

8 Levine, "'Bringing Milkshakes to Bulldogs,'" 28.

9 Barry, Commentary on "How It Feels to Be Forcibly Fed."

10 Scarry, The Body in Pain, 153. Like the soldier who consents to go to war, Barnes "agrees to permit [a] radical self-alteration to [her] body" (112). The fact that her body resists this self-alteration in various ways does not mean, however, that her consent can be fully withdrawn.

11 Barnes, "How It Feels to Be Forcibly Fed," 176, 178.

12 Green, "Spectacular Confessions," 78.

13 Citing the moment in the article at which Barnes, temporarily blinded by the electric light, describes how "all [her surroundings] went out into a great blank" (176), Green concludes of her experience that "there seems to be no position from which woman can look at her own oppression," but this assessment ignores the many other moments, especially after the temporary loss of vision, at which Barnes underscores exactly what she observes of her "oppression."

14 Barry, Commentary on "The Girl and the Gorilla."

15 Barnes, "The Girl and the Gorilla," 180.

16 For the earliest production and publication history of An Irish Triangle, see Barnes, At the Roots of the Stars, 95–96.

17 Messerli, Introduction to At the Roots of the Stars, 9–10.

18 The exact date of Ann Portuguise's composition is unknown, but we can reasonably conjecture that it was written in the early 1920s.

19 Headnote to Ann Portuguise.

20 A note at the end of At the Roots of the Stars declared Sun and Moon Press's intention, in 1995, to publish Ann Portuguise, Biography of Julie Von Bartmann, and a new edition of The Antiphon, but a decade and more later, none of these projected works has appeared in print.

21 Barnes, An Irish Triangle, 97.

22 Mahaffey, States of Desire, 97.

23 Ibid., 98.

24 Barnes, Ann Portuguise, 1–2.

25 See both Messerli and Dalton for further information about the publication and production histories of The Dove.

26 Barnes, The Dove, 148–49.

27 Headnote to Biography of Julie von Bartmann.

28 Barnes, Biography of Julie von Bartmann, 15–16.

29 Eliot, Manuscript notations on The Antiphon.

30 Barnes, "Notes toward a Definition of The Antiphon," 1.

31 Abraham, "'Woman, Remember You,'" 270.

32 Barnes, Note on The Antiphon.

33 Altman, "*The Antiphon*," 284.

34 Though "Barnes 1" sutures together language from both *The Antiphon* and other works by Barnes—and though other pieces in *Barnesbook* also borrow language from the play —I have chosen to focus on this performance piece in particular because it foregrounds the figure of Miranda and, in so doing, comments much more explicitly than any of the other pieces on *The Antiphon*'s themes.

35 Mac Low, Afterword to *Barnesbook*, 47–48.

36 Bernstein, "Close Listening."

37 Barnes, "Cautionary Note" to *The Antiphon*, 5.

CONCLUSION **Other Closets, Other Rooms**

1 Butler, "Imitation and Gender Insubordination," 16.

2 For more information on the Jerome Robbins Theater and its place in the Baryshnikov Arts Center, see Pogrebin, "Baryshnikov Center Gets Resident Theater."

3 Fleche, "When a Door Is a Jar," 254.

4 Puchner, *Stage Fright*, 90.

5 Auerbach, *Private Theatricals*, 4–10.

6 Indeed, Auerbach notes that the Victorian fear of theatricality was predicated on an awareness, if not wholly conscious, that the "volatile self" could "undergo inexplicable changes" in everyday life and that sincerity itself was a theatrical production (114).

7 Halttunen, *Confidence Men and Painted Women*, 172–74.

8 Salvato, "Tramp Sensibility and the Afterlife of *Showgirls*," 636.

9 Noteworthy examples of this valuable critical trend include Strychacz, *Modernism, Mass Culture, and Professionalism*, and North, *Reading 1922*.

10 Scholes, *Paradoxy of Modernism*, 3–4.

11 See McCourt, *Queer Street*, and Newton, *Mother Camp*.

12 Love, *Feeling Backward*, 7.

13 See Salvato, "On the Bubble."

14 One admirable exception, among others, to the tendency that I diagnose is Nealon, *Foundlings*.

15 Such a reading could draw usefully on the innovative genealogy of the Gesamtkunstwerk offered by Matthew Wilson Smith in *The Total Work of Art*.

16 Some of these queer backstage dramas are uncloseted in Robin Bernstein's edited anthology *Cast Out*.

17 Keener, "The Last Words of Dutch Schultz," 156.

18 Humphreys, *Tea Room Trade*.

19 Schultz et al., "The Last Words of Dutch Schultz."

20 Burroughs, *The Last Words of Dutch Schultz*, 17, 19.

21 Edelman, "Men's Room," 152.

22 As Eve Sedgwick observes, "'Closetedness' itself is a performance initiated as such by the speech act of a silence—not a particular silence, but a silence that accrues particularity by fits and starts, in relation to the discourse that surrounds and differentially constitutes it"; *Epistemology*, 3.

WORKS CITED

Abraham, Julie L. "'Woman, Remember You': Djuna Barnes and History." In Broe, *Silence and Power*, 252–70.

Ackerman, Alan. *The Portable Theater: American Literature and the Nineteenth-Century Stage*. Baltimore: Johns Hopkins University Press, 1999.

———. "The Prompter's Box: Toward a Close Reading of Modern Drama." *Modern Drama* 49:1 (Spring 2006): 1–11.

Ackerman, Alan, and Martin Puchner, eds. *Against Theatre: Creative Destructions on the Modernist Stage*. New York: Palgrave Macmillan, 2006.

———. "Introduction: Modernism and Anti-Theatricality." In Ackerman and Puchner, *Against Theatre*, 1–20.

Ahearn, Barry. *Zukofsky's "A": An Introduction*. Berkeley: University of California Press, 1983.

Albright, Daniel. "Pound, Yeats, and the Noh Theatre." *Iowa Review* 15:2 (Spring–Summer 1985): 34–50.

Altman, Meryl. "*The Antiphon*: 'No Audience at All?'" In Broe, *Silence and Power*, 271–85.

The American Poetry Archive and The Poetry Center at San Francisco State University, producers and editors. Outtakes from the NET Film Series *USA: Poetry*, featuring Richard O. Moore's interview with Louis Zukofsky. New York. March 16, 1966.

Amory, Mark. *Lord Berners: The Last Eccentric*. London: Chatto and Windus, 1998.

Archer, William. *Play-making: A Manual of Craftsmanship*. London: Chapman and Hall, 1912.

Athanases, Steven Z. "When Print Alone Fails Poetry: Performance as a Contingency of Literary Value." *Text and Performance Quarterly* 11 (1991): 116–27.

Auerbach, Nina. *Private Theatricals: The Lives of the Victorians*. Cambridge: Harvard University Press, 1990.

Auslander, Philip. *Liveness: Performance in a Mediatized Culture*, 2nd ed. New York: Routledge, 2008.

Backus, Margot Gayle. "'Looking for That Dead Girl': Incest, Pornography, and the Capitalist Family Romance in *Nightwood*, *The Years*, and *Tar Baby*." *American Imago: Studies in Psychoanalysis and Culture* 51:4 (Winter 1994): 521–45.

"Barnes 1." By Jackson Mac Low. Perf. Jackson Mac Low. University of Maine, Orono. June 24, 2004.

Barnes, Djuna. *Ann Portuguise.* Papers of Djuna Barnes. University of Maryland Special Collections.

———. *The Antiphon.* Los Angeles: Green Integer, 2000.

———. *At the Roots of the Stars: The Short Plays.* Ed. Douglas Messerli. Los Angeles: Sun and Moon, 1995.

———. *Biography of Julie von Bartmann.* Papers of Djuna Barnes. University of Maryland Special Collections.

———. *The Dove.* In *At the Roots of the Stars,* 147–62.

———. "The Girl and the Gorilla." In *New York,* 180–84.

———. "How It Feels to Be Forcibly Fed." In *New York,* 174–79.

———. *An Irish Triangle.* In *At the Roots of the Stars,* 95–106.

———. *New York.* Los Angeles: Sun and Moon, 1989.

———. Note on *The Antiphon.* June 7, 1960. Papers of Djuna Barnes. University of Maryland Special Collections.

———. "Notes toward a Definition of *The Antiphon.*" Papers of Djuna Barnes, University of Maryland Special Collections.

———. Unpublished interview with James Scott. April 2, 1971. Quoted in Herring, *Djuna,* 175–76.

Barry, Alyce. Commentary on Djuna Barnes, "The Girl and the Gorilla." In Barnes, *New York,* 180.

———. Commentary on Djuna Barnes, "How It Feels to Be Forcibly Fed." In Barnes, *New York,* 174.

Barthes, Roland. *A Lover's Discourse: Fragments.* Trans. Richard Howard. New York: Hill and Wang, 1978.

Bay-Cheng, Sarah. *Mama Dada: Gertrude Stein's Avant-Garde Theatre.* New York: Routledge, 2004.

Benstock, Shari. *Women of the Left Bank: Paris, 1900–1940.* Austin: University of Texas Press, 1986.

Berners, Lord Gerald. *The Girls of Radcliff Hall.* North Pomfret, VT: Asphodel, 2000.

———. Letter to Gertrude Stein. April 28, 1938. Yale Collection of American Literature.

———. Letter to Gertrude Stein. May/June, 1938. Yale Collection of American Literature.

———. Letter to Gertrude Stein. October 15, 1938. Yale Collection of American Literature.

Bernstein, Charles. "Close Listening: Poetry and the Performed Word." http://epc .buffalo.edu/authors/bernstein/essays/close-listening.html. October 30, 2005.

Bernstein, Robin, ed. *Cast Out: Queer Lives in Theater.* Ann Arbor: University of Michigan Press, 2006.

Bersani, Leo. *Homos.* Cambridge: Harvard University Press, 1995.

Blue Book. Undated. Yale Collection of American Literature.

Boone, Joseph Allen. *Libidinal Currents: Sexuality and the Shaping of Modernism.* Chicago: University of Chicago Press, 1998.

Bowers, Jane Palatini. *Gertrude Stein.* New York: St. Martin's, 1993.

———. *"They Watch Me as They Watch This": Gertrude Stein's Metadrama.* Philadelphia: University of Pennsylvania Press, 1991.

Brecht, Stefan. *Queer Theatre.* Frankfurt am Main: Suhrkamp, 1978.

Bridgman, Richard. *Gertrude Stein in Pieces.* New York: Oxford University Press, 1970.

Broe, Mary Lynn, ed. *Silence and Power: A Reevaluation of Djuna Barnes.* Carbondale: Southern Illinois University Press, 1991.

Brooks, Peter. *The Melodramatic Imagination: Balzac, Henry James, Melodrama, and the Mode of Excess.* New Haven: Yale University Press, 1976.

Burroughs, Catherine B. *Closet Stages: Joanna Baillie and the Theatre Theory of British Romantic Women Writers.* Philadelphia: University of Pennsylvania Press, 1997.

Bush, Ronald. *The Genesis of Ezra Pound's "Cantos."* Princeton: Princeton University Press, 1976.

Butler, Judith. "Imitation and Gender Insubordination." In *Inside/Out: Lesbian Theories, Gay Theories.* Ed. Diana Fuss. New York: Routledge, 1991. 13–31.

Byrne, John. Postscript to Berners, *The Girls of Radcliff Hall,* 95–99.

Carpenter, Humphrey. *A Serious Character: The Life of Ezra Pound.* Boston: Houghton Mifflin, 1988.

Chauncey, George. *Gay New York: Gender, Urban Culture, and the Making of the Gay Male World, 1890–1940.* New York: Basic, 1994.

Churchill, Caryl. *Cloud Nine.* In *Plays: One.* New York: Routledge, 1985.

Classic Stage Company. "History." www.classicstage.org/history.shtml. May 21, 2009.

Cleto, Fabio, ed. *Camp: Queer Aesthetics and the Performing Subject.* Ann Arbor: University of Michigan Press, 1999.

Coleman, Emily. Letter to Djuna Barnes, October 27, 1935. Quoted in Herring, *Djuna,* 58–59.

Conquergood, Dwight. "Rethinking Elocution: The Trope of the Talking Book and Other Figures of Speech." *Text and Performance Quarterly* 20:4 (October 2000): 325–41.

Cox, Kenneth. *In the Shadows of Romance: Romantic Tragic Drama in Germany, England, and France.* Athens: Ohio University Press, 1987.

Coyle, Michael, ed. *Ezra Pound and African American Modernism.* Orono, ME: National Poetry Foundation, 2001.

Dalton, Anne B. "'This Is Obscene': Female Voyeurism, Sexual Abuse, and Maternal Power in *The Dove.*" *Review of Contemporary Fiction* 13:3 (Fall 1993): 117–40.

Davenport, Guy. *The Geography of the Imagination.* San Francisco: North Point, 1981.

———. "Zukofsky's 'A'-24." *Parnassus* 2 (Spring–Summer 1974): 19–23.

Davie, Donald. *Ezra Pound: Poet as Sculptor.* London: Routledge, 1965.

DeKoven, Marianne. *A Different Language: Gertrude Stein's Experimental Writing.* Madison: University of Wisconsin Press, 1983.

Deleuze, Gilles, and Félix Guattari. *A Thousand Plateaus: Capitalism and Schizophrenia.* Trans. Brian Massumi. Minneapolis: University of Minnesota Press, 1987.

DeSalvo, Louise A. "'To Make Her Mutton at Sixteen': Rape, Incest, and Child Abuse in *The Antiphon.*" In Broe, *Silence and Power,* 300–314.

Dolan, Jill. *Utopia in Performance: Finding Hope at the Theater.* Ann Arbor: University of Michigan Press, 2005.

Dworkin, Craig. Email to the author. November 11, 2003.

Dydo, Ulla. *Gertrude Stein: The Language That Rises, 1923–1934.* Evanston: Northwestern University Press, 2003.

Edel, Leon. Editor's foreword to *The Saloon.* In *The Complete Plays of Henry James.* New York: Lippincott, 1949. 641–49.

———. Foreword to *The Complete Plays of Henry James,* 9–11.

———. "Henry James: The Dramatic Years." In *The Complete Plays of Henry James,* 19–69.

Edelman, Lee. "Homographesis." In *Homographesis: Essays in Gay Literary and Cultural Theory.* New York: Routledge, 1994. 3–23.

———. "Men's Room." In *STUD: Architectures of Masculinity.* Ed. Joel Sanders. New York: Princeton Architectural Press, 1996. 152–61.

Elektra. By Ezra Pound and Rudd Fleming. Dir. Carey Perloff. Perf. Pamela Reed, Joe Morton, and Nancy Marchand. Classic Stage Company, New York. November 1–29, 1987.

Eliot, T. S. Manuscript notations on *The Antiphon.* May 1956. Papers of Djuna Barnes. University of Maryland Special Collections.

———. *The Waste Land.* In *Collected Poems, 1909–1962.* New York: Harcourt Brace, 1963. 51–76.

Feingold, Michael. "Ludlam Wise, Pound Foolish." *Village Voice.* November 17, 1987. 109–10.

Fenollosa, Ernest. "Outline of *Aoi No Uye.*" Undated. Yale Collection of American Literature.

Fenollosa, Mary. Letter to Ezra Pound. November 25, 1913. Yale Collection of American Literature.

Feuer, Jane. "Reading *Dynasty:* Television and Reception Theory." Quoted in Chuck Kleinhans, "Taking Out the Trash: Camp and the Politics of Parody." In *The Politics and Poetics of Camp.* Ed. Moe Meyer. New York: Routledge, 1994. 185.

Fleche, Anne. "When a Door Is a Jar, or Out in the Theatre: Tennessee Williams and Queer Space." *Theatre Journal* 47 (1995): 253–67.

Gainor, J. Ellen. "*Elektra* by Ezra Pound: The Classic Stage Company, November 1–29, 1987." *Paideuma: A Journal Devoted to Ezra Pound Scholarship* 16:3 (Winter 1987): 127–31.

Gass, William H. Introduction to Gertrude Stein, *The Geographical History of America*. Baltimore: Johns Hopkins University Press, 1973. 3–42.

Gilman, Sander L. *Jewish Self-Hatred: Anti-Semitism and the Hidden Language of the Jews*. Baltimore: Johns Hopkins University Press, 1986.

———. *The Jew's Body*. New York: Routledge, 1991.

Gledhill, Christine. "The Melodramatic Field: An Investigation." In *Home Is Where the Heart Is: Studies in Melodrama and the Woman's Film*. Ed. Christine Gledhill. London: British Film Institute, 1987. 5–39.

Goldberg, RoseLee. "Performance Anxiety." *ArtForum*. April 2004. http://www.findarticles.com/p/articles/mi_m0268/is_8_42/ai_n6080047. December 12, 2005.

Gould, Evlyn. *Virtual Theater from Diderot to Mallarmé*. Baltimore: Johns Hopkins University Press, 1989.

Green, Barbara. "Spectacular Confessions: 'How It Feels to Be Forcibly Fed.'" *Review of Contemporary Fiction* 13:3 (Fall 1993): 70–88.

Grosz, Elizabeth. "Bergson, Deleuze, and Becoming." University of Queensland, Australia. March 16, 2005. http://www.uq.edu.au/~uqmlacaz/Elizabeth Grosz'stalk16.3.05.htm.

———. "The Time of Architecture." In *Embodied Utopias: Gender, Social Change, and the Modern Metropolis*. Ed. Amy Bingaman, Lise Sanders, and Rebecca Zorach. London: Routledge, 2002. 265–78.

Gussow, Mel. "Stage: Pound's *Elektra*." *New York Times*. November 11, 1987.

Halttunen, Karen. *Confidence Men and Painted Women: A Study of Middle-Class Culture in America, 1830–1870*. New Haven: Yale University Press, 1982.

Hapaz, Clay. Conversation with the author. New York. June 17, 2004.

Hardy, Thomas. *The Dynasts: An Epic Drama of the War with Napoleon*. London: Macmillan, 1924.

Hare, Thomas Blenman. *Zeami's Style: The Noh Plays of Zeami Motokiyo*. Stanford: Stanford University Press, 1986.

Harryman, Carla. Electronic interview with the author. November 2, 2003.

Headnote to *Ann Portuguise*. Papers of Djuna Barnes. University of Maryland Special Collections.

Headnote to *Biography of Julie von Bartmann*. Papers of Djuna Barnes. University of Maryland Special Collections.

Herring, Phillip. *Djuna: The Life and Work of Djuna Barnes*. New York: Penguin, 1995.

Herrmann, Anne. *Queering the Moderns: Poses/Portraits/Performances.* New York: Palgrave Macmillan, 2000.

Hesse, Eva, ed. *New Approaches to Ezra Pound.* London: Faber, 1969.

House/Lights. By Gertrude Stein et al. Dir. Elizabeth LeCompte. Perf. Kate Valk, Suzzy Roche, and Tanya Selvaratnam. Performing Garage, New York. 1999.

Howie, Cary. *Claustrophilia: The Erotics of Enclosure in Medieval Literature.* New York: Palgrave Macmillan, 2007.

Humphreys, Laud. *Tea Room Trade: Impersonal Sex in Public Places.* Chicago: Aldine, 1975.

Irigaray, Luce. *This Sex Which Is Not One.* Trans. Catherine Porter with Carolyn Burke. Ithaca: Cornell University Press, 1985.

Jackson, Shannon. *Professing Performance: Theatre in the Academy from Philology to Performativity.* Cambridge: Cambridge University Press, 2004.

James, Henry. "After the Play." In *The Scenic Art: Notes on Acting and the Drama, 1872–1901.* Ed. Allan Wade. New Brunswick: Rutgers University Press, 1948. 226–42.

———. Note to *Theatricals: Two Comedies.* In Edel, *The Complete Plays of Henry James,* 255.

———. "Owen Wingrave." In *Collected Stories,* vol. 2, *1892–1910.* Ed. John Bayley. New York: Knopf, 1999. 67–102.

———. *The Saloon.* In Edel, *The Complete Plays of Henry James.* 651–74.

———. "Tennyson's Drama." In *Views and Reviews.* Boston: Ball, 1908. 165–208

Johnson, E. Patrick. "Manifest Faggotry: Queering Masculinity in African American Culture." In *Appropriating Blackness: Performance and the Politics of Authenticity.* Durham: Duke University Press, 2003. 48–75.

Kaye, Nick. *Art into Theatre: Performance Interviews and Documents.* Amsterdam: Harwood Academic, 1996.

Keats, John. Letter to George and Thomas Keats. December 21, 27 (?), 1817. In *Selected Letters of John Keats.* Ed. Grant F. Scott. Cambridge: Harvard University Press, 2002. 59–61.

Keener, John F. "The Last Words of Dutch Schultz: Deathbed Autobiography and Postmodern Gangster Fiction." *Arizona Quarterly* 54:2 (Summer 1998): 135–63.

Kenner, Hugh. *The Poetry of Ezra Pound.* Millwood, NY: Kraus Reprint, 1974.

———. *The Pound Era.* Berkeley: University of California Press, 1971.

Killian, Kevin, and Brian Kim Stefans. "The American Objectivists." In *Viz. Inter-Arts Event: A Trans-Genre Anthology.* Ed. Roxanne Power Hamilton. Santa Cruz: University of California Press, 2007. 46–57.

Kurnick, David. "'Horrible Impossible': Henry James's Awkward Stage." *Henry James Review* 26 (2005): 109–29.

Laks, Batya Casper. *Electra: A Gender-Sensitive Study of the Plays Based on the Myth.* Jefferson, NC: McFarland, 1995.

LeCompte, Elizabeth. Interview with Nick Kaye. In Kaye, *Art into Theatre*, 253–60.

———. Interview with David Savran. Quoted in Savran, *Breaking the Rules*, 115–16.

LeCompte, Elizabeth, and Kate Valk. Interview with the author. New York. July 1, 2004.

Leupp, Gary P. *Male Colors: The Construction of Homosexuality in Tokugawa Japan.* Berkeley: University of California Press, 1995.

Levine, Nancy J. "'Bringing Milkshakes to Bulldogs': The Early Journalism of Djuna Barnes." In Broe, *Silence and Power*, 27–36.

Litz, A. Walton. "Pound and Yeats: The Road to Stone Cottage." In *Ezra Pound among the Poets*. Ed. George Bornstein. Chicago: University of Chicago Press, 1985. 128–48.

"Louis Zukofsky: A Performance of 'A'-24." November 15, 1978. Poetry Center and American Poetry Archives.

Love, Heather. *Feeling Backward: Loss and the Politics of Queer History.* Cambridge: Harvard University Press, 2007.

Lucian. "The History of Orestes and Pylades." In *Amores*. Trans. W. J. Baylis. http://www.fordham.edu/halsall/pwh/lucian-orest.html. May 11, 2005.

L.Z. Masque. By Louis Zukofsky and Celia Zukofsky. Perf. Bob Perelman, Carla Harryman, et al. San Francisco State University. November 15, 1978.

MacDuff, William. "Beautiful Boys in *Nō* Drama: The Idealization of Homoerotic Desire." *Asian Theatre Journal* 13:2 (Fall 1996): 248–58.

Mac Low, Jackson. *Barnesbook: Four Poems Derived from Sentences by Djuna Barnes.* Los Angeles: Sun and Moon, 1996.

Mahaffey, Vicki. *States of Desire: Wilde, Yeats, Joyce, and the Irish Experiment.* New York: Oxford University Press, 1998.

Malcolm, Janet. *Two Lives: Gertrude and Alice.* New Haven: Yale University Press, 2007.

Marranca, Bonnie. Introduction to Stein, *Last Operas and Plays*, vii–xxvii.

Marsh, Alec. "Letting the Black Cat Out of the Bag: A Rejected Instance of 'American-Africanism' in Pound's *Cantos*." In Coyle, *Ezra Pound and African American Modernism*, 125–42.

Martins, Susana S. "Gender Trouble and Lesbian Desire in Djuna Barnes's *Nightwood*." *Frontiers: A Journal of Women Studies* 20:3 (1999): 108–26.

Masakazu, Yamazaki. "The Aesthetics of Ambiguity: The Artistic Theories of Zeami." In Zeami, *On the Art of the Nō Drama*, xxix–xlv.

McCourt, James. *Queer Street, Rise and Fall of an American Culture, 1947–1985: Excursions in the Mind of the Life.* New York: Norton, 2004.

Melnick, David. "The 'Ought' of Seeing: Zukofsky's *Bottom*." *MAPS* 5 (1973): 55–65.

Messerli, Douglas. Introduction to Barnes, *At the Roots of the Stars*. 7–11.

Miller, D. A. *Place for Us: Essay on the Broadway Musical.* Cambridge: Harvard University Press, 1998.

Moon, Michael. *A Small Boy and Others: Imitation and Initiation in American Culture from Henry James to Andy Warhol.* Durham: Duke University Press, 1998.

Most, Andrea. *Making Americans: Jews and the Broadway Musical.* Cambridge: Harvard University Press, 2004.

Nealon, Christopher S. *Foundlings: Lesbian and Gay Historical Emotion before Stonewall.* Durham: Duke University Press, 2001.

Neuman, Shirley. "'Would a Viper Have Stung Her if She Had Only Had One Name?': *Doctor Faustus Lights the Lights.*" In *Gertrude Stein and the Making of Literature.* Ed. Shirley Neuman and Ira B. Nadel. Houndmills: Macmillan, 1988. 168–93.

Newton, Esther. *Mother Camp: Female Impersonators in America.* Rev. ed. Chicago: University of Chicago Press, 1979.

North, Michael. *Reading 1922: A Return to the Scene of the Modern.* New York: Oxford University Press, 1999.

O'Hara, Frank, and Larry Rivers. *Kenneth Koch: A Tragedy.* In O'Hara, *Amorous Nightmares of Delay: Selected Plays.* Baltimore: Johns Hopkins University Press, 1997. 121–32.

Olga's House of Shame. By Joseph Mawra. Dir. Mawra. 1964. Something Weird Video, 2003.

"*Olga's White Slaves of Chinatown.*" In *Putrescine: Atrocidades e aberrações cinematográficas.* http://www.diatribe.com.br/putrescine/t_olgawhite.shtml. September 23, 2004.

Ovid. *The Metamorphoses of Ovid.* Trans. Allen Mandelbaum. New York: Harcourt Brace, 1993.

Oxford English Dictionary Online. http://www.oed.com. December 13, 2005.

Packard, Chris. *Queer Cowboys and Other Erotic Friendships in Nineteenth-Century American Literature.* New York: Palgrave MacMillan, 2005.

Parsons, Marnie. "A More Capacious Shoulder: '*A*'-24, Nonsense, and the Burden of Meaning." In *Upper Limit Music: The Writing of Louis Zukofsky.* Ed. Mark Scroggins. Tuscaloosa: University of Alabama Press, 1997. 230–56.

Perelman, Bob. "'*A*'-24." In *The L=A=N=G=U=A=G=E Book.* Ed. Bruce Andrews and Charles Bernstein. Carbondale: Southern Illinois University Press, 1984. 292–93.

———. Foreword to Louis Zukofsky and Celia Thaew Zukofsky, *Bottom: On Shakespeare.* Middletown, CT: Wesleyan University Press, 2002. vii–xiii.

———. Interview with the author. Philadelphia. June 20, 2003.

———. *The Marginalization of Poetry.* Princeton: Princeton University Press, 1996.

———. *Ten to One: Selected Poems.* Middletown, CT: Wesleyan University Press, 1999.

————. *The Trouble with Genius: Reading Pound, Joyce, Stein, and Zukofsky.* Berkeley: University of California Press, 1994.

Perloff, Carey. Introduction to Pound and Fleming, *Elektra,* ix–xxv.

Perloff, Marjorie. *The Poetics of Indeterminacy: Rimbaud to Cage.* Princeton: Princeton University Press, 1981.

Peters, Julie Stone. "Performing Obscene Modernism: Theatrical Censorship and the Making of Modern Drama." In Ackerman and Puchner, *Against Theatre,* 206–30.

Plautus. *Rudens; or, The Rope.* In *Plautus,* vol. 4. Trans. Paul Nixon. Cambridge: Harvard University Press, 1932.

Pogrebin, Robin. "Baryshnikov Center Gets Resident Theater." *New York Times.* September 12, 2007. http://www.nytimes.com/2007/09/12/theater/12theater.htm.

Pound, Ezra. *The Cantos.* New York: New Directions, 1970.

————. Letter to Katue Kitasono. January 30, 1959. Yale Collection of American Literature.

————. Letter to William Carlos Williams. December 19, 1913. In *Pound/Williams: Selected Letters of Ezra Pound and William Carlos Williams.* Ed. Hugh Witemeyer. New York: New Directions, 1996. 22–23.

————. "Noh" *Plays.* In *Translations.* New York: New Directions, 1963. 213–360.

Pound, Ezra, and Rudd Fleming. *Elektra.* New York: New Directions, 1990.

Pound, Ezra, and Louis Zukofsky. *Pound/Zukofsky: Selected Letters of Ezra Pound and Louis Zukofsky.* Ed. Barry Ahearn. London: Faber and Faber, 1987.

Pratt, William. *Ezra Pound and the Making of Modernism.* New York: AMS, 2007.

Preston, John Hyde. "A Conversation." *Atlantic.* August 1935. 187–94.

Puchner, Martin. *Stage Fright: Modernism, Anti-Theatricality, and Drama.* Baltimore: Johns Hopkins University Press.

Quartermain, Peter. *Disjunctive Poetics: From Gertrude Stein and Louis Zukofsky to Susan Howe.* Cambridge: Cambridge University Press, 1992.

Quigley, Austin E. *The Modern Stage and Other Worlds.* New York: Methuen, 1985.

Rabaté, Jean-Michel. *Language, Sexuality, and Ideology in Ezra Pound's "Cantos."* Albany: State University of New York Press, 1986.

Raber, Karen. *Dramatic Difference: Gender, Class, and Genre in the Early Modern Closet Drama.* Newark: University of Delaware Press, 2001.

Reid, Richard. Introduction to Ezra Pound and Rudd Fleming, *Elektra.* Princeton: Princeton University Press, 1989. ix–xx.

Rifkin, Libbie. *Career Moves: Olson, Creeley, Zukofsky, Berrigan, and the American Avant-Garde.* Madison: University of Wisconsin Press, 2000.

Roach, Joseph. *Cities of the Dead: Circum-Atlantic Performance.* New York: Columbia University Press, 1996.

———. "Imagined Communities: Nature, Culture, and Audience Restaged." *Nineteenth Century Theatre* 21:1 (Summer 1993): 41–49.

Robinson, Marc. *The Other American Drama*. New York: Cambridge University Press, 1994.

Román, David, and Tim Miller. "Preaching to the Converted." In Solomon and Minwalla, *The Queerest Art*, 203–26.

Rose, Al. *Storyville, New Orleans: Being an Authentic, Illustrated Account of the Notorious Red-Light District*. Tuscaloosa: University of Alabama Press, 1974.

Rosten, Bevya. "The Fractured Stage: Gertrude Stein's Influence on American Avant-Garde Directing as Seen in Four Productions of *Dr. Faustus Lights the Lights*." Ph.D. diss. City University of New York, 1998.

Ruddick, Lisa. *Reading Gertrude Stein: Body, Text, Gnosis*. Ithaca: Cornell University Press, 1990.

Salvato, Nick. "On the Bubble: The Soap Opera Diva's Ambivalent Orbit." *Camera Obscura* 22:2 (2007): 102–23.

———. "Tramp Sensibility and the Afterlife of *Showgirls*." *Theatre Journal* 58 (2006): 633–48.

Savran, David. *Breaking the Rules: The Wooster Group*. New York: Theatre Communications Group, 1988.

———. *Communists, Cowboys, and Queers: The Politics of Masculinity in the Work of Arthur Miller and Tennessee Williams*. Minneapolis: University of Minnesota Press, 1992.

———. *A Queer Sort of Materialism: Recontextualizing American Theater*. Ann Arbor: University of Michigan Press, 2003.

Scarry, Elaine. *The Body in Pain: The Making and Unmaking of the World*. New York: Oxford University Press, 1985.

Schechner, Richard. *Between Theatre and Anthropology*. Philadelphia: University of Pennsylvania Press, 1985.

Scholes, Robert. *Paradoxy of Modernism*. New Haven: Yale University Press, 2006.

Schultz, Dutch, et al. "The Last Words of Dutch Schultz." October 24, 1935. Recorded by F. J. Long. http://home.swipnet.se/~w-40977/coolpeople/last words.html.

Scroggins, Mark. *Louis Zukofsky and the Poetry of Knowledge*. Tuscaloosa: University of Alabama Press, 1998.

Sebastian, Cyrus. "Stein Soup." Hunter On-line Theater Review. http://www.hot review.org/articles/stein-soup.htm. September 24, 2004.

Sedgwick, Eve Kosofsky. *Between Men: English Literature and Male Homosocial Desire*. New York: Columbia University Press, 1985.

———. *Epistemology of the Closet*. Berkeley: University of California Press, 1990.

———. "Queer and Now." In *Tendencies*. Durham: Duke University Press, 1993. 1–20.

Sellars, Peter. Foreword to Savran, *Breaking the Rules: The Wooster Group*. xv–xvi.

Senelick, Laurence. "The Queer Root of Theatre." In Solomon and Minwalla, *The Queerest Art*, 21–39.

Shikibu, Murasaki. *The Tale of Genji.* Trans. Edward G. Seidensticker. New York: Knopf, 1992.

Sloan, De Villo. "'Crude Mechanical Access' or 'Crude Personism': A Chronicle of One San Francisco Bay Area Poetry War." *Sagetrieb* 4:2–3 (Fall–Winter 1985): 241–54.

Smith, Matthew Wilson. *The Total Work of Art: From Bayreuth to Cyberspace.* New York: Routledge, 2007.

Solomon, Alisa. "Great Sparkles of Lust: Homophobia and the Antitheatrical Tradition." In Solomon and Minwalla, *The Queerest Art*, 9–20.

Solomon, Alisa, and Framji Minwalla, eds. *The Queerest Art: Essays on Lesbian and Gay Theatre.* New York: New York University Press, 2002.

Sontag, Susan. "Notes on Camp." In *Against Interpretation.* New York: Farrar, Straus and Giroux, 1966. 275–92.

Spears, Richard A. *Slang and Euphemism: A Dictionary of Oaths, Curses, Insults, Sexual Slang and Metaphor, Racial Slurs, Drug Talk, Homosexual Lingo, and Related Matters.* New York: Jonathan David, 1981.

Stein, Gertrude. *Byron.* Manuscript notebook. Yale Collection of American Literature.

———. *Byron A Play.* In *Last Operas and Plays.* 333–86.

———. *Composition as Explanation.* London: Hogarth, 1926.

———. *Doctor Faustus Lights the Lights.* In *Last Operas and Plays.* 89–118.

———. *Everybody's Autobiography.* Cambridge: Exact Change, 1993.

———. *Four Saints in Three Acts.* In *Last Operas and Plays.* 440–80.

———. "Identity: A Poem." In *A Stein Reader.* Ed. Ulla Dydo. Evanston: Northwestern University Press, 1993. 588–94.

———. *Last Operas and Plays.* Baltimore: Johns Hopkins University Press, 1995.

———. Letter to Carl Van Vechten. March 1935. Yale Collection of American Literature.

———. Notes to Alice B. Toklas. Undated. Yale Collection of American Literature.

———. "Off We All Went to See Germany." In *How Writing Is Written.* Ed. Robert Barlett Haas. Los Angeles: Black Sparrow, 1977. 137–40.

———. *A Play Called Not and Now.* In *Last Operas and Plays.* 422–39.

———. "Plays." In *Last Operas and Plays.* xxix–lii.

———. *Short Sentences.* In *Last Operas and Plays.* 317–32.

———. "What Are Master-pieces and Why Are There So Few of Them." In *Writings and Lectures: 1911–1945.* Ed. Patricia Meyerowitz. London: Owen, 1967. 146–54.

Stein, Gertrude, and Thornton Wilder. *The Letters of Gertrude Stein and Thornton Wilder.* Ed. Edward Burns and Ulla Dydo with William Rice. New Haven: Yale University Press, 1996.

Straznicky, Marta. *Privacy, Playreading, and Women's Closet Drama, 1550–1700.* New York: Cambridge University Press, 2004.

Strychacz, Thomas F. *Modernism, Mass Culture, and Professionalism.* Cambridge: Cambridge University Press, 1993.

Sutherland, Donald. *Gertrude Stein: A Biography of Her Work.* New Haven: Yale University Press, 1951.

Syros, Christine. "Beyond Language: Ezra Pound's Translation of the Sophoclean *Elektra.*" *Paideuma: A Journal Devoted to Ezra Pound Scholarship* 23:2–3 (Fall–Winter 1994): 107–39.

Szondi, Peter. *Theory of the Modern Drama: A Critical Edition.* Ed. and trans. Michael Hays. Minneapolis: University of Minnesota Press, 1987.

Thomas, Kate. "'What Time We Kiss': Michael Field's Queer Temporalities." *GLQ: A Journal of Lesbian and Gay Studies* 13:2–3 (2007): 327–51.

Toklas, Alice B. Note to Gertrude Stein. Undated. Yale Collection of American Literature.

———. *What Is Remembered.* New York: Holt, Rinehart, and Winston, 1963.

Trask, Michael. *Cruising Modernism: Class and Sexuality in American Literature and Social Thought.* Ithaca: Cornell University Press, 2003.

Tsukui, Nobuko. *Ezra Pound and Japanese Noh Plays.* Washington, DC: University Press of America, 1983.

Twitchell-Waas, Jeffrey. "Tuning the Senses: Cavalcanti, Marx, Spinoza, and Zukofsky's 'A'-9." *Sagetrieb: A Journal Devoted to Poets in the Imagist/Objectivist Tradition* 11:3 (Winter 1992): 57–91.

———, ed. "Z-site: A Companion to the Works of Louis Zukofsky." http://www.z-site.net/.

Villarejo, Amy. *Lesbian Rule: Cultural Criticism and the Value of Desire.* Durham: Duke University Press, 2003.

Waters, John. *Trash Trio: Three Screenplays.* New York: Vintage, 1988.

Whitney, William Dwight, et al., eds. *The Century Dictionary: An Encyclopedic Lexicon of the English Language.* New York: Century, 1895.

Williams, Linda. *Playing the Race Card: Melodramas of Black and White from Uncle Tom to O. J. Simpson.* Princeton: Princeton University Press, 2001.

Wilmer, Clive. "Maker of Songs." *Times Literary Supplement.* June 4, 2004. 9–11.

Wordsworth, William. "The Tables Turned." In *Poetical Works.* Ed. Thomas Hutchinson. Oxford: Oxford University Press, 1936. 377.

Worthen, W. B. "Disciplines of the Text: Sites of Performance." In *The Performance Studies Reader.* Ed. Henry Bial. New York: Routledge, 2004. 10–25.

———. *Print and the Poetics of Modern Drama.* Cambridge: Cambridge University Press, 2005.

Wray, David. *Catullus and the Poetics of Roman Manhood.* Cambridge: Cambridge University Press, 2001.

———. "'Cool Rare Air': Zukofsky's Breathing with Catullus and Plautus." *Chicago Review* 50 2:4 (Winter 2004): 52–99.

———. "'cool rare air': Zukofsky's Breathing with Catullus and Plautus." Unpublished version.

Zeami. *On the Art of the Nō Drama: The Major Treatises of Zeami.* Trans. J. Thomas Rimer and Yamazaki Masakazu. Princeton: Princeton University Press, 1984.

Zukofsky, Celia. "Year by Year Bibliography of Louis Zukofsky." In *Louis Zukofsky: Man and Poet.* Ed. Carroll F. Terrell. Orono, ME: National Poetry Foundation, 1979. 385–92.

Zukofsky, Louis. *"A."* Baltimore: Johns Hopkins University Press, 1978.

———. *Autobiography.* New York: Grossman, 1970.

———. *Bottom: On Shakespeare.* Vol. 1. Austin: Ark, 1963.

———. Letter to Ezra Pound. December 23, 1927. Yale Collection of American Literature.

———. "Poem Beginning 'The.'" In *Complete Short Poetry.* Baltimore: Johns Hopkins University Press, 1991. 8–20.

Zukofsky, Louis, and Celia Zukofsky. *"A"-24.* New York: Grossman, 1972.

INDEX

"A" (Zukofsky), 72, 75, 76, 83–85, 88, 91, 96–98, 193*n*19, 193–94*n*33. See also *L.Z. Masque* (Zukofsky)

Abbey Players, 150

Abraham, Julie L., 170

Ackerman, Alan, 6, 8, 17, 190*n*57, 193*n*24

Aeschylus, 31

African-American soldiers, 57

"After the Play" (James), 23

Agamemnon (Aeschylus), 22, 31

Ahearn, Barry, 75, 77, 83, 84–86, 193–94*n*33

"The American Objectivists" (Killian and Stefans), 63

Amores (Lucian), 48–49

Anger, Kenneth, 2

Ann Portuguise (Barnes), 141, 147–48, 150–55, 163, 164, 198*n*18, 198*n*20

The Antiphon (Barnes): autobiographical elements in, 139; and "Barnes 1," 171–77, 199*n*34; campiness of, 180–81; Eliot's and Barnes's editing of, in 1950s, 165, 181; family relationships in, 166–71; incest and sexual assault in, 139, 140, 167–70, 174–75; lesbian incest in, 141, 168–71; performance of, 171; and predecessor closet dramas, 3; publication of, 165, 198*n*20; setting of, 165–66; World War II setting of, 21; writing style of, 164–65

Antony and Cleopatra (Shakespeare), 73–74

Apollodorus, 191*n*35

Archer, William, 4

Arise, Arise (Zukofsky), 75, 86, 88

Aristophanes, 67

Aristotle, 67, 70

Ark Press, 65

Arnaz, Desi, 134

Arnold, Matthew, 179

Ashbery, John, 63

Atsumori, 35

At the Roots of the Stars (Barnes), 198*n*20

Auerbach, Nina, 23, 179, 180, 199*n*6

Auslander, Philip, 12–14

The Autobiography of Alice B. Toklas (Stein), 2–3, 114

The Awkward Age (James), 24

Awoi No Uye, 39, 43–47

Bacon, 66

Ballet, 118, 123, 134

Barnes, Djuna: as expatriot, 23; family background of, 9; family in works of, 19–20, 147–76; force-feeding of, 142–47, 198*n*13; on gorilla in captivity, 145–47; journalistic "stunt pieces" by, 141–47; lesbian incest in works by, 139–41, 156–65, 168–71; papers of, 17; and Parisian lesbian community, 9; relationship of, with female lover, 11; self-alteration to body of, 198*n*10;